SUCKER PUNCH

SUCKER PUNCH

Boxing films of the 1930s, 40s and 50s

Amanda J Field

CHAPLIN BOOKS

www.chaplinbooks.co.uk

First published in 2023 by Chaplin Books

Copyright © Amanda J Field

ISBN 978-1-911105-69-5

A CIP catalogue record for this book is available from The British Library

Chaplin Books
75b West St
Titchfield PO14 4DG
www.chaplinbooks.co.uk

CONTENTS

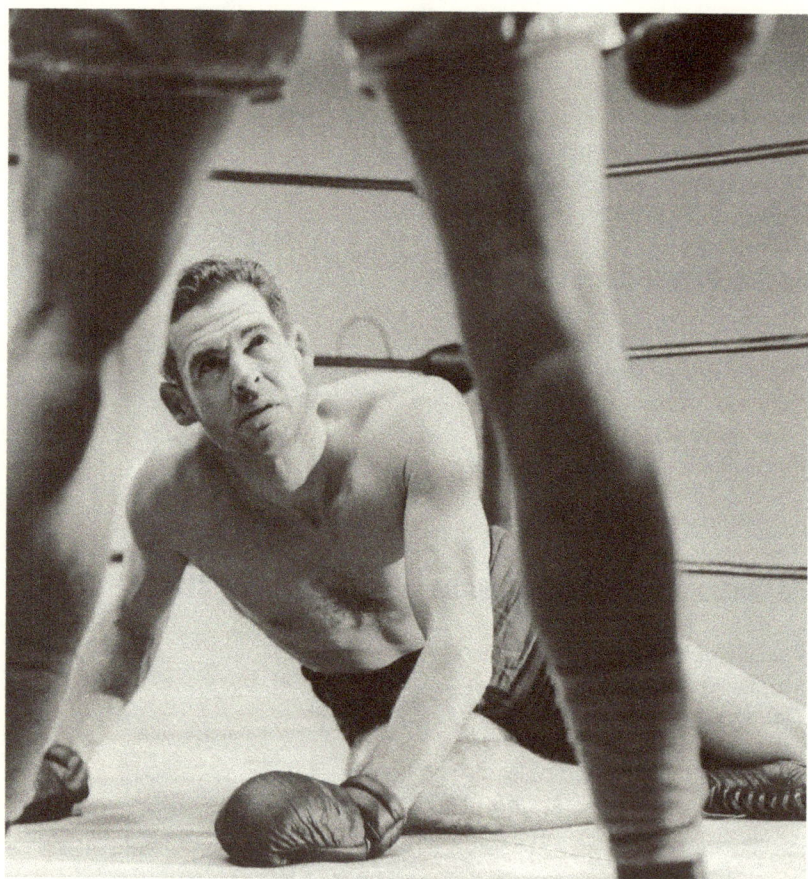

INTRODUCTION

I t would be hardly an exaggeration to say that the history of the movies began with boxing. What better visual spectacle could there be for the new nickelodeons than films full of fast-paced action, with an exciting climax? From the early 1890s, the cameras were on hand to film fights, beginning with unnamed boxers (such as *First Fight Film* in 1894) filmed for the sheer delight of seeing punches swung and knockouts achieved, and quickly progressing to newsreels that documented or 'reproduced' real fights between world-class boxers (such as the *Battle of Jeffries and Sharkey for the Championship of the World* in 1899). Boxing had always been big news with a huge following, particularly in the US: now it could be made to come alive and, what's more, be brought to everyone's home-town. Filmmakers were also quick to grasp boxing's potential for narrative films, with the fight game providing the perfect backdrop to a drama or comedy. The briefest search through silent film listings reveals more than 100 such films. The movies themselves may now be largely forgotten, but the themes are familiar ones because they have been repeated many times over subsequent decades. In fact, these themes can be easily discerned from just a glance through some of the titles, such as *The Battling Fool, Afraid to Fight, Kid Regan's Hands, The Patent Leather Kid,* and - particularly enticing - *The Winning Wallop.* There were comedy tales in which pride takes a fall: in *Bill's Day Out,* for example, a French film of 1911, Bill and his cousin go to a country fair where Bill enters a boxing booth and defeats a black boxer. Treating himself to a big cigar as a reward, he is immediately sick and has to be taken home. There were dramas in which boxing is merely an expedient move in order to reach for a much more worthy goal: in *The Croxley Master,* for instance, a British film of 1921 based on an Arthur Conan Doyle story, a young doctor enters a boxing contest in order to win the money that will allow him to buy a practice of his own: he not only wins the contest, but the girl he loves. And there were films in which the hero is torn between the fight game and a more acceptable way of life, as advocated by the 'good woman'. In the 1924 US film, *The Jazz Bout*, boxer Benny Lane is forced to become a saxophone player in his girlfriend's band, when what he really wants to do is fight Big Iron Parker. When Parker jeers at him, Benny goes ahead with the fight, but gets a real pasting. Only the support of the band, who come along to play jazz tunes such as the 'Angle Worm Wriggle', give him the confidence to win. A glimpse into the future is offered in *The Last Man on Earth* (1924) featuring a 1950s planet without men, culminating in a women's boxing match where the boxers go back to their corners to check on their make-up.

Not all the boxing films from the silent era have been forgotten: some of its real gems have made it into the 'canon' of film studies, such as Charlie Chaplin's 1925 movie *The Champion*, with its balletic fight sequences; Buster Keaton's tale of mistaken identity in *Battling Butler* (1926); and Alfred Hitchcock's remarkable *The Ring* (1927). Other important silent films contained short but memorable boxing sequences, such as Chaplin's expert dodging in the ring in *City Lights*, a silent film made during the sound era (1931); and the fight shots of bruiser Battling Burrows (Donald Crisp) in D W Griffith's *Broken Blossoms* (1919), which - though brief - nevertheless define his character and the nature of the threat he poses to his daughter Lucy (Lillian Gish).

If the birth of boxing films coincided with the birth of the movies, then the arrival of the talkies represented their coming-of-age. In the 1930s, 40s and 50s there were over 130 fight films released. These decades could rightly be called the heyday of the boxing film and they are the focus of this book. The films came from all the major studios, including Warner Brothers, Twentieth Century-Fox, M-G-M, RKO, Universal, Paramount and Loews; and from independents such as Roberts Productions, the unit set up to give a voice to left-leaning film-makers. Even the 'poverty row' studios such as Monogram and Republic, despite the financial handicap and absence of stars (Monogram could boast only The Bowery Boys), secured good distribution for their films.

Some of Hollywood's biggest names starred as boxers, among them Errol Flynn, James Cagney, John Garfield and Kirk Douglas, and some of

City Lights (1931) was a silent film released during
the sound era. Chaplin, in his Little Tramp guise, wears
his trademark bowler hat in the ring

the era's top directors (including Robert Wise, Raoul Walsh, Robert Rossen and Mark Robson), can count boxing films among their credits. Hardly any star or director, however, made more than one fight picture during each decade, the exception being the 'series' comedies which gave regular work to directors like Reginald Le Borg and to actors like Joe Kirkwood, who starred in the majority of the Palooka series. Unlike gangster films, which had become synonymous with Warner Brothers, no single studio dominated production.

Although boxing pictures had been an established part of Hollywood output since the early days of the silents, because they ranged across such a broad range of narrative approaches, from film noir and melodrama, to comedy and animation, they have not been perceived as a distinct genre in their own right.[1] Yet to categorise boxing films simply as 'sports movies' is to do them an injustice: they have a coherence of narrative, characters and visual style which repays careful study and which means that, when viewed as a group, the impact and importance of the boxing genre can be clearly seen.

In or out of the canon

The films examined in detail in this book are not intended to establish or reinforce a particular view of the 'typical' boxing movie, but are offered as examples of the breadth of the genre and the way it has been treated. Even with this (modest) aim in mind, it is worth bearing in mind Rick Altman's warning in *Film/Genre* that:

> nearly every genre critic offers a long list of films but only treats a few of them…It is important to recognise the effective difference between the full list of films identified as the critic's object of study and the far more limited list of films that represent the critic's version of the genre's putative Platonic ideal.[2]

Certainly, some of the films discussed in this book in detail, such as *Body and Soul* (1947) and *The Set-Up* (1949) are recognised as part of the film history 'canon', not because they are boxing films but because they have been retrospectively categorised as film noir, which has become a genre in its own right. Others, such as *Gentleman Jim* (1942) and *The Pittsburgh Kid* (1941), have received little or no critical attention, the latter because it was a low-budget 'programmer' - usually shown as a second-feature on the bill - and therefore not perceived as having any aesthetic value, and the former because, despite lavish production values and the presence of Errol Flynn, it was a period costume drama, a genre that has yet to be treated seriously. Yet all boxing films reward examination: the lesser-known shed light on the more famous (setting them in context); in their recurring themes and narrative structures they provide a composite picture of how the traditional rise-and-fall (sometimes fall-and-rise) fight tale can be told, and they give a valuable insight into both the workings of the film industry and the social attitudes of the times. More importantly they are, for the most part, hugely enjoyable and entertaining.

Reading critical histories of film gives the impression that all boxing films could be categorised as dark melodrama, with the boxer as a tragic hero, but when a filmography of the decades is compiled, a much more complex pattern emerges. Comedy, for example, formed an important element. In 1946 Danny Kaye reprised the role of weedy milkman-turned-boxer that had originally been portrayed by silent comedian Harold Lloyd in *The Milky Way* (1936). The remake was retitled *The Kid From Brooklyn*, shot in Technicolor and featured song-and-dance routines. *Monthly Film Bulletin* praised the 'sparkling direction and the gay clowning' of its star which, it said, made the film 'a first-class musical comedy'.[3] Comedy also

Whereas most writing on the boxing genre has concentrated on dark melodrama, it is important to note that boxing films ranged across many genres., including musical comedy: The Kid From Brooklyn, starring Danny Kaye, is one example

sustained a number of long-running series: the popular Palooka series (1934-1951), which featured hapless boxer Joe Palooka, had eleven outings; Maisie, the feisty 'Brooklyn Bonfire' whose adventures ranged from gold-panning to facing down 'savages' in the Congo in ten films, made a boxing comedy-drama, *Ringside Maisie* in 1941; and the Bowery Boys (*Bowery Blitzkreig* and *Pride of the Bowery* (both 1941)) were never very far from a boxing ring. Comedy boxing also appeared in animated films, which echoed or subverted the tropes of the serious boxing drama: for example, in *To Duck or Not to Duck* (1943), a six-minute cartoon from Loony Tunes, Daffy Duck meets Elmer Fudd in the ring. 'By means more fowl than fair', said *Motion Picture Herald*, 'the ducks ... send Elmer to the floor for a count, but he recovers from a good pasting to rout them all'.[4]

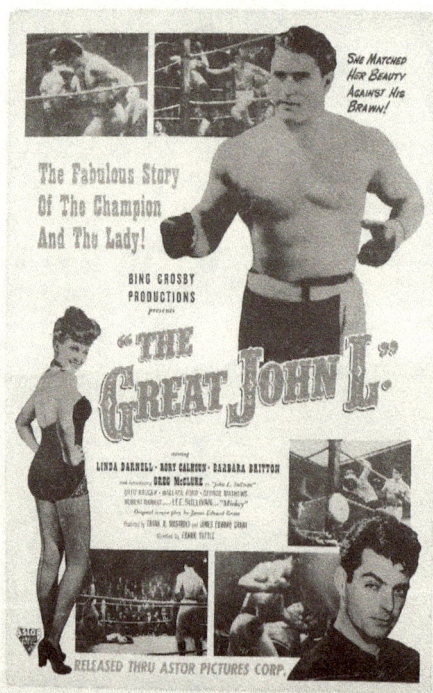

Biopics were a staple of the boxing genre: to attract female audiences, there was usually a romantic angle promoted on the posters

There were dramas that combined boxing with music: in *Golden Boy* (1939) Joe Bonaparte has to choose between fighting and playing the violin; in *Kid Nightingale* - released the same year - Steve Nelson sings operatic arias in the ring; in *City For Conquest* (1940) Danny Kenny fights in order to put his composer-brother through music college; in *Glory Alley* (1952) the fighter - whose trainer is played by Louis Armstrong - falls in love with a New Orleans dancer; and in *Here Comes Mr Jordan* (1941) an angel brings boxer Joe Pendleton - known as the 'Flying Pug' - back to life, only recognisable in his new incarnation by the 'lucky saxophone' he always carries with him.[5] Biopics were a staple of the genre: as well as *Gentleman Jim* (1942), a romantic interpretation of the rise of Jim Corbett through late-nineteenth century San Franciscan society and through the championship, there was *The Great John L* (1945) which tells the story of John L Sullivan, the man who finally lost his heavyweight crown to Corbett. This strand would continue into the 1950s with *The Joe Louis Story* (1952) and *Somebody Up There Likes Me* (1956), the story of Rocky Graziano.

This is not to argue that dark melodrama was absent, but it is most notable in the post-war years, with *Body and Soul, Whiplash* (1948), *The Set-Up* and *Champion* (1949) all focusing on the corruption of the sport and its dirty deals alongside lighter fare such as the Joe Palooka series.

Narrative conventions

So what exactly are the characteristics that combine to make boxing films a genre in their own right? Nick Lacey, in his book *Narrative and Genre*, defines a 'repertoire of elements' which films need to share in order to qualify for genre status: these include characters, setting, iconography, narrative and style.[6] This inevitably results in a certain amount of repetition between films within the same genre - yet as we shall see, this is a key part of their appeal. In *Beyond the Stars: Locales in American Popular Film*, Paul Loukides and Linda K Fuller point out that not only does the audience become accustomed to the conventions of boxing films, 'they need them - as a guide to the ritual being played out in the narrative'.[7] As far as boxing films are concerned, the fight itself may be seen as the central shared characteristic but, although boxing action itself is important and usually provides the climax of the film (and the defining

7

moment of the hero's character development), it is the events that happen outside the ring - or on its periphery - that make the film memorable and give meaning to the fights themselves. This is not to say that everything that happens outside the ring is unique: indeed, part of the interest of the genre stems from the nuances in the way these oft-repeated events are treated. There is no boxing film, for example, that does not dwell on the dressing-room preparations of hand-binding and glove-lacing (indeed some, like *The Set-Up*, barely leave the dressing-room at all); that does not build the sense of occasion through the ringing tones of the fight-announcer; that does not solemnify the fight through the referee's reciting of the rules; use cutaways during the fight to show the reaction of the crowd, whether comic (as in *They Made Me a Criminal*) or blood-thirsty (as in *The Set-Up*); or eavesdrop on the feverish match reporting of the radio commentators (as in *Champion*). The ritualistic nature of these details is essential to the fight film and arguably more central than the fight itself, which is often dealt with in a perfunctory manner and offers little variation in filming. The build-up to the championship fight is also invariably handled in the same way from film to film, through a montage sequence which uses newspaper headlines, whirring train-wheels, city signposts and a series of knockout punches to chart the boxer's rise up the rankings. As Carmen Ficarra points out, these sounds and images may be cliches, but they 'comfort us with their easy familiarity'.[8] Indeed, familiarity and repetition is essential to the genre-film. Only by repeating key images and elements of narrative-style does the genre accrue symbolic meaning that is easily (and economically) understood by its audience. As Thomas Schatz makes clear in *Hollywood Genres*, the qualities that have been traditionally viewed as artistic shortcomings, such as the predictability of the plot 'assume a significantly different value when examined as components of a genre's ritualistic narrative system'.[9]

The plot-range of boxing films is necessarily narrow. Zucker and Babich, in their book *Sports Films*, cynically but accurately sum up the typical narrative trajectory: 'a slum boy rises to be a contender, but he either loses his virtue to a vamp or is corrupted by gangsters and falls, only to make a comeback at the end aided by the pleas at the ringside of the sweetheart he's left behind'.[10] A more sophisticated tracking of the typical narrative has been charted by Leger Grindon, who has sought to break down the rise-and-fall pattern of the boxing film into a ten-stage 'master plot'. The result is a structure that fits most boxing movies like a glove, beginning with the discovery phase, in which the protagonist is found to have a talent for fighting; and moving through the family-versus-ambition crisis that drives him into the ring; the promise displayed in his first victory; his rise to fame; the deal made with a crooked promoter; subsequent debauchery; the winning of the title fight and the eventual resolution or epilogue. Grindon acknowledges that some works 'may portray only a part of this narrative pattern, but still operate within the conventions of the genre'.[11]

Tony Williams, writing in the *Quarterly Review of Film and Video*, feels that semantic similarities are not enough and that the incoherence of the genre stems from the lack of a 'stable, syntactical set of elements'. He also offers the interesting view that the sporadic nature of Hollywood's output was influenced by concerns about the way boxing movies 'negate(d) key ideological components within an American Dream of Success'.[12] This could be interpreted as being about the way that boxing sometimes seems, to its protagonists, as a route to overcoming societal obstacles (such as overcoming racial prejudices) but rarely seems to fulfil that hope.

The price of victory

Thematically, all boxing films are essentially about winning - but the way the fighters win, the motivation behind winning and the price they pay for victory are the variables. Some win on sheer merit: with Jim Corbett in *Gentleman Jim* (1942), it is the fighter's dancing feet that keep him out of range of the swinging punches delivered by more traditional pugs schooled in bare-knuckle boxing. Other boxers have their fights fixed right from the beginning of their careers, such as milkman Burleigh Sullivan in the comedy *The Milky Way* (1936) and 'Wild Man of the Andes' Toro Moreno in *The Harder They Fall* (1956). Other boxers start winning because they realise exactly what they are battling against: the stereotypical dim pug played by Aldo Ray in *Pat and Mike* (1952), a Katharine Hepburn/Spencer Tracy vehicle, loses every fight until Pat explains that if he sees the opponent as himself, he will win. As Leger Grindon points out, the ring opponent is often a 'phantom antagonist representing an inner weakness or fear residing in the boxer himself'.[13]

In terms of motivation, winning can be about personal pride, showing the world that they are 'someone' after all, as with Midge Kelly in *Champion* (1949), whose punches are filled with resentment against a world in which they seem to have no place. Sometimes it is about racial pride: in *Body and Soul*, corrupt boxer Charley Davis comes to realise that his mother's words early in his career were true - he needs to fight for a good reason, not just for money. In his final fight, when he refuses to take a dive, winning could be interpreted as a Jewish point of honour, a gesture of solidarity with the East Side community in which he grew up (even though his Jewishness is never made explicit in the film). Often, the motivation is a woman: in *The Set-Up*, veteran fighter Stoker Thompson wants to prove to his wife that he can break his losing-streak and be a man she can be proud of, the irony being that she needs no convincing - like other boxing-film wives, who constitute the moral force of the genre, she just wants him never to fight again. The quality that all the winners share is their hunger: 'if other fighters have a flame burning inside them,' says poet and film noir chronicler Nicholas Christopher, then the champion 'has a bonfire, stoked by some fury he could never define. Maybe not even acknowledge'.[14]

In serious drama, the price boxers pay for victory is their soul, a Faustian bargain that uses money, women and fame as the lure. This Faustian element is made explicit in *Champion*, when a new manager invites Midge Kelly to admire the view from his high-rise office. Gesturing to the expanse of New York ('the capital of the whole world') that lies before him, he tells Midge: 'it's all yours if you want it.' Midge is more than willing to pay the price. In most films, the final selling-out is averted through the boxer's own actions, often by defying the faceless gangsters who demand they take a dive in a crucial fight: they win and are prepared to take the consequences. Their reward for standing firm against corruption is the regaining of their pride, the freedom to give up the fight game, and the winning back of the woman in their lives, the girlfriend or wife left behind in their search for fame and fortune.

Money is at the heart of professional boxing, but is rarely a fighter's sole motivation (there are plenty of other people willing to make it their sole motivation, notably the managers, 'fixers' and people like journalist-turned-publicist Eddie Willis in *The Harder They Fall*). As Nicholas Christopher says: 'never far from the sweet science is the art of the fast buck'.[15] Ronald Bergan, in his book *Sports in the Movies*, goes so far as to liken the business to prostitution, with the manager as pimp, the gym as brothel and the crowd as the clients (which in its assignment of the crowd to an active, rather than a passive/voyeuristic role, is interesting in itself).[16] Bergan's analogy may be overly cynical or pessimistic, but it certainly holds good for the distribution of wealth: in every case, it's the fighter who gets swindled, and the promoters and fixers who walk away with the lion's share. All the promoter has to do is make sure the boxer gets just enough taste of the big money to keep him fighting; and to deliver an authentic-looking match that will convince the 'clients' that they are getting their money's worth. Films are usually very specific about the amount of money involved (either the prize money or the money on offer to take a dive) and this serves to signal the attitude of the film towards the fight business. In light comedy, for example, the amounts are often ludicrously small, implying that corruption is petty and harmless, though small amounts when cited in serious drama (such as the revelation that Stoker's manager in *The Set-Up* will fix a fight for as little as 40 dollars) can highlight the small-time seediness of the business.

'Kill him!'

If money is at the heart of professional boxing, then its lure is often symbolised by women. Women (but only 'other' women) are frequently the prize for winning, with the genre chock-full of glamorous gold-diggers who are experts at 'following the money', backing only the winners, and moving seamlessly onto the next promising young fighter as soon as they sense a losing-spell. These women are inevitably blonde, over-dressed (witness Babs in *The Pittsburgh Kid* in her veiled hats and fur muffs), predatory and high-maintenance. Above all, they are city women, and their names reflect this (Goldie, Babs, Nina, Babe). They often have showbusiness jobs, such as nightclub singer Fluff in *Kid Galahad*, show-girl Rose in *Iron Man* (1931) or chorus-girl Evelyn in *King for a Night* (1933). They make a fine contrast with the neatly dressed, dark-haired wives and girlfriends (Peggie, Pat, Connie, Norma, Marie) who love the hero only for who he is, not for how much money he has: 'we only like to ride with the winners,' says Babs in *The Pittsburgh Kid*. Leger Grindon reminds us that, unlike the predatory women, whose appeal is to the body, the 'good woman's' appeal is to the soul and to the 'uplift of the spirit under the rubric of family, religion, or the arts'.[17] These women have unassuming jobs: Kid Curtis' wife Peg in *The Square Ring* works in a teashop, as do the women in *There Ain't No Justice* and *Champion*. Often, though not always, these 'good women' come from the country, not the city, reinforcing the idea prevalent in boxing movies that the country equates with health and community, and the city with corruption and greed. It is the role of these 'good women' to have their advice ('give up the fight game') ignored until the climax of the film - and the role of the gold-diggers to be passed coldly by once the hero has achieved redemption. During the fights themselves, the 'good women' sit at the ringside - or by their radio sets - recoiling with every punch as if they have been struck themselves; the gold-diggers sit forward in their seats, shouting 'kill him, baby.' Frank Krutnik, in his article 'Something More Than Night,' maintains that the femme fatale is never the cause of disorder

Glamorous gold-diggers are contrasted with the 'good women' who the fighter has cast aside in his rise up the rankings. They dress ostentatiously, usually come from the city and relish the fight spectacle. Rose (Jean Harlow) plays the fighter's cheating wife in Iron Man (1931): she leaves him when he's losing and only returns when he is winning

'but she does service as the principal scapegoat for far less tangible anxieties about identity, gender and economic status'.[18] Although he is writing about film noir, his comments are equally applicable across the boxing-film spectrum. The femmes fatales are always collected - as trophies - on the boxer's rise up the ranks: once his anxieties have been worked through or laid to rest, usually through the achievement of championship status with its attendant wealth, fame and power, they are no longer needed. Part of the appeal of these women is the way they encourage the boxer to exert his masculinity, through fighting, aggression out of the ring, and through sex. They free him from any demands to be the sensitive, caring, conventional companion that the 'good woman' requires.

Women introduce another aspect to the goal of 'winning' (winning in love as well as winning in the ring) and make us question who is actually the victor in many of these films. Ultimately, it is not the boxer himself: his victor status is, at best, temporary and often illusory. He may have undergone some catharsis during the film, regaining his integrity, making a moral stand, or realising where his true loyalties lie, but in the end the only possible outcome (and this applies to comedy as well as melodrama) is to quit the fight game. Quitting is the price he pays to win back the 'good woman'. When gangsters break Stoker Thompson's hand in *The Set-Up* after he refuses to take a dive, it is clear he will never fight again. Had he lost this last fight, shamed as well as broken, the film could only have ended in his death: but he won, a fact he repeats over and over again to his wife as he lies beaten and bleeding in the gutter. Her reply: 'we both won tonight' indicates that it is a new life, and not death, that awaits them. Her wish has come true - that he quit the fight game - and he is now able to accede to that wish, not just because of his broken hand, but because his pride and integrity have now been proven beyond any doubt. This rite of passage that all boxers seem to have to endure is reminiscent of the breaking-in of wild horses to make them suitable for riding and reinforces the animal/primitivism themes that run through many boxing movies. Like wild horses, the boxers are 'tamed' and domesticated - but their spirit is somehow broken in the process. Just what kind of new life of suburban domesticity awaits Stoker and his wife is unimaginable. It is interesting that an overt masculinity, which has its visual manifestation in the boxing ring, is usually presented as a weakness - something to be overcome rather than celebrated. Joyce Carol Oates, in her impassioned treatise *On Boxing* believes that boxing is 'a celebration of the lost religion of masculinity all the more trenchant for its being lost'.[19] She is writing from a 1980s perspective, when definitions of what constitutes male masculinity were being called into question, but interestingly her comment could easily be applied to the boxing films of the 1940s, which seem to share this poignant sense of a 'lost religion'.

Bodily display

In Hollywood movies, women are traditionally thought of as the object of the audience's gaze, but with boxing films, where the masculine body is overtly on display - active, muscular, half-naked - in a way it is rarely shown in other genres, it can be argued that it is the boxer himself who is the recipient of the gaze (something which has implications for sexuality, the 'object' usually being sexualised). Richard Dyer points out that semi-nakedness in non-boxing movies of this period (governed as they were by the Production Code) was usually only possible when motivated by the plot or when dealing with 'natives' - Paul Robeson in *Sanders of the River* (1935) appears with naked torso because he is a tribesman and, of course, he is black, thus making his nakedness more 'acceptable'; Johnny Weissmuller in the Tarzan films wears only a loincloth, but this is excused by his classification as a 'primitive'.[20] In the boxing genre, the principal male characters appear half-naked throughout much of the movie, whether training at the outdoor camp, waiting in the dressing-room or fighting in the ring. Their bodies are their living, and the camera is always there to record every movement, every change, sometimes to the extent of fetishisation, as happens with Kirk Douglas' body in *Champion*, or with Errol Flynn's body in *Gentleman Jim*. As David Davis says, in a survey of boxing-film history on the Moviemaker website: 'actors line up to play boxers primarily because it gives them yet another excuse to go to the gym, work-out and preen'.[21] Right from the beginning of *Gentleman Jim*, it is clear that it is Flynn's body that is the focus of the gaze, not that of his female co-star Alexis Smith, who remains cloaked in Victorian flounces and frills while Flynn's body is gradually and titillatingly stripped of its clothing. Flynn begins by sparring in his bank clerk's suit at the Olympic Club, works out in long leggings and vest, then fights bare-chested and even, at one point in an illegal dockside match, falls into the water,

Errol Flynn's body is sexualised and made the object of the gaze in
Gentleman Jim *(1942)*

climbing out soaking wet to resume the fight, in a scene which is clearly designed to call attention to, and sexualise, his body. In *Champion*, there are many low-angle shots of Kirk Douglas' body in the ring, leaning against the ropes, as he awaits the beginning of his fights, and in scenes at his country training camp.

In many boxing films, it seems that the studios were caught between overt sexualisation of the boxer's body and working to *de*sexualise it. They did this in two main ways, the first being what could be called distraction or deflection techniques, constantly cutting away from fight-scenes to show comic reaction-shots of the crowd. This might be understandable in comedy boxing films such as *Palooka*, or *Ringside Maisie*, but it is done even in dark melodrama. In *They Made Me a Criminal*, for example, the climax is the fight between Johnnie Bradfield and Gaspar Rutchek. This is a crucial fight, not just because Bradfield wants to win, but because he is

Constant cut-aways to the crowd during a fight serve to limit the level of brutality shown on screen, but also deflect from the erotic spectacle of half-naked men in the ring. The cutaways are often used for comic effect, as in this shot from
They Made Me a Criminal (1939)

on the run, wanted for murder, and at the ringside is the policeman who has been tailing him, convinced he's the fugitive. All he really knows about Bradfield is that he's a southpaw - a left-handed boxer - and much of the tension of the fight comes from the fact that, in order not to be identified, Bradfield is fighting right-handed - and taking a beating. Despite the darkness of the mood, the scene has constant cutaways from the action to show the Dead End Kids in the stadium audience, feinting with their fists in imitation of what's happening in the ring, and a punching Grandma Rafferty knocking off the hat of the man seated in front of her - shown not once but again and again. Arguably the purpose of these cutaways might be to limit the level of brutality shown on screen - but perhaps there is also a nervousness on the part of the studios to any sustained images of the half-naked fighters.

The second way of desexualising the body was through seeking to neutralise its erotic power. This was sometimes done by feminising the fighter; sometimes by constructing him as a wild animal - a primitive creature - and sometimes by portraying him as childlike, his bodily urges something that 'cannot be helped'.

An example of feminisation is the lead character in *Golden Boy*, in which Italian-American Joe Bonaparte has to choose between boxing and playing the violin for a living - between brute masculinity and a sensitive femininity. which the dialogue of the film makes explicit as being a choice between the values of the jungle (the body), and the values of the nuclear family (the soul). In some of the shots where the son agonises about this choice, the nuclear family is present not just in the figure of his father, but in the presence of an image of the Blessed Virgin Mary, part of the Holy Family, on the wall behind them. Leger Grindon, who has written extensively about the boxing genre, says: 'In order to cultivate his soul, the boxer must take on attributes associated with the female'[22] and, in the case of *Golden Boy*, that is exactly what he eventually does. These attributes help prevent Joe's body being too uncomfortably the object of the sexual gaze. The musician/boxer dichotomy was, incidentally, also later used in other films including *The Joe Louis Story*, *Here Comes Mr Jordan*, *Kid Nightingale* and, with a slight twist, in *City For Conquest*.

Fighters are often compared, visually or in the dialogue, to animals, something that makes them somehow not responsible for their sexuality, and therefore less threatening. They are 'primitives' (a bit like the 'natives' mentioned earlier) and as such their sexuality is shown to be just a basic urge that will be 'trained out of them' once they 'evolve'. In *The Set-Up* (1949), the rather sinister manager, Mr Roberts, says 'I like fighters better than horses', thus categorising both as dumb animals; and in *Kid Monk Baroni*, Hellman tells the trainer not to 'overfeed' Baroni, as if he is a kept animal.

Fighters are also portrayed as having a childlike quality, something that is emphasised again and again to defuse and rationalise their greedy desires for money, sex, drink, food and expensive clothes. Boxers (their names often include the word 'Kid' such as Kid Nightingale, Kid Galahad, The Miracle Kid, The Pittsburgh Kid, Kid Dynamite, Kid Monk Baroni), are also shown to be simple-minded and docile: in *Palooka* (1936), as Joe Palooka comes round from a knockout punch, he calls out for his mother. When Charley Davis hits the big-time in *Body and Soul* (1947) he expresses childish joy at the luxuries of his new world, parading in front of the mirror in his new overcoat, and - in a scene reminiscent of Tony Camonte bouncing on the bed in *Scarface* (1932) - expressing a delight at the built-in bar in his apartment. More often, it is the boxer's manager who confers the status: in *The Harder They Fall*, one of the managers remarks that his fighter 'couldn't even go out and buy a pair of shoes without me'; and in the only boxing-related sequence in noir melodrama *I Wake Up Screaming* (1942), promoter Frankie Christopher (Victor Mature) says fondly of his fighter 'I raised him from a little pup,' thus neatly conflating the concept of fighter-as-child with allusions to fighter-as-animal, a notion that is made explicit in the King Kong-analogies that form an intrinsic part of Toro Moreno in *The Harder They Fall*.

Many fight films include scenes in the dressing-room - indeed, some films, including *The Set-Up* and *The Square Ring,* barely emerge from the dressing room at all - where fighters lie prone on the couch, clad just in their shorts, and have their bodies massaged. Their passive position has the potential to objectify their bodies, but the nature of the 'handler' (the name of this role is significant because it harks back to the animal analogy) - mitigates any possible homoerotic qualities the scene might have. The boxers have become like children, having their wounds tended by a parent-figure, like Danny Felton (Jack Warner) in the 1953 film *The Square Ring*.

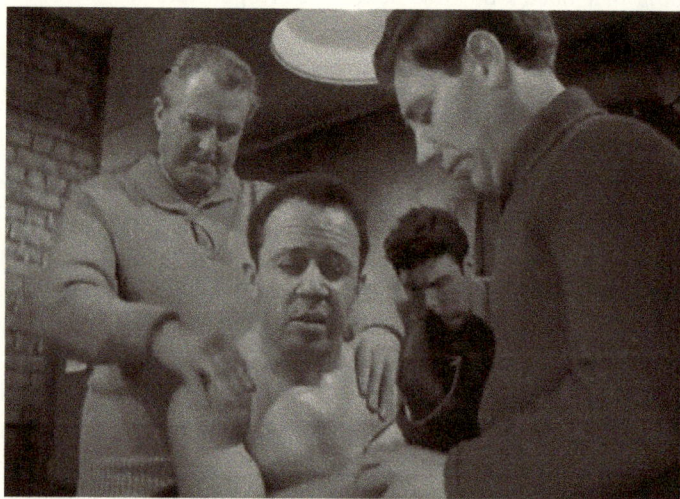

Danny (Jack Warner), the 'handler', takes on a non-threatening parental role as he tends to the boxers' bodies in The Square Ring *(1953)*

Intimate touching of the boxers' bodies, therefore, has become neutralised.

The gaze need not always be sexual: it can be for laughs instead, as the weedy bodies of Harold Lloyd in *The Milky Way*, George Formby in *Keep Fit* (1937) and Charlie Chaplin in *City Lights* (1931) demonstrate. *City Lights* is not a boxing film, but does contain a boxing sequence which, as well as being the funniest scene in the film, has spawned many imitators. It is also represents a useful link between the days of silent cinema, where boxing films grew up, and the talkies, where they came of age. Sound had been introduced in 1928, but Chaplin held out against the tide, believing that talkies were a passing fad - and championing the superiority of the silent screen.

In *City Lights*, the Little Tramp (Charlie Chaplin) falls in love with a blind flower girl. She thinks he's rich and will pay for an operation to cure her blindness, but the Little Tramp hasn't got a cent. Among other adventures to earn some 'easy money', the Tramp enters the boxing ring for a challenge match. He sits in the dressing room, pale, thin and half-naked, wearing shorts, boxing gloves - and his bowler hat, which is not taken off him until he enters the ring (the character of Happy in *The Square Ring* was to use the same device, wearing his flat cap until the very last moment, and Harold Lloyd kept on his trademark spectacles throughout his fights as Burleigh Sullivan in *The Milky Way* (1936)). The Tramp has no real worries because his fight is fixed, the money being split 50/50 with his opponent, who has promised not to punch too hard - corruption here seen as beneficial to all parties. But the plans go awry when the Tramp's opponent flees town after receiving a telegram telling him that he is wanted by the police. At the last moment, the Tramp is matched with another fighter, a real bruiser who insists on 'winner takes all'. Watching a boxer go through a 'lucky' prefight routine that involves kissing a rabbit's foot and making signs in the air with a horseshoe, the Tramp does the same: just how 'lucky' the routine was can be judged from the fact that the boxer is carried unconscious back into the dressing room just moments after he left it. Now there's no escape; the Tramp enters the ring and begins the perfect comic boxing match, contriving to place the referee between him and his opponent at all times, only emerging from time to time to land a quick blow. By Round Two, both boxers are walloping the referee instead of each other and several times the referee has to point the opponent back towards the Tramp. Without the protection of the referee, real fighting ensues; the Tramp windmilling his fists at great speed and both boxers are knocked out, getting up alternately at the count. Eventually, the Tramp is defeated and carried back out to the dressing room. The sequence ends as he lies unconscious on the couch, his gloves hung on a hook above his head. As he wakes up, one of the gloves falls off the hook, knocking him out once more. The fight is the point at which Chaplin's use of mime and body-language demonstrate the eloquence of silent cinema, with the Tramp twisting and turning in coy, nerve-wracked, effeminate gestures, the very opposite of the manly types who share the dressing room with him (and cast some dubious glances his way).

The very opposite of the sexualisation of the boxer's body: Charlie Chaplin is coy and effeminate in City Lights *(1931)*

Yet sexualisation seems to be the norm: when Mrs Frost, the femme fatale in *There Ain't No Justice* (1939), sees Tommy Mutch in the ring she actually licks her lips. But from an audience point of view, who is actually doing the 'looking'? Contemporary reviewers almost always categorised boxing movies of this period as being for men (thinking perhaps of the 'action scenes') and frequently made a point of citing the love story as being the element that would appeal to the women. Posters and lobby-cards similarly separated out the action-scenes from the love-interest. This supposes that the display of the male body was either not an element deemed to appeal to women, or - more plausibly - that such an appeal could not be spoken about. Miriam Hansen, writing about early boxing films, believes the latter is true, with the films affording women 'the forbidden sight of male bodies in semi-nudity, engaged in intimate and intense physical action'.[23] In other words, boxing action legitimises the way the male body becomes the object of the gaze. In Polly Card's view (in an unpublished study of the reception of early boxing films), such display is clearly a source of erotic pleasure.[24] But what about the reaction of the male members of the audience to this display of the body? Again, it is the action itself which displaces or counteracts any potential sexual appeal. The fight is something which Joyce Carol Oates calls 'the obverse of the feminine, the denial of the feminine-in-man,' but she acknowledges that this 'feminine-in-man' is something 'that has its ambiguous attractions for all men'.[25]

Sometimes the boxer's feminine side is allowed to show through, softening his hard-man image and constituting perhaps a less threatening masculinity. Music is often used to symbolise the feminine side of the fighter's character: in *Here Comes Mr Jordan* (1941) the hero is a saxophonist, in *Kid Nightingale*, an opera singer and in *City For Conquest* Danny Kenny fights to raise money for his musician brother. *Golden Boy* is constructed as a battle between the masculine and feminine sides of the hero's nature, boxing (the masculine) being associated with aggression and corruption; and musicianship (the feminine) being associated with sensitivity and family values. That they might co-exist is a concept that the film quickly dismisses: it is clearly stated that a man has to choose. Needless to say, the violin - together with its implied values - eventually wins out over the fight game.

The big fight

In many of the films discussed in this book, the boxing action - although crucial to the plot development and to understanding the character of the

21

boxer himself - is dealt with in a surprisingly perfunctory manner. Apart from a few token knockout punches, or a scene at the open-air training camp, it is often the climax of the film before any sustained fighting is shown. Certainly this technique helps build suspense, but the lack of boxing action until late in the film also reveals the filmmaker's intentions: to win hearts and minds, a boxing film has to be about more just boxing, with the events outside the ring bearing what Joan Dean calls 'some emblematic relationship' to the fight itself. Cultural critics go further, she says, 'reading' the fights symbolically as battles between 'good and evil, brutality and dignity, black and white, instinct and intelligence, body and soul.' Dean obviously has some sympathy with these views: without this perspective, she says, boxing movies would simply be about 'watching some guy bite off another guy's ear'.[26] Then again, perhaps that is the whole point. Even the most poetic of writers on boxing, Joyce Carol Oates, believes that 'boxing really isn't metaphor, it is the thing itself'.[27]

Perhaps this concept is too bald, too prosaic, for the filmmaker, who seems constantly to be striving for the perfect poetic touch that will lift the fight into another realm. Usually this touch is perceived to lie not in the fighting itself, but in looking away to the ritual that surrounds it - from the referee's call for a fair match, to the clocking-up of the round-numbers on the board: anything rather than a continued focus on the action. The ringside crowd, for example, is usually given equal 'weight' in terms of screen-time. The mood of this crowd (by the climax-fight, usually rapacious and baying for blood) helps to set the emotional tone of the fighting. Early in the film, they can be cheerful and light-hearted, echoing the easy victories of the rising boxing-star: by the championship match, their mood is always darker, reflecting the more visceral nature of the fighting which is inevitably tinged with a determination or doggedness that is missing from earlier bouts. The animalistic nature of the crowd is sometimes emphasised through extreme close-ups of their shouting mouths, which seem ready to devour the boxers themselves. 'The human animal has not changed much from the days of the Roman arena,' said the *New York Times* after viewing *The Set-Up*. 'The squared ring is an area where blood is expected to be spilled and when it is not the crowd yells its displeasure'.[28] It is in the championship fight, too, that the camera at last shrugs off the distancing-aspect of the ropes that surround the ring, usually moving from midshot to close-up as the camera enters the ring itself to move more fluidly, following every punch and telegraphing every moment of pain. Although cinematographers such as James Wong Howe are often credited with innovation in filming fights - Howe wore roller-skates to achieve this fluidity and realism in *Body and Soul* - getting in close to the action was said to be Mushy Callahan's suggestion. In 1933 the ex-fighter told Jack Warner, head of Warner Brothers studio, that prize fights on screen looked unrealistic, because the distant camera only picked up roundhouse swings of the 'rusty gate' variety. If the camera moved in, it could photograph 'left jabs, right crosses, hooks and chops and upper cuts'.[29] Warner took Callahan's advice.

In Body and Soul *(1947), director of photography James Wong Howe got close to the action, shrugging off the distancing effect of shooting from outside the ropes*

Low angles emphasise the snapping-back of the boxers' heads with every blow, sweat spraying into the lights above, the darkness of the stadium outlining their pale bodies in the too-brilliant whiteness of the lights. Point-of-view shots enable the film's viewer to seem (safely) on the receiving end of the punches. There is almost a relish in the way the camera shows the suffering of the fighters, as Kasia Boddy points out, 'like the attention given by Renaissance artists to the crucified Christ'.[30] Sound plays an important part too, not just in the cries of the crowd but in the sickening sound of fists making contact. As if this might be too much for the film audience to bear (and, indeed, in sustained sequences such as the fight in *The Set-Up*, it is), extensive use is made of cutaways - to the reactions of the crowd, to the fighter's family listening on the radio at home, to the fighters and handlers waiting in the dressing-room, and to other distancing mechanisms such as the ringside commentators delivering their radio broadcasts. In some films, this technique is highly successful (for example, illustrating the difference in reaction between the 'good woman' and the gold-digger to the fighting) - in others, it serves as a distraction (particularly with comic cutaways during a particularly tense and serious fight).

It is in the shots of the crowd that we can see the true appeal of the fight game. The crowd is a far cry from the amusing scene in *Gentleman Jim*, where Jim Corbett fights an exhibition match at the Olympic Club in front of an audience of crinolined ladies, applauding each round with white-gloved hands. The crowd are there to watch winners because they themselves are losers and they derive a vicarious heroism through the spectacle of the match. William Hazlitt's 1822 essay 'The Fight' spells out the allure in a description whose culminating phrase contains no irony:

> to see two men smashed to the ground, smeared with gore, stunned, senseless, the breath beaten out of their bodies; and then, before you recover from the shock, to see them rise up with new strength and courage, stand steady to inflict or receive mortal offence...this is the most astonishing thing of all: this is the high and heroic state of man![31]

The people viewing this spectacle as 'heroic' are likely to be those described by Nelson Algren in his boxing novel *Never Come Morning*. In the crowd is:

> the troubled salesman behind the sucker bet and the frayed collar, the housewife getting in secret debt to the dead-pan sheet writer beside her, the jobless youth rejected by the navy and hoping to make the army, the ex-middleweight from Fargo with a restaurant and a daughter who wouldn't wait on trade, the linotyper whose wife sat invalided on a suburban sun porch...the professional

blackjack dealer's mistress and the poolroom idler.[32]

This chilling picture of the underbelly of society, no-hopers gathered together to get their 'fix' of vicarious violence, is something that filmmakers have proved squeamish about: despite all its blood-thirsty cries, only the depiction of the crowd in *The Set-Up* comes close. Sometimes the plight of the crowd is used as a metaphor for what is happening in the ring. In *I Wake Up Screaming*, in which sports promoter Frankie Christopher (Victor Mature) is framed for a murder he did not commit, he sits high up in the stands with girlfriend Jill Lynn (Betty Grable). The only view of the boxers is a distant longshot, taken from Frankie's point of view. 'They look so little, I don't know which is which,' says Jill, drawing attention to just how small and insignificant are herself and Frankie. Like the boxers, they are pawns in a game being played for much higher stakes. In a sense, the identity of the boxers does not matter to the crowd: the fighters are, as Leger Grindon says, 'a vehicle for entertainment, strictly a commodity' and the crowd remain unmoved by their humanity.[33]

Ethnic groups

It wasn't just the crowd that came from the disenfranchised of society. The fighters themselves, usually dirt-poor, came from marginalised ethnic groups, to whom the appeal of big money and social acceptance was obvious. Promoters saw ethnic animosities as good for business, says Kasia Boddy, often pitching 'a Jewish fighter against an Irishman or an Italian fighter against either'.[34] Though the films are good at portraying the poverty of the fighters, their interpretation of ethnic status is more patchy, ranging from stereotypical representations through to performances that give little or no indication of ethnic background, the character often eclipsed by the star's familiar screen persona. In *Gentleman Jim*, for example, Jim's family are quintessentially Irish, defined through their love of fighting, drinking and religion, but the hero himself - played by Errol Flynn - exhibits none of the signs of ethnicity in accent, dress or naivety that his brothers display. Sometimes this works by implying that the second-generation immigrants have become pure American (thus in *The Ring*, Tommy distances himself from the stereotypical image of the

Mexican that his father embodies, though the 'Anglo' world still sees him as a 'dirty Mex'). In *Body and Soul*, Charley Davis is Jewish, but you would have to listen very attentively to just two lines in the dialogue to realise it; in *Somebody Up There Likes Me*, the opposite is true, with Paul Newman emphasising his character's Italian background. In literature, unlike film, 'star' personae do not influence or refract the portrayal of characters, and arguably a more historically accurate picture emerges. Nelson Algren, for example, describes entire fights where the participants are referred to only by their ethnic group: the Jew, the Pole, the Negro, the Greek referee and the young Italian announcer.[35] In the book *The Life of Jimmy Dolan*, by Bertram Millhauser and Beulah Marie Dix, the fighter, his girlfriend Goldie and his pal Jojo are all Jewish (indicated through their use of Yiddish words like goy, kike and ganef) and when Peggy first sets eyes on Jimmy, 'she sees an Ishmaelite, if ever there was one'.[36] In the film that was based on this book, *They Made Me A Criminal*, all traces of Jewishness have been eliminated, racial epithets like 'Guinney' and 'Chink' have been dropped, and the Irish, Mexican and Negro child-polio sufferers have been replaced by the Dead End Kids, who offer a non-specific racial background more identified with New York's East Side than any particular racial group. Given that, in this era, Hollywood studios were dominated by Jewish movie moguls, this elision of race is intriguing and perhaps indicates that what was acceptable on the stage, or in literature, was not acceptable - or not such good box-office - for filmgoers.

According to Nicholas Christopher, the list of boxing champions is just as revealing of the immigration patterns to the US as any government document. 'Irish fighters predominate at the turn of the century,' he says, 'then we see a sudden mixture of Italian, Polish, German and Swedish fighters, a host of Jewish champions in the 1930s, and beginning in the 1940s the large wave of African-American fighters'.[37] Hollywood may have reflected - overtly or not - this historical pattern, but had a problem when it came to the influx of black boxers. In fact, even the fight-game itself did not accept black fighters easily. When Jack Johnson became the first black heavyweight champion in 1908 (having finally overcome the informal 'bar' put up by John L Sullivan and his successors, who refused to fight 'negroes'), it triggered a spate of race riots and lynchings, according to boxing historian Harry Mullan. Twenty years went by before there was another black championship challenge: it was only after the success of Joe Louis that the boxing world acknowledged that colour would never again be a consideration.[38] The reality was much slower to be reflected by Hollywood: Joe Louis would have to wait until 1953 before his success was acknowledged in *The Joe Louis Story*. Until then, black fighters were cast only in cameo parts (such as Harlem's unnamed 'Chocolate Drop' contender in *Golden Boy* in 1939), though there was a strong supporting role for Canada Lee as Ben in *Body and Soul* in 1947. As with other genres, black actors had to turn to independent production companies if they wanted to achieve starring roles as boxers. These companies made films with an all-black cast for all-black audiences - but despite the popularity of the fight game, there were very few such movies made: two of them were *Keep Punching*, a 1939 film directed by John Clein in which boxer Henry Jackson (Henry Armstrong, who had won featherweight, lightweight and welterweight titles the year before this film) is betrayed by an old school friend who arranges to have his drink spiked the day before his championship bid; and the 1940 Oscar Micheaux film *The Notorious Elinor Lee*. Micheaux's main career was in the silent era and his was the only black filmmaking company to survive the Great Depression. 'Even if he was not a winner,' says G William Jones, 'he was always a contender'.[39] *The Notorious Elinor Lee* is the story of heavyweight contender Benny Blue (Robert Earl Jones), whose contract is sold to Elinor Lee (Gladys Williams), a wealthy but corrupt woman who teams up with another crook to fix Benny's fights. The film may now be forgotten but it had a high-profile premiere in Harlem 'complete with gold-engraved invitations, floodlights, a carpeted sidewalk' and a well-known black aviator, Col Hubert Julian, as master of ceremonies 'in formal dress, top hat, white silk gloves and a flowing cape'.[40] At least it was one way of avoiding being typecast: in *Body and Soul*, it is interesting to note that the black fighter is portrayed as the victim, dying as a result of the greed (and punches) of white men. Aaron Baker says that the black characters have something in common with the representation of women in classic Hollywood films: they are present in order for the white male to achieve self-definition through fighting. In other words, they appear as supportive helpers to the white fighter, or as obstacles that the protagonist has to overcome. He sees some shift in this attitude after World War II, possibly because of the importance of black Americans to the war-effort and to the wish to portray America as a democratic nation. Whereas in the 1939 film

27

Golden Boy, the Chocolate Drop has no speaking part and appears only briefly, in *Body and Soul*, Ben Chaplin plays an important role that places him at the moral centre of the film. Yet even by the 1950s, the time of *The Joe Louis Story* and *The Ring*, black athletes are shown to 'lack the discipline and autonomy central to the favored masculinity in most sports films,' he says. They may have the ability as fighters but are forced to 'accept the control of white mentors because of a lack of strategic skills'.[41]

Stereotype or archetype?

As we have seen, compared to other genres, boxing movies offer a fairly rigid structure of narrative, character and visual content (there are only so many ways to chart a boxer's rise/fall and to film the fight scenes), and this results in the source of viewing pleasure being concentrated on the small differences, the nuances, between each film; and on the recognition of particular stereotypes. It is often thought that stereotypes detract from the emotional draw of a film, being only 'cardboard cutouts', but in fact - as Christine Gledhill points out - they actually offer shortcuts to individualised characters who authenticate recognition. In the best boxing movies (many of which are featured in this book), these characters transcend the stereotype, distilling its qualities to create an archetype, something Gledhill describes as 'trans-individual, trans-historical, and trans-cultural: a figure whose reappearance can be used to chart relations between past and present, and between different cultures'.[42] This is an interesting point: given that the figure of the boxer is the single constant in these films, the way he is portrayed over the three decades should provide an insight into changing attitudes and a changing society. Charting any real shift, however, is not as easy as it might first appear: for a start, every writer on film seems to have a particular agenda (often coloured by the established film 'canon') that can skew an accurate reading. By examining only certain films - usually those which have been critically acclaimed - and omitting others, a partial picture emerges that is then taken for a complete one. For example, it would be easy to accept the view, expressed by Nicholas Christopher, that the boxer is the 'prototypical, existential noir hero' or by Tony Williams that 'the Boxing Hero is both a tragic and melodramatic figure' - but this interpretation ignores the fact that, throughout the 1930s, 40s and 50s, around a third of the boxing-film output was comedy (and a good deal more could be classified as light drama with not a 'noir' hero in sight).[43] Christopher's view probably derives from only half a dozen of the 130 or so boxing films made over these decades. Critical snobbishness is also a problem in achieving a balanced view of the genre: as Steve Neale points out in *Genre and Hollywood*, intellectuals, critics and reviewers have always been patronising about Hollywood films 'on the grounds that they were commercially produced, that they were aimed at a mass market, that they were ideologically or aesthetically conservative, or that they were imbued with the values of entertainment and fantasy, rather than those of realism, art or serious aesthetic stylisation'.[44] With this kind of damning indictment of mainstream Hollywood product, what chance does the genre-film have?

The concerns about entertainment and fantasy can be seen in Ronald Bergan's analysis of the boxing genre. Bergan expresses the view that too many fight films concentrate on a rags-to-riches, Cinderella-like tale that belies the reality of the fight game, where glory and riches are usually an illusion. He praises films like *The Harder They Fall* and *The Set-Up* for showing an alternative to the traditional Hollywood happy-ending tale whose only purpose, he believes, is as 'an effective sop to the have-nots to passify their discontent'.[45] Whether the films had such an overt motivation is debatable, but it is significant that the films he mentions are post-war pictures, a period when audiences were certainly less convinced by escapist, sentimental tales. This may have been a reaction to the shock of the war or, as Grindon believes, have stemmed from a more complex set of factors which included 'the crisis of the Hollywood industry brought on by the HUAC investigation and subsequent blacklist, the Paramount decrees, and the decline in profits' and resulted in boxing films with a bleaker tone'.[46] Certainly, as Thomas Cripps points out, there was a post-war trend towards 'message movies' and film noir.[47] Message movies exposed some social dysfunction and called for reform - *The Harder They Fall* might fit into this category, with journalist Eddie Willis (Humphrey Bogart), once complicit in the corruption of the sport, determined in the end to expose it - whereas the film noir, with what Cripps describes as 'unremitting despair at its core' offered a pessimistic picture of an unredeemable situation (*The Set-Up* would be an example of this category).[48] The main change Cripps identifies in postwar films, as opposed to prewar, is a focus on inner failings and inner frailty rather than on the world outside. Robert Sklar notes much the same trend, seeing threats as no longer emanating from external sources, but lying closer to home 'in the veiled malevolence of trusted intimates, in one's own innermost thoughts'.[49] This surely is the epitome of the boxer in serious drama, fighting not just his opponent, but his inner demons, able to trust no-one, for - just like the boxer himself - everyone around him is vulnerable to corruption and betrayal. It is a vision of a paranoid world which can be glimpsed in films like *Body and Soul* and *Champion*.

In 1948, one exhibitor - E A Boldus from Conway, New Hampshire, was moved to write to the trade paper *Motion Picture Herald*, complaining about this new trend. Citing *Body and Soul* as well as *Cry of the City*, *Key Largo*, *Naked City* and *Sorry Wrong Number* - all of which were released in 1948 - he said that these 'dozens of pictures with crime themes and vicious characters and stars drinking throughout the story are terrible to show to…young people as examples of the American way of life. Fellow exhibitors, let us all join in and tell Hollywood that such pictures are not entertainment for the masses. What the public wants is good wholesome stories'.[50] On the other hand, 1948 was notable for releases such as *Mr Blandings Builds His Dream House*, *Easter Parade*, *Here Come the Huggetts*, *Alias a Gentleman* and *The Three Musketeers* - plus two comedies in the *Palooka* series - all of which could be described as 'wholesome stories'.

Again, we must be wary of generalisation: message films, for example, were not always rallying cries for social reform - they could be simply a call for individuals to 'pull their socks up,' a notion prevalent in the 1950s particularly to highlight youth/delinquency problems. *Somebody Up There Likes Me* (1956), for example, is ostensibly about a young man trying to find his place in a world not of his making (the theme of many earlier boxing films), but the fact that many of his East Side friends end up in prison, and even in the electric chair, indicates that what is being debated here is not an individualised problem (Rocky Graziano's 'inner demons'), but a generational one of disaffected, alienated youth. The point is somewhat undermined, however, by the film's insistent 'message', which is not so much that we are *all* responsible for the youth of today, but that individuals can and should try to rise above their upbringing through the use of their talents. Another problem with generalisations about shifts in

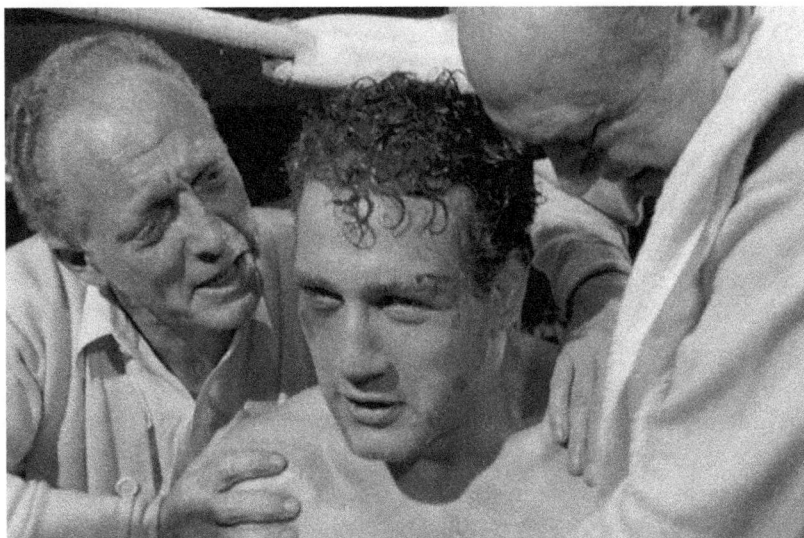

Message films were not always rallying calls for social reform. In Somebody Up There Likes Me *(1956), Rocky (Paul Newman) is shown to rise above his upbringing through the use of his talents*

attitude in 1950s boxing films is that production was much diminished compared with the 30s and 40s, with only half-a-dozen or so boxing movies made in the second half of the decade - hardly a representative sample. In fact, spotting any major trends over three decades is an uncertain process, with hard-edged, bleak dramas being interspersed with escapist comedies at every turn. Inevitably, there is also considerable overlap in style, theme and tone as one decade turns into the next: this means that the construction of separate sections for films from particular decades - which is the way this book is organised - is somewhat arbitrary. The noirish atmosphere of *The Set-Up*, for instance, released in 1949, gives it a distinctly 40s 'feel', but the style and tone of *Champion*, made the same year, has more affinity with 1950s films. The war also disrupted the viewing of many movies: *Golden Boy*, for example, was first released in 1939 and then re-released after the war in 1947. To what extent, then, can it be categorised as a 1930s movie? Audience perceptions and interpretations of the film must have changed when they saw it post-war (the decision of the 'golden boy' to put home and family before fighting would have different connotations when viewed in 1947), and this rather calls into question critics' belief that the war acted a watershed, with audiences casting off fairytale stories in favour of hard-hitting realism. The truth cannot be quite that simple, even if some of the postwar films exhibit little of what Joan Mellon calls the 'sunny optimism' notable in *Gentleman Jim*. The idea that 'the man of assured physique' can rely on success and fame had been replaced, says Mellon, by the idea that 'the athlete's physical ability only renders him vulnerable to malevolent predators'.[51] Yet this overlooks the fact that eleven Palooka comedies were made in the post-war period, along with films like *Mr Hex* (1946) and *Fighting Fools* (1949) - both Bowery Boys romps - and the Danny Kaye comedy *The Kid From Brooklyn* (1946). Discounting these films in favour of only considering darker drama as characteristic of the era distorts the overall picture and arguably does not accurately mirror the experience of cinema audiences at the time who would have viewed both A- and B-movies.

After the 1950s, the boxing genre went into a decade of hibernation, due to a combination of factors, including the prevalence of black fighters and Hollywood's reluctance to mirror this in film, and the rise of television. Although in 1962 there was a remake of *Kid Galahad* (starring Elvis Presley) and the release of *Requiem for a Heavyweight* (starring Anthony Quinn), it was not to reclaim itself as a genre until the 1970s with the emergence of the *Rocky* series.

The final word must go to *On the Waterfront*, a critically acclaimed 1954 film directed by Elia Kazan. Nominated again and again in polls of the 'best boxing movies of all time', it is not included in this book, for the simple reason that it is a crime drama about racketeering, not a boxing film. There is no boxing action shown on screen and although Terry

Malloy (Marlon Brando) is an ex-prizefighter who took a dive in his last fight, there is actually only one line of dialogue that refers to boxing, as he sits in the back of a cab with his brother Charley (Rod Steiger). Perhaps the iconic 'I could have been a contender' line has expanded in the popular imagination.

---

[1] Leger Grindon was first to identify them as a distinct genre

[2] Altman 1999 p24

[3] *Monthly Film Bulletin* Dec 6 1946 p170

[4] *Motion Picture Herald* Mar 27 1943 p1227

[5] Joe Pendleton (Robert Montgomery) is killed when his light aeroplane crashes. Mr Jordan (Claude Rains), the angel in charge of the newly dead, discovers the death is a mistake: Joe is not scheduled to die until 1991. The solution is to put Joe's soul into the body of someone about to die, firstly a rich, nasty-minded playboy who Joe transforms into a generous loving man, and then - as Joe misses boxing - into the body of KO Murdock who magically rises from the canvas after being shot in the ring for not taking a dive

[6] Lacey 2000 p133

[7] Loukides and Fuller, 1993 p185

[8] Ficarra, https://www.moviemaker.com/the-best-boxing-movies-of-all-times-3227/

[9] Shatz 1981 p15

[10] Zucker and Babich1987 p54

[11] Grindon 1996 p55

[12] Williams 2001 p305

[13] Grindon 1996 p61

[14] Christopher1997 p174

[15] Christopher 1997 p173

[16] Bergan 1982 p14

[17] Grindon 1996 p61

[18] Krutnik 1997 p95

[19] Oates 1987 p72

[20] Dyer 1992 p146

[21] www.moviemaker.com

[22] Grindon 1996 p61

[23] Hansen 1991 p1. Kasia Boddy makes much the same point: after 1920 it 'became increasingly fashionable for women to attend boxing matches … boxers were sex symbols and women were no longer coy about admitting it'. Boddy 2008 p219

[24] Polly Card, 'The Reception of Early Boxing Films', 2002 MA dissertation, University of Southampton

[25] Oates 1987 p76

[26] article no longer on internet

[27] Oates 1987 p102

[28] *New York Times* Mar 30 1949 p31

[29] Pressbook for *Kid Nightingale*

[30] Boddy 2008 p277

[31] Hazlitt 1927 p160

[32] Algren 1988 p262

[33] Grindon 2011 p20

[34] Boddy 2008 p170

[35] Algren 1988 p260

[36] Millhauser and Dix 1948 p43

[37] Christopher 1997 p174

[38] Mullan 1997

[39] Jones 1991 pp 26 and 30

[40] Sampson 1995 p166

[41] Baker 2006 p24-26 and 73

[42] Gledhill 1995 p81

[43] Christopher 1997 p175; Williams 2001 p309

[44] Neale 2000 p10

[45] Bergan 1982 p14

[46] Grindon 1996 p65

[47] Cripps 1997 p217

[48] Cripps 1997 p215

[49] Sklar 1994 p255

[50] *Motion Picture Herald* Nov 20 1948 p42

[51] Mellon 1977 p164

GOLDEN GLOVES - FILMS OF THE 1930s

RELIANCE PICTURES
presents

JIMMIE
DURANTE
LUPE
VELEZ
STUART
ERWIN

in

Palooka

BY HAM FISHER

with
MARJORIE RAMBEAU
ROBERT ARMSTRONG
MARY CARLISLE
WILLIAM CAGNEY
THELMA TODD

Directed by
BENJAMIN STOLOFF

Produced by EDWARD SMALL

Released thru
UNITED ARTISTS

The Einstein of the Squared Circle

Palooka (1934)

When Joe Palooka hit the screen in 1934, he was already a well-known figure to millions of Americans, through the comic strip by Ham Fisher which first appeared in American newspapers in April 1930. The term 'palooka', meaning an incompetent boxer, had been around even longer: it can be heard in some of the early Popeye cartoons, but Fisher imbued it with affection when he applied it to his 'gentle giant' heavyweight fighter who always seemed to be a failure. The strip appeared for more than 50 years, finally being laid to rest in 1984, and the character was to have spin-offs into radio, film, merchandise, and later television.[52] Fisher's Palooka is a tall, well-built blond-haired man with the figure of a Greek god, but he's a simple soul, and simply too nice for the fight game. In one strip, in 1938, he gets a two-dollar lesson from a veteran, Nifty Hawks: 'gee, it's swell. It's all timin' an' sorta rhythum, ain't it?' Joe says, successfully trying out a swing move. But when he learns that the old fighter has lost everything in the Wall Street Crash and has no money to buy food for his children, he is happy to pose as a 'dumb cluck', pretending that it will take him all week to learn the move and thus ensuring that the fighter gets several days' pay.[53]

The character's first screen appearance, in *Palooka*, directed by Ben Stoloff for Reliance, one of the 'poverty row' studios, is a knockabout comedy with a happy ending and some moral lessons thrown in along the way. Joe Palooka (Stuart Erwin) is the son of middleweight boxing champ Pete Palooka (Robert Armstrong), whose persistent womanising drives his wife Mayme (Marjorie Rambeau) to take baby Joe and move out to the country, away from the bad influence of his father and the temptations of

Two frames from a 1938 Palooka strip cartoon by Ham Fisher: Palooka is a simple soul, too nice for the fight game

the city. She exchanges her feather boas for modest frocks, and swaps her showbiz career for selling chicken-eggs to her rural neighbours. Twenty years on, and Joe is a good-natured farm-boy with a demure girlfriend, Anne (Mary Carlisle), who he can never quite get around to kissing. His life changes when, on the way to the railway station, he intervenes in a roadside dispute, punching what turns out to be the boxer 'Dynamite' Wilson and impressing fight-manager Knobby Walsh (Jimmy Durante) who immediately signs him up. After a series of fixed fights, Joe beats the champion, Al McSwatt (William Cagney), who is too drunk to fight properly. Joe is seduced by the money, the city and Nina (Lupe Velez), a glamorous gold-digger, and - carried away by his own hype - ill-advisedly agrees to a rematch with McSwatt. Sober, McSwatt makes mincemeat of Joe, whose boxing career is over in Round Eight, and he returns to his mother, the countryside and his childhood sweetheart.

Throughout the film, the darker side of boxing (fixed fights, gangsters and double-crossing managers) is present, but is dealt with relatively lightly and never impinges on the certainty that everything is going to turn out well for Joe. This light touch belies the film's somewhat difficult birth: according to the *American Film Institute Catalog*, the script was problematic, with many writers being called to work and rework it (five writers are named in the credits), and the appointment of two directors - Alfred Werker and William Beaudine - was announced before production finally went ahead with Ben Stoloff.[54] Beaudine would have been an interesting choice. Known as 'one-shot Beaudine' because of his ability to

38

turn out films quickly and cheaply, he directed more than 350 films in his career across a wide variety of genres, including a number of the Bowery Boys movies. He did not specialise in comedy, but then neither did Alfred Werker, whose output was largely unremarkable (though he did direct *The Adventures of Sherlock Holmes* for Twentieth Century-Fox in 1939). Stoloff began in comedy shorts for the Fox Film Company, but by the time he was offered *Palooka* he was specialising in westerns, directing Tom Mix and Buck Jones: the year before *Palooka* went into production, he worked on *Destry Rides Again*. The final directing/scriptwriting combination produced a film whose popular success can be judged from the fact that it spawned a series of nine 'shorts' from Vitaphone, eleven B-movies from Monogram, and then 25 TV shows. *Palooka* is one of many run-of-the-mill Hollywood films which seem to have been disregarded by film historians: it has received no critical comment or serious examination despite its role in spawning a long-running series.[55] This is partly due perhaps to its B-movie status: at 86 minutes running-time, it would have been shown as the 'second feature' on a double-bill, and one which exhibitors paid a flat fee to rent, rather than a share of the box-office. B-movies were usually made quickly and cheaply, had lower production values than prestige pictures, and often featured little-known stars, though clearly Jimmy Durante's presence in *Palooka* would have been a box-office draw. The film did achieve good reviews on its release - the trade paper *Variety* praised the number of laughs and said that, in this respect, 'Palooka is the nearest approach to a Marx Bros. picture that's been around'.[56] The British fan magazine *Picturegoer* was less enthusiastic, praising its 'boisterously amusing' qualities but noting that it 'deals in caricatures rather than real character values'.[57]

The star of the film is ostensibly Stuart Erwin as Joe Palooka, a plump, fresh-faced young man who exudes innocence. Erwin had a prolific film career which began at the birth of the talkies in 1928: he appeared in nearly 70 films in the 1930s alone, and in 1955 switched to television where the Stu Erwin show ran for 129 episodes. In *Palooka*, however, he is really just a stooge for Jimmy Durante who, as boxing manager Knobby Walsh, spends the entire film in a frenzy of gesticulation, malapropism and wise-cracking. His performance turns what would otherwise be an unremarkable but charming film into a screwball comedy. Durante was a well-established film actor, appearing in 16 films before *Palooka* (from

1921 on), but this was his first big break into mainstream Hollywood comedy. He had built a reputation as Hollywood's 'No 1 pinch-hitter and flop-picture saver,' according to *Variety*: 'It got to be that any time a picture looked about dead in the sixth reel, in walked Durante, who always reached first base'.[58] This time, Durante was in the picture from the start, and it clearly paid off: as Frederick Romano points out in his *Boxing Filmography*, 'it was Durante and not the boxing vignettes that [was] the picture's intended showpiece.'[59] This is reflected in the fact that the film was released under the title *The Great Schnozzle* for the UK market: one of the posters features Durante at its centre, holding all the other characters in his arms, thus positioning him unequivocally as the star. Any reference to boxing is completely absent from the poster: instead, under the strapline 'Come on! Schnozzle's the screen's new perfect lover, with a heart as big as his nose', the copy emphasises romance and comedy. 'Wow!' it says. 'It's a landslide of howls as Durante inka-dinka-doo's his way into every woman's heart'.[60] In the pressbook, a publicity handbook issued by the studio and designed to provide cinema managers with promotional material, 13 different catchlines for the film are suggested: every single one mentions Durante and almost all make jokes about his nose, but not one of them mentions boxing. The leading man does not even get a look-in, though the pressbook does see some editorial potential in the presence of James Cagney's brother, William, in a supporting role, as high-living boxer Al McSwatt.[61]

It is, perhaps, just as well that the publicity did not promote *Palooka* as a boxing film, as the three fight scenes are brief, and rely heavily on long-distance stock-footage of boxing-arenas (using stock-footage - re-using existing footage that had been shot for another film or, perhaps, a newsreel - was a good way of making a tight budget go further), intercut with conventionally filmed midshots of the fighters, and many cut-aways to the crowd, the commentators and the family listening at home on the radio. The only dynamic quality comes from the fact that the fight scenes are speeded up to give them more impact.

Palooka is a film that offers an unambiguous moral: the city - all 'gasoline and carbon monoxide fumes' as Joe excitedly describes it - is a bad and corrupting influence, whereas the country is good, innocent and protecting. This moral is one which - though not so loudly proclaimed - is present in many boxing films of the classic Hollywood era including *Kid*

Galahad (1937), *They Made Me a Criminal* (1939), *The Pittsburgh Kid* (1941) and *Body and Soul* (1947). The moral polarities of the country and the city are paralleled in *Palooka*'s female characters: sophisticated city-girl Nina, whose preferred milieu is the nightclub, is a fickle gold-digger or (as Joe Palooka's mother succinctly puts it) 'a little tramp', her corrupting influence being underlined by the fact she is 'foreign', whereas country-girl Anne, with the ribbon she wears in her simply-styled hair, her Puritan collars and neatly tailored suits and her attachment to Joe's mother, is loyal and undemanding.

We learn Joe Palooka's heritage right at the beginning of the film, when Joe is just a baby: his mother Mayme is a tough-talking showgirl, leader of the American Beauty Chorus, and his unreliable and absentee father, 'Goodtime' Pete, is a boxer about to secure the middleweight championship.[62] In this first fight scene, the camera stays back in the second row of spectators, filming the fight from their point of view, with the action visible through the ropes. It is a short sequence which ends with Pete knocking out his opponent. Rounds in the ring are followed by rounds of drinks with glamorous blondes, one of whom his wife socks pleasurably in the eye, before she announces that she is leaving Pete. The film then skips to 20 years later: we find Mayme has retired to the country - along with her black housekeeper, Crystal (Louise Beavers) - to run a farm, though she still retains plenty of in-your-face city-attitude, berating one of her customers who is complaining about the size of the eggs ('what were you expecting - eggs the size of watermelons?'). Joe, meek and naïve, is obviously destined to spend his life on the farm, marrying his sweetheart Anne - the 'nice girl with nothing much to do', as *Variety* described her character. When Joe is signed up as a fighter, Knobby declares 'I'll make you the Einstein of the squared circle,' having evidently misinterpreted Joe's level of intelligence (which is plain enough to the audience). This is the way that many film fighters get signed up: singing waiter Steve Nelson in *Kid Nightingale* (1939) is spotted as a potential boxer when he socks a troublesome customer on the jaw; milkman Burleigh Sullivan is mistakenly thought to have knocked out a prize-fighter in a scuffle in *The Milky Way* (1936) and farmboy-turned-bellhop Ward Guisenberry floors a professional fighter in defence of Fluff in *Kid Galahad* (1937).

We do not see Joe's first fight, the camera staying in the dressing room to allow it to focus on a monologue from Knobby, who hears the shouts of the crowd and believes that his 'Einstein' must be winning. Joe is carried to the dressing-room unconscious. When he comes round, he calls out for his mother, emphasising his simple country background, and explains that his opponent had asked him to go easy on him out of consideration for his wife and kids. Knobby, undeterred by Joe's performance, sets up a fight against the champion, Al McSwatt, an arrogant night-clubbing boozer, because McSwatt's manager is looking for a 'sure thing'. Joe is a laughing-stock before the fight even gets underway, getting his boxing-gloves tangled in the sleeves of his tartan dressing-gown. Against McSwatt's compact, muscular physique, Joe's body looks pale and flabby. The fight, mostly shown in low-angle shots, is interrupted by cutaways to the ringside and to Mayme at the farm, sitting with Anne and Crystal, the unsophisticated nature of the latter two being shown by the way they talk back to the radio, with Anne saying 'hello Joe' into the loudspeaker as Joe gives a post-match interview. Joe wins the fight by delivering a series of blows to McSwatt's booze-filled stomach, knocking him down and taking the champion's title. At the ringside, watching the contest (and yelling 'kill him, baby, kill him!') is McSwatt's girlfriend, a figure familiar from almost all boxing movies: the glamorous, exotic, hard-hearted temptress with an infallible instinct for following the money - always a carefully drawn contrast in dress, make-up and manner with the down-home girl that the champ has left behind. In an instant, as soon as McSwatt is floored, Nina Madero smiles and pats her hair, ready to set her sights on the new champion. Nina is played by Lupe Velez, a Mexican singer and dancer who found her niche playing in comedies, notably opposite Laurel and Hardy in *Hollywood Party*, released the same year as *Palooka*, but is probably now best remembered for her tempestuous but brief marriage to Johnny Weissmuller, star of the Tarzan films.

Joe's innocence can prevail only a little longer, but it's highly enjoyable while it does: after he watches Nina's song-and-dance performance at the Paradise Club, for which she wears a dress split to the waist at both back and front, he is lured back to her lavish apartment, which is funded by McSwatt. Her attempted seduction fails and he confesses that what he desires most is a cheese sandwich. By the next scene, however, Joe is hooked, appearing in a swell's costume, carrying Nina's pet pooch, and with Nina, dressed in furs, on his arm. They are posing for advertisements in an early form of celebrity endorsement: first

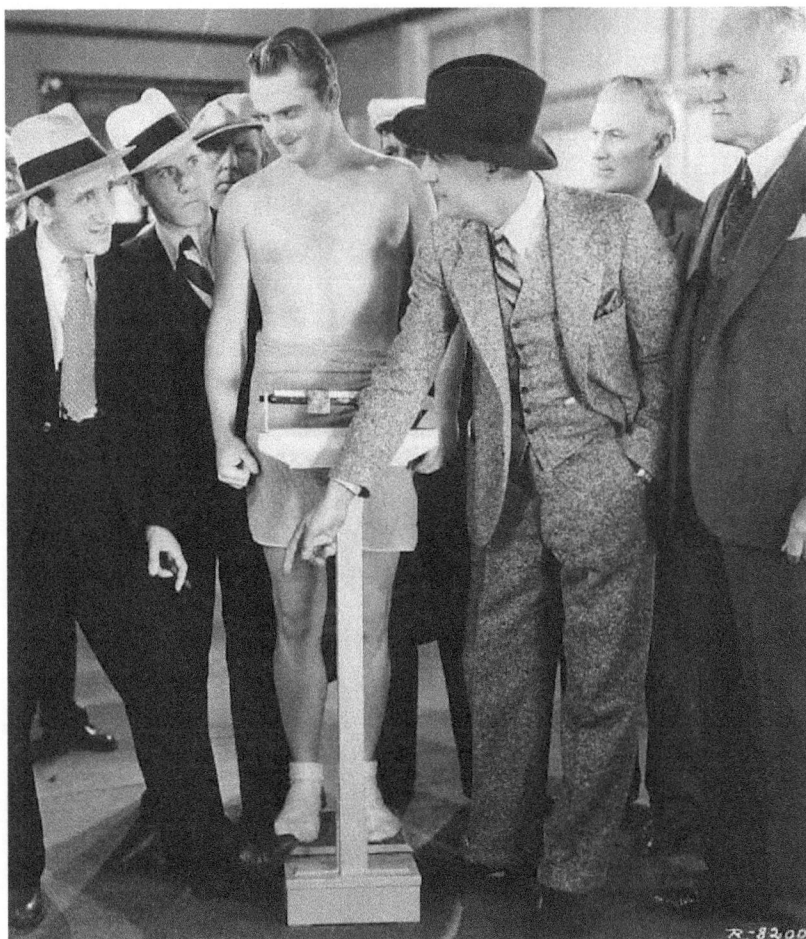

The star of Palooka *was not Stuart Erwin, who played the title role, but Jimmy Durante (pictured left, fixing the weigh-in, with William Cagney as champion fighter McSwatt on the scales): in the UK the film was released as* The Great Schnozzle

he is seen in a passionate embrace with Nina to advertise 'Doctor Gray's Gargle' and then swinging a golf club clad only in his underwear. Joe has now become a man of fashion, with a doting French butler, Alfonse, and a visiting manicurist who offers to give him more than a manicure if he invites her back later.

Joe's subsequent fights are not shown on screen - just the newspaper headlines marking his victories all around the country, match-results that Knobby has engineered by paying a bunch of 'mugs' to take a dive. Joe is more interested in champagne and jewels than fighting, and even Knobby is known to partake of a bottle of champagne or ten - the trigger for the centrepiece of the film, when a drunken Knobby, thrown out of the Paradise Club, breaks the plate-glass window of The Song Shop in order to play the piano that is on display in the window. Durante sings his own composition, *Inka-Dinka-Doo* (a song that would become his theme-tune for the rest of his life), and his clowning, now ostensibly 'on stage', seems set in its rightful context.

Mayme may have moved to the country, but has not lost her street-smarts. 'Don't small-town me,' she says when Knobby implies she is a country girl, and she is equally forthright with Nina, warning her that she's 'on to all the tricks'.

In a drunken moment, Joe accepts McSwatt's challenge of a rematch, and enlists his long-absent father, Pete, to help him get ready, unwilling to believe what Knobby has told him: that all his previous fights have been fixed. The Cagney family connection is amusingly exploited at the photo-shoot before the fight: McSwatt taunts Joe and they are about to trade ugly punches. 'You dirty....' says Joe, but is interrupted by the photographer asking them to pose. They turn to the camera and smile ingratiatingly while the flash goes off. '....rat,' continues Joe, swinging his fist at McSwatt.

The 'big fight' is the only sustained footage of boxing in the whole film. Romano is critical of the film's boxing sequences, calling them 'sub-par and over-reliant on stock footage of crowd scenes'.[63] Certainly the establishing shots, of the exterior of Madison Square Gardens, and the long-distance shot of the packed interior of the stadium, are stock-footage, but at least we see more of the action in this fight, even if the filming style is conventional and the punches look to be without any weight behind them. Joe floors McSwatt in Round One, when McSwatt goads him, and the challenger is only saved by the bell. After cutaways to typewriters, ticker tape and wire machines sending match reports, there is a sign for Round Four. This is a sustained sequence, with an authentic-looking punch by McSwatt as he floors a bloodied Joe. Round Five is not shown - instead we just see the numbers flicking through 6, 7 and 8 in sequence. When the camera returns to the action in the ring, it stays behind McSwatt as he delivers bruising punches, until the towel is thrown in. Joe's boxing career comes to an end, though ironically, he actually does knock out McSwatt - in the dressing-room after the match.

Joe returns to his sweetheart Anne and to his mother's farm (now with a sign proclaiming it to be the 'Palooka Inn' featuring 'Southern Cooking' and now with errant father Pete back in residence), where he receives a huge wad of money sent by Knobby. An honest manager? Well, not entirely. Before the fight, Knobby told Blackie, a notorious gangster, to put all his money on Joe, but put his own shirt on McSwatt: he has to skip town to avoid Blackie, but does the right thing by Joe.

It's the perfect circle, even if Joe is not quite Einstein: he has learnt his lesson and is back where he belongs, in the protectiveness and innocence of the countryside. In a neat end-piece, Knobby visits Joe and Anne at the farm, revealing that he is now McSwatt's manager and that Nina (once more wisely following the money), is now Knobby's wife. The final shot is of their baby, bundled up in Nina's arms. It has Durante's face.

In 1936 and 1937, Vitaphone issued nine Palooka shorts, directed by Lloyd French, but it was 13 years before a major follow-up series was produced, by which time Hal Fisher's comic strip was America's most popular, reaching an audience of 40 million every week. The character was not entirely absent from the screen during these years: in 1943 *Palooka* had a theatrical re-release (cut to 65 minutes), but was clearly showing its age. *Kine Weekly* thought its humour and sentiment to be, like the costume of the women characters, 'a little old-fashioned' but advised exhibitors that they thought it was still good for 'an occasional tear and laugh in family and industrial company'.[64] When Monogram - known for their B-movie series, which included the East Side Kids and Charlie Chan - decided to take on Palooka, it launched a nationwide talent search, with 20,000 hopefuls applying to play the hapless but lovable lead. The contest was won by golfer and former amateur boxer Joe Kirkwood, who played throughout the entire run, beginning with *Joe Palooka, Champ* in 1946 through to *Joe Palooka in Triple Cross* in 1951, and then on television for a further 25 episodes in 1954-1955. Despite all this popular exposure, the Palooka name is probably best remembered as a line in *On the Waterfront* (1954) when Terry Malloy (Marlon Brando) tells his brother Charlie (Rod Steiger) that taking a dive in a fight had been a 'one-way ticket to Palookaville'.

The Lion and the Mouse
The Milky Way (1936)

Given the potential for visual gags offered by the fight film, it was not surprising that it attracted the top three comedians of the silent era - Buster Keaton, Charlie Chaplin and Harold Lloyd. But only Lloyd was to make a boxing talkie: *The Milky Way*, released in 1936, stars the comedian as a meek-and-mild milkman ('he could whip his weight in cream!' reads the poster) who embarks accidentally on a boxing career and becomes middleweight champion of the world.[65] It was one of Harold Lloyd's last pictures - he retired in 1938 - and unfortunately serves to highlight just how good he was in silent films - and how curiously charmless he was revealed to be in talkies. This might be more a problem of the age, rather than the medium. As Andrew Sarris writes in his book *You Ain't Heard Nothing Yet*, Lloyd 'seems not to have transcended his own time as the pushy go-getter of the Jazz Age.' Sarris softened his opinion of Lloyd over the years, feeling it unfair to bracket him with Keaton and Chaplin because Lloyd, he thought, belonged more in mainstream comedy. However he still clearly felt that Lloyd had outstayed his welcome, noting that his antics were viewed as somewhat baffling by Thirties audiences.[66]

Although supporting characters - particularly Veree Teasdale as the feisty Ann Westley - are given some sharp one-liners, most of Lloyd's own jokes in *The Milky Way* are rooted in slapstick or farce: this could easily have been made as a silent film, and might have gained something in the process. Despite co-writer Frank Butler's insistence that the days of 'comedy business for comedy's sake' in film were on the way out, and that what audiences wanted was for a 'gag (to) progress the story', this intent did not seem to translate onto the screen. 'The funniest material', said

Butler, 'consists of incidents that can and do happen to all of us', yet the high-comedy moments in *The Milky Way* run the gamut of unlikely situations, from trying to fit a horse into the back seat of a taxi, to floating down from a train-carriage roof using an umbrella as a parachute.[67]

Harold Lloyd in a publicity still for The Milky Way. *A giant cut-out of him in his Sunflower Dairies uniform was used in Woolworth stores, which sold Milky Way Cocktails as part of a film tie-in*

From a critical point of view, the film has been somewhat overshadowed by its remake, *The Kid From Brooklyn*, released in 1946 and starring Danny Kaye.[68] Kaye was on the upward swing of his career - he was to make *The Secret Life of Walter Mitty* the following year - and was perhaps therefore more newsworthy than a silent comedian who was perceived to have had his day. *The Milky Way* was reviewed favourably in the press at the time, however, with *Film Weekly* calling it a 'slick piece of comedy entertainment' whose fight-sequence ('one of the funniest screen battles on record') also manages to poke fun at the serious boxing drama.[69] As hardly a single punch is thrown throughout the film, the reviewer was clearly in generous mood. *Monthly Film Bulletin* described it as a 'rattling fine comedy' and *Kine Weekly* were adulatory, rating it was Lloyd's best film, whose 'new and hilarious gags' would ensure that Lloyd had the box office at his feet.[70]

Lloyd had switched to Paramount in 1925 after working with Hal Roach on a series of shorts released through Pathé, culminating in the highly successful feature *The Freshman*. After initial attempts to mirror Chaplin's Little Tramp character, Lloyd had developed a successful screen persona of an eager, young, bespectacled American who would allow nothing to get in his way. He made four talkies prior to *The Milky Way*, including *Feet First* (1930) and *Movie Crazy* (1932).

The Milky Way, based on a successful Broadway stageplay of 1934 by Lynn Root and Harry Clork, was directed for Paramount by Leo McCarey, a comedy specialist who began his career as an assistant to Tod Browning at Universal, moved to Hal Roach's studio where he teamed Stan Laurel and Oliver Hardy together for the first time, and went on to have a prolific career as writer, director and producer. He wrote around 100 screenplays and directed in excess of 100 films, notably *Duck Soup* (1933) for the Marx Brothers, *The Bells of St Mary's* (1945), and *Going My Way* (1945), the latter winning him a hat-trick of Oscars - for Best Picture, Best Director, and Best Screenplay. *The Milky Way* seems to have been problematic, costing a million dollars and taking seven months to produce though, as Romano says, Lloyd was well known for his 'excruciatingly long projects.'[71] Even with success at the box office, it was still to make a loss.

In *The Milky Way*, Lloyd plays Burleigh Sullivan, an ironically named weedy milkman for Sunflower Dairies.[72] Clearly not a star member of the team - at a recognition ceremony he is the only member of staff not to get a commendation - Sullivan appears to be an embarrassment to the boss, hiccuping during the speeches and baffled as to how the dairy can boost its sales. His life is transformed when he goes to collect his sister Mae (Helen Mack) from the restaurant where she works, and ends up rescuing her from the attentions of two drunken revellers. Sullivan, resplendent in his white uniform, black bow tie and peaked cap, is half the size of the other men, but in the ensuing fracas one of the men is knocked out with a punch. It's

Milkman Burleigh Sullivan (Harold Lloyd) is mistakenly thought to have knocked out Speed McFarland (William Gargan), the middleweight champion of the world

not until the next day that Sullivan realises the import of what has happened: the man on the ground was Speed McFarland (William Gargan), middleweight champion of the world, and it appears to have been Sullivan's punch that did it. Already the newspapers are making much of what they have dubbed the 'Lion and the Mouse' incident, discrediting the boxer's reputation and making his manager, the excitable Gabby Sloan (Adolph Menjou), apoplectic.[73] Sullivan denies he punched anyone, but Gabby must clear McFarland's good name - and he sees a way to do it, gaining the maximum publicity into the bargain. He signs Sullivan up to be a boxer, fixing his debut fight so he knocks out the daunting-looking Tornado Todd in the first round (keen-eyed viewers may spot Anthony Quinn in the crowd, in his first screen appearance). More fixed fights follow on a barnstorming tour, until it's time once again for Sullivan, now known as 'The Tiger' as presumably 'The Mouse' would hardly have been a crowd-pulling name, to meet McFarland in the ring. This time it's for real - or it would be, if Sullivan's sister hadn't conveniently drugged McFarland at the last possible minute. Now a world champion and a proven publicity-draw, Sullivan gives up the fight business in order to become a partner in the dairy.

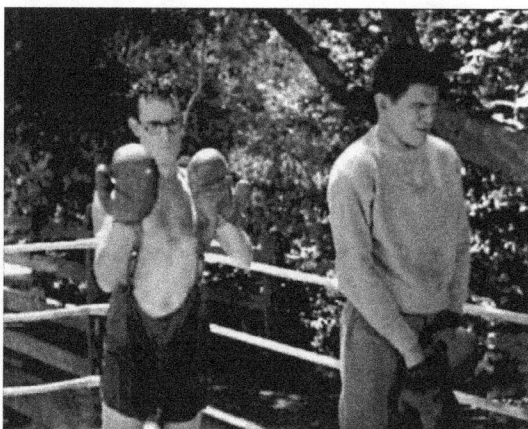

Sullivan (Harold Lloyd) arrives at the practice ring soaking wet, but the effect is comic - a contrast to Errol Flynn's wet body in Gentleman Jim *(1942)*

As a story, it doesn't offer anything particularly new, and most of the gags stem from Lloyd's slight stature - 'he's not much to look at, folks,' says one of the fight commentators as Sullivan struggles to get through the ropes and into the ring. Like Chaplin, he retains his defining characteristic in the ring itself: in Chaplin's case in *City Lights*, this was his bowler hat; in Lloyd's case, it is his glasses. A giant pair of glasses dominates one of the posters, with scenes from the film reflected in both lenses.[74] And as with Chaplin, much is made of Lloyd's body, which is the very opposite of the expectation of what a boxer's body should look like. At Gabby Sloan's country retreat, where Sullivan trains, the usual tropes of the genre are parodied: as Sullivan runs joyfully to the training ground, Gabby's girlfriend Ann compliments him on his appearance: he is wearing oversized baggy shorts held up with braces over his naked and under-developed chest. Delighted by her praise, Sullivan runs on, leaping a hedge only to land in the pond and have to arrive at the practice ring soaking wet. The 'gaze' is thus drawn to his body in exactly the same way that it would be to Errol Flynn's wet body in *Gentleman Jim* (1942) where he falls from the ring into the dock - but with very different results.

In the ring, McFarland's sidekick Spider (the gravel-voiced Lionel Stander) attempts to train him, but it's clear that although Sullivan excels at ducking - a survival skill acquired when he was picked on at school - he doesn't know how to throw a punch. When asked to put up his hands, Sullivan puts them into the air in a gesture of surrender. In the end, Ann teaches him by asking him to pretend that he is dancing with a girl, moving his feet and then punching in time to imaginary music: 'tra, la, la-la, boom boom!' Sullivan becomes enchanted with the idea, even tapping out the rhythm on the roof of his bunk on the overnight sleeper compartment of the train. Scenes of actual fighting, however, are notably absent from the film. While a bottom-of-the-bill fight is shown in some detail, with cut-aways to a horrified and cringing Sullivan cowering in the audience, his own (fixed) bout against Tornado Todd, together with its knockout punch at the end of the first round, is heard only through the radio commentary as McFarland and Mae listen at home. In fact, we only see him throw a punch once, in his first sparring bout with Spider, during which Sullivan rains punches down ineffectually on Spider's head while Spider stands there unperturbed. Publicity material for most boxing films is quick to emphasise how much training the actor had in order to box authentically, or to cite his early amateur interest in boxing, but its inclusion in relation to *The Milky Way* where the protagonist is demonstrably not a fighter, is surprising. According to the film's pressbook, Lloyd took lessons at a Denver gymnasium, reaching the semi-final of the Colorado State amateur boxing tournament, but withdrawing 'due to parental disapproval'.[75]

Other conventions of the 'serious' boxing film are included: Sullivan has a 'lucky' pre-fight routine, and a lucky charm: a lock of hair from his milk-horse's tail; fights are fixed but seemingly in a good-natured way; and Sullivan's rise to championship status is told through a montage of newspaper headlines and train-wheels - the only element missing from the montage being the knockout punches that usually characterise these sequences.[76] Instead, we see the novelty costumes that Sullivan has chosen to wear in the ring.

Plenty of slapstick is derived from Sullivan's job as a milkman, from his ability to control his horse and cart with a crafty series of whistles, to his trying to conceal a pony (and its whinnying) in the back of a taxi-cab without the driver noticing. In fact it is his relationship with his horse, Agnes, that leads Sullivan to meet his future wife Polly (Dorothy Wilson). When Agnes collapses in the street, Sullivan rushes to an apartment building, pressing all the bells in the effort to get help. Inside Polly's apartment, he phones the vet, explaining that Agnes is lying in the gutter and, yes, she's definitely had a lot to drink. Once he's cleared up any misunderstandings about exactly who Agnes is, his relationship with Polly progresses smoothly, barring of course Sullivan's botched exit from the apartment during which he walks into cupboards and into closed doors before he finally escapes.

When he becomes a fighter, Sullivan turns out to have a knack for publicity that obviously did not exhibit itself when he worked for Sunflower Dairies. He takes to heart Gabby's comment that 'colour is what makes a man stand out from the crowd', embarking on a series of headline-grabbing stunts such as arriving at a hotel with a lion on a leash; or greeting his homecoming celebration crowd by appearing on the roof of the train and floating down to the platform on an opened umbrella.[77] The dairy boss is impressed and buys out Sullivan's contract, using Sullivan to front his latest venture - the Milk Fund, a charity for 'tiny tots'. The socialite promoting this charity was modelled on the estranged wife of William Randolph Hearst, Millicent, who from 1921 onwards had promoted high-profile matches to raise money for the 'Free Milk Fund For Babies' which supplied the poor of New York with milk. Knowing that he will be the 'babies' champion' overcomes Sullivan's qualms about continuing with the championship fight: he has recently convinced himself that he has a 'Jekyll and Hyde' character and that he needs to 'destroy the tiger' within him. This comparison of a boxer with a wild animal, while done for laughs in *The Milky Way*, again alludes to a convention of fight films: Charley Davis in *Body and Soul* (1947) is likened to a tiger, Toro Moreno in *The Harder They Fall* (1956) is billed as the Wild Man of the

Harold Lloyd's glasses were his trademark and he keeps them on in the ring, just as Chaplin wears his bowler hat into the ring in City Lights

Andes, and *Kid Monk Baroni* (1952) acquires the 'Monk' nickname because his face resembles that of a monkey.

The film has plenty of pace (Lloyd claims he lost 15lbs during its production), and the jokes come thick and fast: in a particularly glorious moment, an irate Gabby pulls the telephone from its socket and hurls it through his office window - whereupon its trajectory takes it straight through the window of the jewellers' opposite and sets off all the alarms. In fact, Menjou's performance as Gabby is one of the highlights of the film: Graham Greene admired the way he 'strides noisily and victoriously through this picture ranting, raving, wheedling, double-crossing'.[78] Menjou's well-established star persona was that of a suave and sophisticated, if somewhat roguish, dandy, and this fashion-plate image is alluded to when Ann jokingly tips his hat forward over his face and he positions it carefully back at the right angle. 'But the 'drawing-room' parts for which he became typecast during the silent era and into the talkies,

53

disappeared when in 1934 he was cast as a bookmaker in *Girl in Pawn*. After that, he played 'beachcombers, actors, a broken-down theatrical producer, racketeers and gamblers'.[79]

The theme of the film lent itself to local exhibitor promotions, particularly milk tie-ins. Woolworth's stores around the UK sold The Milky Way Cocktail, which came in 11 different flavours and was marketed through a window-display featuring a cardboard cut-out of Harold Lloyd as Burleigh Sullivan. Other ideas suggested in the pressbook included a milkman's delivery race, a milking contest, and lucky-numbered milk bottle-tops. [80]

Despite all the antics and a strong supporting cast, Lloyd himself remains strangely uncharismatic. When the talkies were first introduced, he said: 'I can only hope that when the time comes, I shall not try to fool either the public or myself, but will bow my way out as gracefully as I can'.[81] This film demonstrated that the time had come for him to do just that.

The Clean Kid from the Farm
Kid Galahad (1937)

Boxing and mobsters are never far apart in films of the 30s and 40s, but *Kid Galahad* makes this overt, not just in its casting of Edward G Robinson as racketeer and boxing manager Nick Donati, and of Humphrey Bogart as his rival, Turkey Morgan, but in the way the marketing draws specifically on Robinson's gangster screen persona, the posters referring to him as 'Little Caesar'. Robinson had starred in *Little Caesar* in 1931 and Warner Brothers, who made *Kid Galahad*, were well known for their gangster pictures.

Kid Galahad was based on a serialised story in the *Saturday Evening Post* story by Francis Wallace which ran from April - May 1936 and was published as a book later that year. Wallace covered sports for the *New York Post* and the *New York Daily News* before writing for the *Saturday Evening Post* and was the author of 17 books, a number of which went on to be made into films. Wallace did not write the screenplay for *Kid Galahad*: that was the work of Seton Miller, a prolific screenwriter who had worked on *Scarface* (1932) and would go on to write *G-Men* (1935) and *Here Comes Mr Jordan* - another boxing picture - in 1941 and enjoyed a long contract with Warner Brothers.

In the film, Nick Donati and Turkey Morgan are nattily dressed rival New York gangsters with an interest in prize fighters, at loggerheads over a perceived betrayal of an agreed dive: a betrayal that cost Donati thousands of dollars. Their rivalry will cost both men their lives at the end of the film.

Donati expects complete obedience from his fighters, firing them whenever they disobey his orders and not allowing them to speak to the press - Donati reserves that privilege for himself, wining and dining those that can get him good coverage, and persuading them not to print stories that might damage his reputation. Fighters are just commodities to Donati: 'a fighter's a machine,' he tells his girlfriend Fluff (Bette Davis), 'not a violin player'. In this way, he dimisses any 'art' there might be to fighting, let alone any sensitivity or even humanity. He discovers his new fighter when he sees bellhop Ward Guisenberry (Wayne Morris) - a man he has just mocked for his name - flatten boxer Chuck McGraw (William Haade) with a single punch while serving drinks at a three-day party. He signs up Guisenberry - a Florida farm boy who is looking to earn enough money to buy his own farm - and Fluff dubs him Kid Galahad, due to his good manners and strapping good looks. The Kid follows Donati's instructions to the letter and rises through the ranks with an eye to becoming world heavyweight champion. Along the way, Fluff falls in love with the Kid, but the Kid is in love with Donati's young sister Marie (Jane Bryan), a Convent girl he met when staying on the farm belonging to Donati's mother. Angry at discovering the relationship, Donati deliberately gives the Kid the wrong instructions in his challenge fight for the world heavyweight championship, betting a huge sum on him to lose and recommending that Turkey does the same; only a last-minute desperate plea by Fluff and Marie makes him relent. He tells the Kid to change tactics and the Kid knocks out the champ. Turkey Morgan has been betrayed and there is a shoot-out in the shower room after the match.

To gain the maximum audience for boxing films, posters do not always show fight scenes and, in the case of *Kid Galahad*, some versions do not mention boxing at all. On one, above an image of Bette Davis in a slinky evening gown, hands on hips - is the catchline 'Will you be able to take it…when these dynamite dealers start dishing it out?'. The dynamite dealers, pictured alongside, are Robinson and Bogart, neither of whom are boxers and both recognisable to the audience as gangsters. The only picture of Kid Galahad himself is at the bottom of the poster, in a smiling head-and-shoulders shot alongside Jane Bryan as Marie, the only match implied being a love-match. Though there are encoded references to fighting ('take it', 'dishing it out' and so on), these words could also refer to gang turf-wars, and the main marketing proposition of the poster in fact is a love story: 'Out of a million dames', reads the marketing copy, 'Little Caesar had to pick on The Marked Woman for his playmate - and does she play rough! It's a match the devil himself must have made! And a picture

EDWARD G. **ROBINSON** · BETTE **DAVIS** · HUMPHREY **BOGART**

IT'S A KNUCKLE-RAW
JOLT TO THE JAW!

SLUG 'EM-MUGG 'EM-KILL 'EM AND KILL 'EM AGAIN! THE CRIME-CRAZED GREED OF THE UNDERWORLD KING!

"KID GALAHAD"

...WAYNE MORRIS ...... MICHAEL CURTIZ · WARNER BROS. ......

There is little to indicate on the posters for Kid Galahad *that this is a boxing film: audiences associated Bogart and Robinson with gangster pictures. The drawn guns and the tagline about the 'underworld king' just serve to reinforce this*

the whole world is bound to cheer!' The copy therefore draws on Bette Davis' feisty and tough-talking star persona ('The Marked Woman' is a reference to her previous Warner Bros film, in which she starred - again alongside Humphrey Bogart and Jane Bryan - as a hostess at a mob-owned clip-joint), and suggests that the picture is about gangsters (to appeal to the male audience) and about love (to appeal to the female audience). *Variety* felt that there was indeed 'more than the usual amount of romance for a slugfest', because most fight films 'have been poison to the girls'.[82] None of the US lobby cards show fight scenes: one shows Bogart and Robinson confronting each other with guns and a 'flash' across the card reads 'the crime-crazed greed of the underworld king'. Only the lobby cards for the South American market (the film was called *Campeon de Nacimiento - Birth of a Champion*) show fight scenes in the ring.

This approach is entirely at odds with the material produced by the studio for the pressbook or campaign book, which describes *Kid Galahad* unequivocally as a 'prize-ring drama', suggests that though 'we're not stressing the fight feature in either advertising or exploitation', local cinema owners could set up a boxing ring on the back of a flat-bed truck and drive around the town, using 'a couple of fast stepping lads who box a round or two at busy corners', with a loudspeaker so that the 'ref' can plug the film between rounds. The studio also wrote template letters that fight promoters and fans could send to their local newspaper, promoting a controversy about whether fight-fixing was really so widespread in the business.

The film was directed by Michael Curtiz, who was born in Hungary and came to Warner Brothers in the late 1920s aged 38 after a prolific early directing career in Europe, much of it in the silent era. Throughout the 1930s and 40s he directed a huge range of films that spanned many genres (mostly notably, perhaps, *Casablanca* in 1942). *Kid Galahad* was his only boxing picture, although he worked with its stars on a number of films: Edward G Robinson in *The Sea Wolf* in 1941; Bogart on six films including *Angels with Dirty Faces* in 1938; and Davis in *The Cabin in the Cotton* in 1932, *20,000 Years in Sing Sing* in 1933 and *Jimmy the Gent* in 1934. He also had an uncredited role as co-director, with Lloyd Bacon, in *The Marked Woman*.

According to Alan K Rode, Michael Curtiz spotted the unknown Wayne Morris on stage at the Pasadena Playhouse theatre and had producer Hal Wallis sign him to Warner Brothers.[83] Initially he was cast in a boxing B-movie, *The Kid Comes Back*, but the release of this film was put back in order to cast him in *Kid Galahad*, a film with a much bigger budget and a stellar cast. This does not seem to have been a shrewd move on the part of the studio, because once Morris had appeared alongside such top box-office names, it would surely seem a downward step for him to be seen to take the lead in a B-movie. *The Kid Comes Back* was released later that same year to favourable reviews, however, and although Morris made two other boxing pictures (*The Kid From Kokomo* released in 1939, which also cast Morris as a country boy good with his fists, and *The Big Punch* released in 1948, where he turns down a professional boxing contract in order to become a church minister) he never did become the A-list star that the studio had anticipated, partly because his screen career was interrupted by war service. Clearly they had trumpeted their ambitions for Morris: in

Frank Nugent's review of *Kid Galahad* for the *New York Times* he calls Morris 'Warners' latest astronomical discovery' and remarks on his 'natural and easy performance', saying that with 'that cornfed look we habitually blame on Iowa' he is almost 'too happily cast'.[84] *Variety* said rather dryly that 'he looks like the boy who won all the prizes at the YMCA, including scripture lessons'.[85] His 'to-be-looked-at' quality as the Kid is emphasised in his first scene, where he is working as a bellhop and is summoned to Donati's hotel suite to help serve drinks. The party-girls swarm all over him, tearing off the gold buttons from his bellhop jacket. Donati laughs at him until the Kid floors heavyweight champion Chuck McGraw with one punch, when McGraw insults Fluff. Donati immediately wants to sign him up. When Turkey Morgan takes out a knife and slashes the Kid's trousers below the knee, making him look ridiculous, it works as a kind of symbolic castration and a forerunner of the violence that will ensue.

It was a studio convention that any actor playing a boxer on screen would be trumpeted in the pressbook as having trained hard, possessing real talent (often having boxed at college), and able to fight his corner against any seasoned professional. Wayne Morris was no exception. Ostensibly talking to a reporter who has come to watch the film being made at the studio, trainer Mushy Callahan, who coached the actor during the fight scenes, says of Morris: 'I could take him out to the Olympic Club or the American Legion stadium tomorrow night, and match him against any professional heavyweight in the preliminaries'.[86] Certainly Morris looks the part, but the pressbook article, in praising these looks, contrasts him to the 'spindly-legged, anemic looking, thin-chested but pretty movie heroes who, in days gone by, used to portray heavyweight prize fighters'. Unless the writer is thinking of comic boxers, such as Harold Lloyd and Charlie Chaplin, it's hard to know who is being referenced.

Monthly Film Bulletin praised the fight scenes, calling them 'intelligible and thrilling, having nothing in common with the dull or gruesome fights frequently shown on the screen' though they do not say which films they had in mind. *Variety* said that 'the ring battles are superb' and that Morris's 'faking is excellent, with some of the punches and falls, so realistic they hurt'. The Kid's first fight scene opens in the dressing room where he is waiting to be called: he looks apprehensive as a fighter is carried in, unconscious. He is to fight McGraw's brother in a four-round

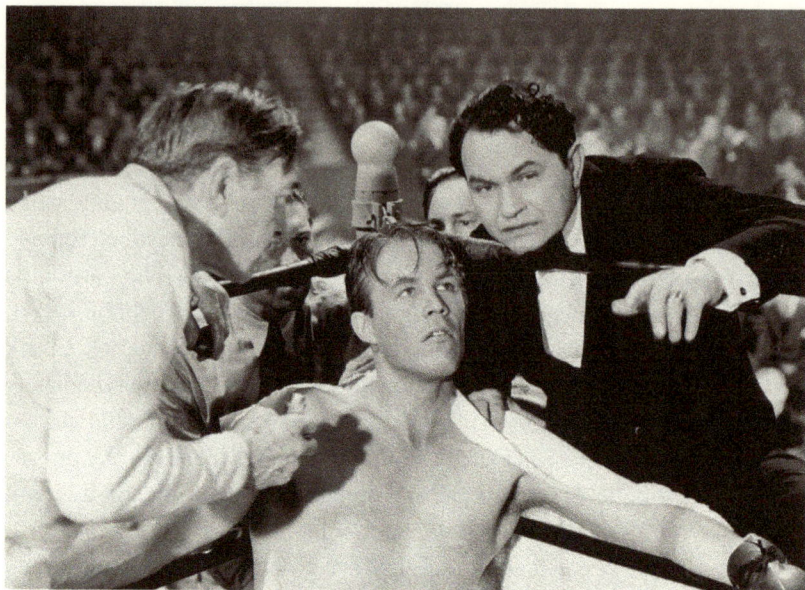

Kid Galahad (Wayne Morris) looks bemused as Nick Donati (Edward G Robinson) and Silver (Harry Carey) give him contradictory advice

preliminary, during which the camera stays in longshot, cutting away to Turkey, Donati and Fluff watching from the ringside. McGraw is a slugger and knocks the Kid to the floor, but there is then a cutaway to Fluff telling Donati to stop the fight, so that the Kid's knockout victory punch does not appear on camera. It's not until the fight against Tim O'Brian that the camera moves in for close-ups of the two fighters' faces after O'Brian taunts the Kid with Fluff's name, in the same way that the Kid - previously holding off and dancing around to dodge punches - has closed in.

The trigger for the championship fight against Chuck McGraw is the press finding out that the Kid's love-interest is Donati's sister, something that Fluff inadvertently lets slip to a reporter. Whereas he previously wanted to wait, to allow the Kid more training time, Donati tells Turkey that he's ready for the fight now, wanting to punish the Kid. Even though McGraw is out of shape - which we learn through a scene where the champion is drunk and partying with two young women - Donati has no doubt that he will win, especially if he tells the Kid the wrong tactics to use in the fight. Donati wagers 50,000 dollars on McGraw to win and tells

Turkey what he's done. Turkey immediately bets 150,000 dollars - an extraordinary amount of money in 1937 when the average wage was less than 1,000 dollars a year.

The 15-round championship fight is a tense scene with Donati and trainer Silver (Harry Carey) yelling contradictory advice at the Kid, Donati howling at him to 'get' McGraw and Silver telling him to stay away. By Round Two, the Kid is being knocked to the floor again and again by powerful punches from McGraw. As with all boxing movies, only the first couple of rounds are shown before there is a montage of punches, round-numbers, shots of radio commentators, cutaways to the crowd and to the Kid resting between rounds, looking bemused. Fluff is at ringside to support Marie, and they plead with Donati not to kill the Kid. It's the reality check that Donati needs: he tells the Kid to change tactics and the Kid dances around the ring, running McGraw ragged. Again there are more round-numbers until the Kid's knockout punch. The viewer knows this is not good news when police start arriving.

The final scenes are in clear-cut gangster, film noir territory, taking place in the shadowy corridor outside the Kid's dressing room, with wire-screens in the background. When Turkey Morgan draws his gun, we see

only his shadow silhouetted on the brick wall behind him. He enters the dressing room by using one of his henchmen to shoot a random punter to cause a distraction. His dress has been flamboyant throughout the film, but for this final scene he wears a dark suit and dark fedora.

As Turkey Morgan (Humphrey Bogaart) draws his gun to kill Donati, only his shadow is shown on the wall: the wire mesh and stark lighting indicate we are in film noir territory

In a shootout in front of the Kid and Silver, Turkey and Donati fire at each other, Turkey dying immediately but Donati living long enough to wish Marie and the Kid happiness and to tell Fluff she's 'always been swell'.

Afterwards, Fluff walks out alone into the shadowy New York night, her future uncertain.

The film includes many of the tropes of the genre that were already becoming familiar in boxing movies: as well as the montage of newspaper headlines and round numbers to indicate the Kid's ascendancy, it also includes the contrast between city and country, with the city associated with violence and corruption, three-day parties, loose women, drinking, gambling, mobsters and violence, and the country as wholesome where fresh air and honest toil signify 'old-fashioned' moral and family values.

Costume indicates Fluff's change of heart. Gone are the revealing dresses: when she tells Donati she is leaving him, she wears a dark-coloured tailored suit, more akin to the costumes of the 'good woman' who form the moral centre of the genre

Fluff - her nickname is deeply ironic as there is nothing 'fluffy' about her character - is tough-talking, blonde, cynical and dressed extravagantly. A former nightclub singer who gave up her career to be with Donati, she is cleverer than him but appears devoted to him, despite his constant suspicions and jealousy. *Variety* noted that the script 'adroitly avoids any line or allusion that could identify (Fluff) as the mistress of Robinson, who, however, is constantly walking into her apartment with a proprietory air'.[87] When she tells Donati that she is quitting, because her unrequited love for the Kid means she can't bear to be around him, her costumes signal her change of heart: gone are the revealing dresses with floaty fabrics and plunging necklines, to be replaced by dark-coloured tailored suits, much more analogous to Marie's way of dressing. This makes her portrayal more nuanced than the typical 'good-time girl' of the genre and symbolises her love for the Kid, who represents the values of the country. The division between the values of city and country is also signalled through the fact that whereas the mobsters call her 'Fluff', the Kid never does, always referring to her by her proper name, Louise. Country and city also meet through the unexpected friendship between love-rivals Fluff and Marie.

The country is the home of Nick Donati's mother (Soledad Jimenez) and sister Marie, a dark-haired, modestly dressed, Convent-educated young woman coded as the 'good girl'. There is an emphasis on family and healthy fresh-air life; and on traditional values - Donati's mother wears old-fashioned ankle-length dresses, for example. Here, Donati is addressed as 'Nicky' and whereas when seen in New York, he is wholly American (apart from one short scene where he speaks in Italian to his barber), at the farm he is wholly Italian.[88] When he arrives, there is a lengthy scene between him and his mother in which all the dialogue is in Italian, mostly about her cooking. He inhabits a different persona from his New York persona, and is keen to ensure that Marie is not 'tainted' by any connection to the fight business - and presumably the gangster business. As the older brother, he presumes to dictate who Marie can see and to control her life, something which Marie eventually resists in order to follow her love for the Kid. Scenes in the country are filmed in daylight and mostly outdoors; scenes in the city are filmed at night, usually in enclosed spaces such as the boxing arena and dressing room, the inside of taxi-cabs, or the inside of hotels. Artificial light, neon lights and deep shadows prevail. When Fluff takes the train back to New York with the Kid, they travel on the evocatively named Orange Blossom Special, thus taking a little bit of the country back with them to the city.

Although thematically there is nothing new about *Kid Galahad*, the presence of the three stars - Bogart, Robinson and Davis - and the ready-made screen personae and audience expectations they bring with them, lifts this film. Through it all, as *Variety* said, 'Miss Davis is the thread that sews and holds the story together … doing a laugh-clown-laugh through the last half of the picture.'[89] The film took 1.5 million dollars at the box-office and helped to catapult Bogart (who was paid substantially less than the other two stars) into the big-time. He was to make one more boxing film - *The Harder They Fall* - in 1956: his final film.

Help Yourself is My Slogan
They Made Me a Criminal (1939)

R eleased in 1939, *They Made Me a Criminal* was another of Warner Brothers' forays into more serious boxing drama - apart from *Winner Take All* (1932) - a James Cagney film - and *Kid Galahad* (1937) they had, until now, mostly concentrated on boxing comedies such as *Hold Everything* (1930); *Dumbells in Ermine* (1930); *The Irish in Us* (1935) again with James Cagney, and *Cain and Mabel* (1936), which was a vehicle for Marion Davies. In *They Made Me a Criminal*, traces of the genre's comic heritage still remain, with the film's noirish mood interrupted, rather than balanced, by the clowning of the Dead End Kids (later known as the East End Kids and then as the Bowery Boys). Thus the dark side is somewhat diluted, though the ending stops short of sentimentality, with considerable ambiguity remaining about whether boxer Johnnie Bradfield has really achieved redemption.

Despite the film's unevenness, its direction by Busby Berkeley shows considerable flair. It was Berkeley's eleventh film as director - he had been a choreographer for many more - but his first major drama. Though the film was well-received by contemporary reviewers, later critics have tended to view the choice of Busby Berkeley as a mistake on the part of Warner Brothers: Larry Swindell says that in those days the studio had not thought highly enough of his abilities to assign him to a drama and that even in his dance films 'there would be a Mervyn LeRoy, a Lloyd Bacon or an Archie Mayo to guide the story line'.[90] It is true that the heyday of the musical at Warner Brothers came to an end around 1938 (Berkeley had directed spectacular song-and-dance numbers in all Warners' musicals from 1933 onwards, beginning with *42nd Street*) leaving Berkeley looking for work: he was to move to M-G-M the following year.

The film was billed as the successor to the highly acclaimed Paul Muni vehicle, *I Am a Fugitive From a Chain Gang* (1932), the structure of the title mirroring that of the earlier film, and exhibitors were even provided by Warner Brothers with a letter to send to influential groups in their community explicitly linking the two films and reminding cinemagoers of 'the hundred emotions that rocked them as they watched' Paul Muni six years earlier. One poster even used the strapline 'I am a fugitive' over the title.[91] *They Made Me a Criminal* was promoted as a 'most daring' film and though it was common for publicity-writers to emphasise any drama's shock value, the slogan 'I'd rather be LASHED by whips than tortured by freedom I can never have!' (with the word 'lashed' in as large a typeface as the film's title) promised something rather more than the film delivered. It was John Garfield, however, who was the key to its box-office success. Garfield had only appeared in one film before this: *Four Daughters*, released in 1938 and directed by Michael Curtiz, in which Garfield was cast as cynical Mickey Borden, the disruptive interloper in a family of four musically gifted young women. The posters for *They Made Me a Criminal* referred to this first screen role: alongside a photograph of Garfield the copy reads: 'the boy who was hailed in *Four Daughters* as 'Dynamite the screen has never known before! … now blazes to new and even greater heights'. A strapline opposite says: 'the most sensational find of 1938 becomes the most sensational star of 1939!'.[92] The repetition of the word 'sensation' emphasises not just Garfield's box-office appeal but alludes to his screen persona too. He was, according to Nicholas Christopher, Hollywood's 'first smoldering anti-hero, sexy, up-from-the-streets, brash and dangerous' - in other words, the perfect star persona to play a boxer.[93] Garfield went on, in 1947, to play the lead in the more critically acclaimed *Body and Soul*, an unrelievedly dark film, but it was his portrayal of Johnnie Bradfield in *They Made Me a Criminal* that undoubtedly shaped him for the role.

Unlike many boxing dramas and films noirs, *They Made Me a Criminal* is told sequentially, with no flashback. Yet the beginning closely resembles the flashback-films, with Johnnie already a success - no rags-to-riches story here - giving his opponent a high-speed pasting in the ring. Southpaw Johnnie is everybody's model of a clean-cut American and good sportsman, helping his opponent to his feet, grinning broadly and innocently, giving a disingenuous radio interview during which he says hello to his mother, and reminding the guys in the dressing room that he

John Garfield has been described as Hollywood's 'first smoldering anti-hero, sexy, up-from-the-streets, brash and dangerous'

doesn't smoke or drink. Just as this is shaping up to be something out of *Boy's Own Paper*, or reminiscent of Joe Palooka, the scene cuts to Johnnie's hotel room where the boxer is revealed to be blind drunk in the arms of the glamorous Goldie (Ann Sheridan), who is described in the shooting-script as 'a freshly prepared blonde with artificial eye-lashes that could span the Atlantic'. Johnnie is expounding his philosophy of life: 'it's a sucker's game, clean living,' he declares, as it is revealed that everything just witnessed is a lie. Lying, plus a keen eye for suckers, will become a *leit motif* of the film right through to the very last line of dialogue. The play on which the film was based, by Bertram Millhauser and Beulah Marie Dix, was called *Sucker* and had opened off-Broadway in New York in 1933; in its turn it was based on a 1938 book by Millhauser and Dix, *The Life of Jimmy Dolan*, later retitled *Hot Leather*.[94] No-one comes out of this drunken hotel-room scene well - when a reporter visiting the suite overhears Johnnie's remarks about suckers, he threatens to print what he's heard and, in the ensuing scuffle, Johnnie's manager, Doc (Robert Gleckler), cracks the reporter over the head with the nearest bottle. The man dies, and Doc and Goldie flee, leaving Johnnie passed out on the floor. They pause only to steal his watch and car-keys - clearly, they are in accord with his view about suckers. In the first tinge of film noir, the car, pursued by the police through the night, plunges off the road and explodes in a ball of fire. Because he is wearing Johnnie's watch, Doc is wrongly identified by the police, and the newspaper headlines - a key stylistic ingredient of film noir - reveal that the 'runaway killer' is 'dead in smash-up'. Now officially dead, Johnnie is advised by his crooked lawyer to 'stay dead', advice that comes at considerable cost as the lawyer has just fleeced him of nearly 10,000 dollars (after all, how can Johnnie complain?). Clearly, the sucker mentality is widespread and can cut both ways. Overnight, Johnnie goes from a cheery, well-dressed, devil-may-care figure to a hunted, unshaven fugitive, the collar of his suit turned up and his hat pulled low. He may be a champ, but he's now longer calling the shots, and is in the power of any sucker that cares to take advantage.

In common with many boxing dramas, which open with a gripping fight sequence, that's the last to be seen of any in-the-ring boxing action until the end of the film: instead, the film concentrates on character and plot - and on building the obligatory romance. The pursuit of Johnnie by Monty Phelan, a maverick policeman who alone is convinced that Johnnie is alive and guilty, is somehow incidental, particularly as there is no cutting back and forth between pursuer and the pursued. The progress of Phelan (played by Claude Rains who had starred alongside Garfield in *Four Daughters*) throughout most of the film is not shown and therefore any tension of a chase is absent. This structure echoes that of the book on which the film was based, though the character of Phelan (called Phlaxer in the book) is infused with Rains' star quality, which gives it a more dapper and determined air than the defeated, discredited detective described by Millhauser and Dix, with his 'slack face like a low comedian's after a lifetime of mugging'.[95]

Armed with a new identity as 'Jack Dorney', Johnnie hits the road looking for work. In a particularly haunting Depression-style montage sequence, his progress is charted westwards across the map of the country, riding freight trains, staying in 60c lodgings and 15c doss houses, and getting fleeced of the last of his money in a bar. Throughout the sequence, close-ups of his shuffling feet mark out the state-lines until he reaches Arizona, where he is thrown off the roof of a freight train by the guard and treks through the empty sun-baked desert. It is this unshaven, sweat-soaked image of him that interestingly dominates one of the posters for the film, rather than the boxing sequences or even the romance. Location shooting, in the 100-degree temperatures of the Palm Desert - the film was said to have melted in the camera - lent the picture an authenticity unmatchable by a studio-based set. Exhausted, Johnnie arrives at the Rancho Rafferty date-farm where he's told 'if you wanna eat, you gotta pick,' a proposition that Johnnie concludes is a game for suckers, pointing out, as he walks proudly away, that he owns two limosines - only to collapse a few paces further on. In its publicity for the film, Warners said that Johnnie's journey across the US was one that John Garfield had done himself eight years before as a 'young lad', travelling from New York's East Side to California to work on the fruit farms. Drawing parallels between star and screen-character was a much-used tactic, though the studio acknowledged that hopping freight trains on the way back became too tough-going: unlike Johnnie, Garfield took a bus home once he'd got as far as Nebraska. The experience, however, said the publicity material, 'was one of the best investments ... Garfield ever made'.[96]

Much of the rest of the film concerns Johnnie's stay at the date-farm, a curious mix of city and country. Though run by a stereotypical Irish grannie, Grandma Rafferty (May Robson), the main protagonists are the granddaughter Peggy (Gloria Dickson), a city girl transplanted to Arizona - homely in her gingham frocks but with a hard urban edge - and the Dead End Kids (Leo Gorcey, Huntz Hall et al, whose last film for Warner Brothers had been *Angels With Dirty Faces*, released in 1938), a group of New York street boys sent to the farm to reform. The country is thus constructed as a place of healing, but also a place where Johnnie can make meaningful contact with other people: pitting him against the perceived innocence of real country folk would have left little scope for any meeting of minds. But Johnnie is an unconventional role-model for the boys or romantic partner for Peggy: he is relentless in his lying and cheating right through to the final scene of the film, teaching the boys dirty fight tricks, and confiding to Peggy on their first date that he'd like to stop the car in a quiet layby but that honourable intentions form no part of his plan. He exudes an easy charm which is turned on and off and will, but the influences of the country and of a 'good woman' make none of the expected dramatic transformations in his character: he remains an urban

Rafferty's Date Farm is a mix of country and city. Grandma Rafferty (May Robson) is a stereotypical Irish grannie, but granddaughter Peggy (Gloria Dickson) is a city girl transplanted to Arizona. Together with the urban presence of the Dead End Kids, it enables Johnnie to make meaningful contact with other people

smartass, tough and street-savvy. The enduring image of Johnnie is of him chewing a match, hat tipped back on his head, condemning all suckers and saying: "help yourself' is my slogan'. At this stage, it's hard to see him as an innocent man that 'they' have made into a criminal: in fact it's tempting to think he would have become a criminal at some stage anyway had he remained in New York. Indeed, the 'they' - Doc and Gloria - referred to in the title have played such a small part in the film that the blame somehow seems to lie with the whole of society or the 'establishment', and in this way *They Made Me a Criminal* prefigures the social-problem films that would become prevalent after the war. One of the posters makes this culpability explicit: over a photograph of Garfield as a fugitive is the strapline: 'you stand accused, America!...As long as any man can cry They

Made Me a Criminal'.[97] Some small character reformation is glimpsed when Johnnie rescues the Dead End Kids from being trapped in an irrigation tank where they go to swim - but as he led them there in the first place, lying to Peggy about where they were going, any real reformation is questionable.[98]

Many boxing movies feature open-air, countryside training-camps as a key part of fight preparation, and as an antidote to the evils of the city. These usually portray boxers, trainers and seconds as equal partners in the team (sitting down together at the same bench to eat), and often provide an opportunity for women to watch and encourage the sparring, whereas women are either absent or out of place in the city gyms. In *They Made Me a Criminal*, once Johnnie decides to sign up for a boxing challenge to win 500 dollars against barnstormer Gaspar Rutchek, he enlists the help of the Dead End Kids. This provides an excuse for some comic interludes with the Kids rigging up a home-made shower built out of a sieve, and robbing an upper-class boy of his camera and smart clothes, pawning them in order to buy Johnnie new boxing gloves. But suddenly, the deal is off: Tommy (Billy Halop), one of the Kids, has taken a photograph of Johnnie in the ring in his characteristic southpaw stance and the picture has won three dollars in a newspaper competition. Even though this is happening in Arizona, we are expected to believe that, back in New York, the detective Phelan spots the picture and recognises his escaped fugitive: a 'ludicrous coincidence,' says Ronald Bergan in his book *Sports in the Movies*.[99] Even more unbelievably, Johnnie passes by the boxing venue at the exact moment that Phelan is there buying his ticket for the fight - and thus knows he's being followed. After lying and attempting to wriggle out of his commitment, Johnnie decides to go ahead with the fight in order not to let the Kids down, thus exhibiting his first small sign of compassion, even though he knows it means Phelan will arrest him. In his bedroom, we see his shadow on the wall as he practises his new, right-handed stance: a stance he believes will fool the detective.

They Made Me a Criminal saves its big fight sequence until last: this is a well-filmed match that was shot in the 'Barn', an amateur boxing arena near Burbank that used to be the home of the former heavyweight champion James Jeffries.[100] After a tense build-up in the dressing room, the mood is under-mined by fairly static camerawork of the fight itself, and by the constant cutting away to the comic antics of the Dead End Kids and

Grandma Rafferty in the crowd as they egg on Johnnie, Grandma in her excitement knocking off the hat of the man in front of her again and again. Lending an air of menace is the presence of Phelan in the front row, suit immaculate, hat set at a precise angle, watching and smiling as Johnnie consistently comes off worse against the hairy, animal-like Gaspar 'Wild Bull' Rutchek (185-pound professional boxer Frank Riggi who also played a fighter in Garfield's other boxing movie, *Body and Soul*, as well as appearing in *Knockout* (1941), *Ringside Maisie* (1941) and *The Kid From Brooklyn* (1946)). The attempt to fight right-handed is just not working: Johnnie ends each round on the deck. By Round Four, as Johnnie once again lies winded, Phelan brings his face close and tells him to box with his left: 'I know who you are,' he tells him. Thus released, Johnnie resumes his normal style but he has left it too late and, after some brave punches, he's carried unconscious out to the dressing room. The game is up, a situation that is underscored by Johnnie's lying prone on the bench,

'I know who you are,' whispers Phelan (Claude Rains) as Johnnie is decked by Gaspar 'Wild Bull' Rutchek (Frank Riggi)

half-naked and vulnerable, while Phelan stands over him, formally dressed and powerful - it's Johnnie who is the sucker now.

Johnnie continues telling lies right to the end, calmly explaining Phelan away as his new manager who's taking him on a barnstorming tour. Peggy is not fooled and the fact that Johnnie makes no attempt to make his lie seem realistic implies that he is either lying to preserve his pride or that lying is his automatic reaction to any situation, rather than an indication of consideration for Peggy. In the dark and murk of the railroad night, Phelan and Johnnie cross the tracks to board the train that will take him East - and to prison. Sitting on the empty platform, Phelan eventually confides that the murdered reporter was slugged with the right hand - it couldn't have been Johnnie. He's seen with his own eyes that Johnnie just can't punch with his right. Phelan boards the train, but pushes Johnnie away at the last minute, granting him his freedom. The train snakes away into the distance as Johnnie expresses his gratitude: 'sucker,' he says. Given this parting shot, it's hard to see how *Variety* could have interpreted this film as being about a 'cynical scrapper who's softened up by romance'[101] or how both *Kinematograph Weekly* and *Film Weekly* perceived it to be a 'regeneration melodrama' with a tough character reformed 'through decent treatment'.[102] Phelan tells Johnnie that he was only caught because he was a 'sucker' for Peggy and the Kids. But this does not equate to reform, and any regeneration is the merest flicker. In fact, if anyone achieves redemption it is Phelan: ten years before, he had convicted an innocent man: when Phelan looks at Peggy as Johnnie says goodbye, it reminds him of how the wife of the man he convicted looked when her husband was taken away, 'her mouth all twisted up'. By denying himself the kudos of arresting Johnnie he is making amends for his guilty past.

This redemptive aspect is absent from the book on which the film was based. In the book, the detective sits at the ringside but cannot concentrate on the fight, as he is daydreaming about his triumphant return to New York with the escaped murderer, and the admiration this will engender in his superiors. When the fight is over, and the stadium empties, he is found still in his seat - dead. There is no opportunity for him to decide to let Johnnie go. And if the film is sentimental in terms of coding the Dead End Kids at the date-farm as 'lovable rogues', needing only a good male role-model in order to reform, then the book is almost mawkish in its depiction of the six child polio victims who are looked after by Grandma and Peggy and who become slavishly devoted to the fugitive.

They Made Me a Criminal was 'boffo' (ie highly successful) at the box office according to John Garfield's biographer Patrick McGrath and 'went a long way in shaping Garfield's 'young fugitive' image'.[103] Despite the disaffected anti-hero persona - surely, a good decade before its time and a prefiguring of the James Dean / Marlon Brando school of anti-hero - the film was not perceived by contemporary critics as breaking new ground. *Motion Picture Herald* said that Garfield played a 'Cagney-like role, differently but very effectively'. It praised the film's realism, commenting that 'there is no sugar coating' on the portrayal of Johnnie Bradfield.[104] While *Monthly Film Bulletin* found the film's 'spontaneity and simplicity' to be refreshing, *Film Weekly* felt it was 'really only hokum disguised with considerable neatness'.[105] It's true that the plot doesn't stand up to any close examination, the boxing sequences are not particularly exciting, and the film veers uncertainly between melodrama and comedy. What lifts the film above the ordinary, however, are the noir touches, the echoes of the Depression, the fresh take on the interpretation of city versus country, and Garfield's panache. Robert Sklar felt it to be a 'quiet but subtly powerful performance' which built a self-assured character who 'can make mercurial swings to laughter or anger and gradually reveal[s] a vulnerability that has no trace of self-pity.'[106] Garfield became an established star, appearing in six films in 1939 alone, and then working steadily throughout the 1940s, starring notably in the noir thriller *The Postman Always Rings Twice* (1946) and in *Gentleman's Agreement* (1947), a film that, through its depiction of race relations, helped break the Production Code. He didn't take on the part of a boxer again until 1947, when *Body and Soul* secured his critical reputation. He died in 1952.

Johnnie has gone from the high-life of drink and fast living (above) to defeat at the hands of Rutchek (below). It is Johnnie who is the 'sucker' now

The Singing Swinger
Kid Nightingale (1939)

In 1939, the same year that Warner Brothers released *They Made Me a Criminal*, with its uneasy mix of melodrama and comedy, they issued a film which drew more sure-footedly on their boxing heritage - *Kid Nightingale*. This enjoyable, lighthearted B-movie from former film editor George Amy features a boxer-singer (the boxer-musician theme would also show up in Columbia's *Golden Boy* (1939) and *Here Comes Mr Jordan* (1941)). Like *Palooka*, *Kid Nightingale* makes fun of the fight rackets - its fixed fights and greedy managers - but is unusual in that its protagonist, Steve Nelson, is shown as incorruptible. This incorruptibility stems not from rectitude but from sheer lack of interest in what money or fame can buy: Steve is interested only in singing and will put up with boxing for just as long as it takes for him to land singing lessons with the world-renowned Rudolfo Terrassi.

John Payne was cast as Steve Nelson, a tall, good-looking singing waiter at Soxie's Tavern. A well-aimed punch designed to shut up a couple of drunks who are interrupting his rendition of *Dancing With Tears in My Eyes* results in a melee, and Nelson and a customer are thrown out. The customer, who has witnessed the punch, is down-on-his-luck boxing manager 'honest' Skip Davis (Walter Catlett). Davis is desperate to find a heavyweight contender so he signs up Nelson on the strength of that one punch, rechristens him Kid Nightingale and sets him up with a series of fixed fights. Steve's impressive physique and his habit of including an aria or two at his matches draw a large female audience and he remains unaware that all his fights are fixed. Still sure that he would rather sing than box, Steve is tricked into a championship bout by being promised singing lessons from a top voice-trainer. In his anger at being double-crossed, he actually knocks out the champ.

Payne had been a singer before beginning a movie career with Sam Goldwyn: he then worked for a number of studios including Warner Bros, who saw him as a successor to Dick Powell, before signing with Twentieth Century-Fox the year after *Kid Nightingale* was released. Fox were to place him in supporting parts in musicals, where what the *New York Times* called his 'spirited baritone' could be shown off to advantage. He went on to appear in a wide range of musicals, dramas and Westerns right through the 40s and 50s, including the boxing 'backstage musical' *Footlight Serenade* (1942).

There is precious little boxing shown on screen in this film, which although fast-paced, concentrates more on the developing romance between Steve and Judy (Jane Wyman), the reaction of women to the rise of Kid Nightingale, and on the comic rivalry between two boxing promoters - Mike Jordan (Ed Brophy) and Charles Paxton (Charles Brown) - vying for the top slot. There is a standout performance by Walter Catlett as Skip Davis, one of those indomitable types who wear a straw boater and keep a flower in their lapel, and it is interesting to speculate whether Phil Silvers, in developing the Sgt Bilko character, was influenced by Catlett's performance, as they share many of the same acting mannerisms. Catlett, who had a vaudeville background and a prolific film career, often played blustering characters - he had appeared as the policeman, Constable Slocum, in the screwball comedy *Bringing Up Baby* in 1938 and was to go on to portray the theatre manager in James Cagney's *Yankee Doodle Dandy* in 1942. In *Kid Nightingale*, Skip Davis - he calls himself 'Honest Davis' - is a fraud: the kind of man who keeps bouncing back with yet another scam, yet the frauds being so petty and so unsuccessful that he remains pure comedy.

When Skip takes Steve to meet promoter Mike Jordan, Steve wanders around the building while the other two men negotiate. Seeing little to hold his attention in the boxing gym, he follows the sound of piano music to a room where a 'fatties keep fit class' is being held (Skip refers to them as 'the blimps'). Playing the piano for the class is Judy - blonde, wholesome-looking, and dressed in a short skirt and Breton striped top with a scarf knotted at her neck. Steve leans in the window and the two sing a duet, *Hark Hark the Meadowlark*, the prelude to a romance. Jane Wyman, who plays Judy, had signed with Warner Brothers in 1936 and from 1939 onwards began to get better parts in A and B features. In the same year as she made *Kid Nightingale*, she also appeared in another boxing film, *The Kid from Kokomo*, opposite Wayne Morris and though she is perhaps best remembered today as the wife of Ronald Reagan, she was to achieve critical success in the ground-breaking 1945 film *The Lost Weekend,* as the wife of an alcoholic. It is the romance and the singing that is emphasised in the trailer for *Kid Nightingale*: 'Shut the doors! Love's coming through the window!' says the trailer, calling Jane Wyman 'winsome' and only making veiled references to boxing ('grand opera gets a new swing treatment') until the end.

Publicity for Kid Nightingale *emphasised romance and singing, rather than boxing action*

Steve is signed up by Jordan's rival, Charles Paxton, who buys a half-share in him for 100 dollars (the use of such small amounts of money throughout the film implies that any 'racket' is really just a harmless bit of fun). It's not that he thinks Steve can box - and anyway all his fights will be fixed - but he's witnessed the scene in the dressing room when Steve takes off his shirt, revealing an impressive set of shoulders, manly chest and narrow waist. The reaction of a visiting posse of society ladies - all hats, fur coats and lorgnettes - is unmistakable: this boxer appeals to the 'dames' and that means box-office.

There is actually very little boxing action in the film, beyond a few punches and some montage shots at the training camp (where women have eagerly paid 25 cents admission in order to watch). In Steve's first fight, against Rocky (William Haade) - a washed-up fighter paid to take a dive - there is no music, only ambient sound, which enhances the impact of the scene. The fight is slow-paced and awkward: Steve shows himself to be useless until Skip (under the pretence of re-lacing Rocky's glove) laces it to the ropes, giving Steve time to administer a knockout punch. 'He doesn't know a right hook from a fishhook,' says Paxton, but realises that Steve could earn him big bucks because of his sex appeal. In a three-round challenge to all comers, with 100 dollars in prize money, Steve knocks out every challenger. Steve then embarks on a barnstorming tour, told through the usual montage of punches and newspaper headlines, shots of women in the crowd and young women listening at home on the radio. He is accompanied everywhere by a band that comically strikes up 'Listen to the Mocking Bird' every time he achieves a knockout. His popularity grows and, by the end of the tour, when the 'Singing Swinger' returns to New York, more than 10,000 squealing women are waiting to greet him at the train station.

Unusually for a boxing film, there is no gold-digging 'bad girl' to lure the fighter away from his true love, and Steve seems completely unfazed by all the female attention, so focussed is he on his future singing career. He remains unfailingly pleasant and naive throughout, though he knows that his popularity gives him useful leverage over Skip and Paxton. So he insists on having singing lessons from top Italian coach, Rudolfo Terrassi, or he'll quit fighting and marry Judy. Skip is equally eager to please, especially as the championship fight is coming up: it's just that if he can find a corner to cut, it's too hard to resist. And he sees the ideal candidate

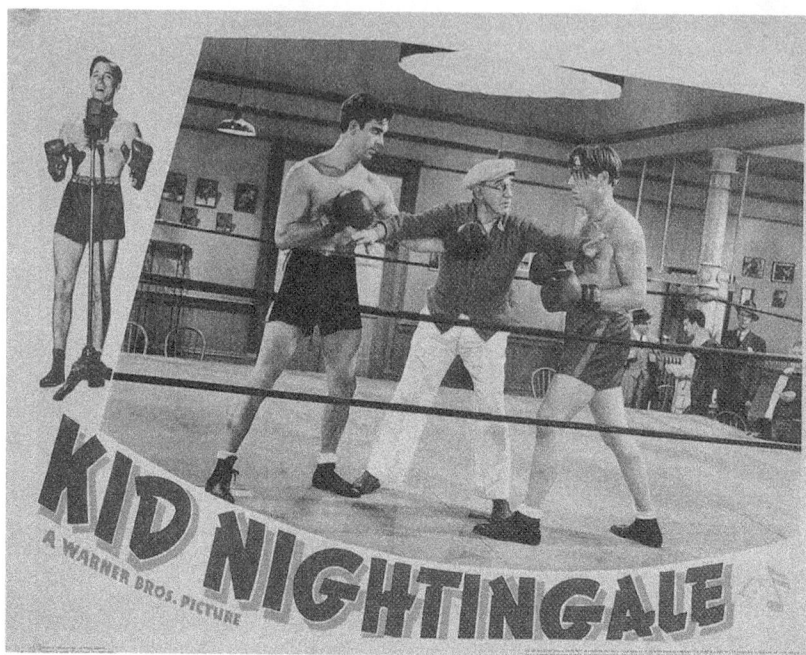

Skip 'Honest' Davis (Walter Catlett, centre) is a fraud, but his frauds are so petty and unsuccessful that they remain pure comedy

for a 'fake Terrassi' in old-time New York-Italian boxer Strangler Columbo (Harry Burns) who, for a few bucks, is happy to impersonate the singing coach. He tells the Kid exactly what he wants to hear: that he'll have a date at the Met soon, but only if he keeps up his exercise - and stays single. The ruse only becomes apparent at the championship fight, where Steve sees both the real and the fake Terrassi at the ringside.

It seems a rule of the genre that the final fight is always given added status and tension by including the announcer's build-up (Steve is announced as the 'whipoorwill of the ring'), reporters typing, the referee's instructions and the boxers' pre-fight handshake. These tropes are present, but any tension here is immediately dispelled, to good comic effect, by two devices: the fake Terrassi coming face-to-face with the real one, and the desperate attempt by the musicians to pick exactly the right moment to play Steve's signature tune, intended to accompany a knockout punch. The fight (against an uncredited opponent) begins with long-distance and overhead shots, then moves to a ringside point-of-view, with lots of cutaways. Steve knocks down the champion numerous times, and each time Steve is punched, he comically utters an operatic note. Eventually both fighters fall to the floor, with Steve lurching to his feet just in time to be crowned champion, to the promoters' surprise.

Payne was trained for the fight scenes by Mushy Callahan who had been with Warner Brothers to advise screen-boxers since 1933 and had coached Wayne Morris for *Kid Galahad*. The studio said that one of the difficulties with Payne was that he looked 'too handsome to have received many punches', so Callahan matched him with the equally good-looking 'and as yet unmarked young heavy' Bill Haade (who appeared in the film as Rocky Snyder), teaching Payne to 'roll away from the punches' so that the fight looked good without damaging 'high-priced jaws'.[107] A prolific bit-part player, Haade had appeared in *Kid Galahad* two years previously as Chuck McGraw and was also to feature in a couple of the Joe Palooka film series.

'The End' comes up so quickly that you could be forgiven for thinking that the final few seconds were accidentally left on the cutting-room floor - the audience is left to assume that Steve will give up the fight game, become an opera singer, and marry Judy. Or perhaps, as *Today's Cinema* pointed out, the fact that Steve demonstrated that he is 'no mere stooge as a fighter' means that his eventual career 'remains in the air.'[108]

There may be rather more singing than boxing action in *Kid Nightingale*, but nevertheless Payne's bare-chested body is displayed for the titillation of the female cinema audience as well as the ringside women. Many of the stills from the film, which would have appeared in editorial coverage as well as in cinema lobbies, are moody, low-angled shots of John Payne sitting in the corner of the boxing ring, his legs spread towards the viewer and light falling on his chest. It would be hard to guess from these stills that the film is a light comedy and not a film noir. The posters for the film focus much more on the romance: on one, the lovestory is foregrounded through the use of a close-up of Steve and Judy about to kiss. To their right is a picture of Steve clad in boxing shorts and gloves, his arms outspread as he sings at a microphone; it is only in the background that small illustrations of fight scenes are depicted. The publicity for the film made much of its dual-appeal to male and female audiences with the twin themes of singing and boxing appearing on all the

Many of the publicity stills for Kid Nightingale *are moody, low-angled shots of John Payne, emphasising his bare-chested body*

materials. Some advertisements were aimed directly at women: one shows a photograph of John Payne embracing Jane Wyman: Payne is wearing his boxing robe and has his back to the camera, while Wyman smiles directly at the viewer over his shoulder. The tagline above reads: 'Girls! Here's one guy you have to handle with gloves! … Boxing gloves!' Although each advertisement and poster used an action shot of Payne delivering a powerful punch in the ring, the musical theme was given equal prominence. This is a slightly different approach to that used to promote *Golden Boy*, where the romance was foregrounded and on a number of the publicity materials, the violin does not appear at all. The twin themes gave plenty of scope to the copywriters, with lines like: 'when he swings...look out for your heart!...and your chin' and 'meet the sock-a-bye baby with the rock-a-bye voice!'.[109] Local exhibitors were urged to create some 'ballyhoo' for the film by holding a singing contest among local prize fighters or dressing up a street-corner choir in boxing gloves. Stills of the 'fat girls' were offered so that exhibitors could run a weight-loss competition with prizes going to the women who lost the most weight in one week.[110]

Overall, the film succeeds because of its unpretentiousness, its breezy manner and the looks and persona of John Payne. At previews in Los Angeles, *Motion Picture Herald*, which categorised the film as 'farce', says the audience 'went wild with laughter'.[111] Much of the humour hinges on farce or slapstick rather than on clever dialogue (and there's the tendency to keep repeating a gag or funny line in order to milk the most from it), but the film was judged by *Kinematograph Weekly* as being 'capital light entertainment for the family' with some 'good scraps'[112] and by *Today's Cinema* as a 'reliable proposition for the masses.'[113] The humorous treatment of the rackets behind the sport, with promoters being portrayed as lovable rogues, the money involved as pitiably small and the fighters immune to real corruption, arguably trivialises the issues - but, then again, laughter and ridicule can quite often be the best weapons.

Knees Up Mother Brown
There Ain't No Justice (1939)

In a genre dominated by Hollywood, the British boxing film *There Ain't No Justice* can certainly hold its own, in a way that *The Square Ring*, also made at Ealing some 16 years later cannot. Compared to *There Ain't No Justice*, the later picture looks like a pale imitation of American boxing films, tired, stagey and derivative, whereas *There Ain't No Justice* is fresh, lively and engaging. The film - a second feature - was not particularly well-received at the time, either from a critical perspective or at the box-office. British class snobbery seems to be at the bottom of this: *Film Weekly* gave it a largely favourable review, undermined by its dismissal as 'pleasantly homely English fare.'[114] *Kinematograph Weekly* remarked condescendingly on how interesting are its 'cross-sections of low-life,' showing 'the proletariat at home, at work and at play'.[115] Only *Monthly Film Bulletin* seemed to be enthusiastic: the film, said the magazine, 'is an extraordinary vital and accurate picture of everyday, working-class life as it is lived, and not as it is imagined. It has humour, pathos, racy dialogue, and in numerous slight but deft touches, reveals Cockney wit and grit.'[116] In the US, the Cockney wit was a problem, not an attraction: *Variety* thought *There Ain't No Justice* could be made more fast-moving by cutting the running time, but worried that 'the beginning contains too much cockney conversation to be readily understood by the majority of theatregoers'[117] and *Motion Picture Herald* said it was 'designed for the London primitives' but missed its target, falling into a 'hotch-potch of synthetic Cockneyisms and 'Golden Boy' burlesques'.[118]

Like many British dramas, *There Ain't No Justice* is about class, the central characters being a working-class family from Notting Dale (now renamed as Notting Hill). As Marcia Landy points out in her book *British*

Genres, the film uses boxing as a metaphor for intraclass and interclass conflict, with the working-class males more likely to use 'brawn rather than brains' in the struggle against (their) oppressors'.[119] The film was directed by 25-year-old Pen Tennyson, a promising director (great-grandson of the poet Alfred Lord Tennyson) with an interest in social-problem drama: he went on to make *The Proud Valley* (1940), the pro-nationalisation coal-mining drama set in Wales and starring Paul Robeson. Tennyson was to die early in the Second World War in a plane crash (he was in the Fleet Air Arm), so never had the opportunity to fulfil his potential. He had already been spotted by Alfred Hitchcock, for whom he worked as an assistant on *The 39 Steps* in 1935, and was a protege of Michael Balcon. *There Ain't No Justice* is a confident picture that does not pull back from controversial themes and contains one of the best fight scenes of the genre. Its dedication - 'to the small-time boxer' - is indicative of its social conscience. George Perry, in his book *The Great British Picture Show*, feels that *There Ain't No Justice* was one of the few pre-war films - along with *Bank Holiday* (1938) and *Storm in a Teacup* (1937) - that relied on accurate observation of the British people, genuinely borrowed nothing from Hollywood and could have heralded the beginning of a unique national cinema. That it came to nothing is, he says, because 'bread and butter has always counted in the cinema for more than social consciences....it was the box-office subject which could equally well have emerged from the studios of Hollywood that drew audiences and profits'.[120]

The film was scripted by James Curtis, from his own novel of the same name that was published in 1937.[121] Curtis was British and was also the author of *They Drive By Night*, a 1938 novel which became a critically

THERE AIN'T NO JUSTICE

H499
ACE BOOKS
2'6

London's boxing underworld—the parasites who live on the exertions and agonies of the victims of the ring.

JAMES CURTIS

In James Curtis' books, criminals are unromanticised and the protagonists doomed

acclaimed film noir. The focus on class was characteristic of Curtis' work: though apparently from a middle-class background, he was drawn through his left-wing politics to the working-class world and particularly to the unfairness of society. Matthew Sweet, in choosing *There Ain't No Justice* as one of the 'lost classics' of British film, said that Curtis had a 'pinprick-sharp ability to commit a (dirty) world to the printed page'.[122] His language is that of the street; his criminals are unromanticised and his protagonists doomed.

It is ironic, therefore, that *There Ain't No Justice* was categorised as a 'comedy-drama' or 'boxing drama' on release, and in hindsight is pure romance: the romance of the portrayal of a safe, ordered, companionate community, where family ties are paramount, and from which corrupt forces can be expelled. Part of this romantic modern-day perception stems from the fact the film was released in 1939, just a few weeks before war was declared, yet contains no mention of the increasingly tense world situation (a silence common to all British pictures of the time). This serves to isolate the film in a kind of timelessness, despite contemporary notes being struck by, for example, the presence of a milk-bar and the portrayal of Len, an untrustworthy proto-spiv. The presentation at a local party of a pigeon-fanciers' prize, followed by everyone linking arms and joining in a boisterous rendition of *Knees Up Mother Brown*, presents a picture of unsophisticated fun where generations are united not just by class, but by the 'village' in which they live. Charles Barr, who has written extensively on Ealing, notes that 'the London neighbourhood is presented with real warmth'.[123]

There Ain't No Justice tells the story of Tommy Mutch (Jimmy Hanley), a young motor mechanic whose friendship with old-time boxer Harry 'Punchdrunk' Dunn (Mike Johnson), leads to him becoming a fighter. His motive is money (he only earns £2 a week at the garage), but all he craves is a home of his own - and to get married. His romance with Connie (Jill Furse) does not always go smoothly: she disapproves of his boxing and is jealous of the seductive scheming of Mrs Frost (Sue Gawthorne), mistress of boxing-promoter Sammy Sanders (Edward Chapman). Tommy does well in the early stages of the fight business, but when he learns that fights are routinely fixed, he walks out. The need to raise money for his sister forces him back into Sammy's clutches, and into a fight where he is supposed to take a dive. In the end his integrity shines through: he wins the fight and the girl, and walks away from boxing forever.

These may be familiar themes, but they are exceptionally well-handled with none of the parade of 'characters' that were to populate *The Square Ring*. Jimmy Hanley excels in the part of Tommy with his natural, confident acting style and unforced manner (he was to star in other Ealing vehicles such as *The Blue Lamp* (1951)). At 21 years old, he is younger than the protagonists of many boxing movies - and thus more credible as a fighter just starting out. His big grin, London accent (he addresses all women as 'ducks') and gutsy attitude mark him out from the start: the role 'looks as if it had been written to order for him', said *Variety*.[124] Giving Harry - who is as sharp as they come, despite his 'punchdrunk' nickname - a lift to the boxing stadium in his employer's car, Tommy is involved in a car-crash and a full-scale punch-up with the other driver ensues, with Harry shouting encouragement just like a trainer at the ringside. Watching the fracas is Mrs Frost, epitome of the blonde, over-dressed gold-digger with a fake cut-glass accent to match. She clearly likes what she sees.

Tommy (Jimmy Hanley) shows that he is handy with his fists - and not just in the boxing ring

Tommy takes up with a girl he meets at a party: Connie (dark-haired and modest of manner) works in the milk-bar alongside Tommy's sister Elsie (Phyllis Stanley). When Tommy gives her a ride home using his father's pony and trap, we see that Connie - though working-class - comes from a better neighbourhood: her mother's house has a front garden and picket fence; creeper grows up the wall and a carriage-lamp gives a soft glow. The house would not be out of place in the country. A cut from this scene to Tommy's home reinforces the difference: Tommy's family's terraced house is set right on the pavement; inside, a small child (Tommy's little sister) is screaming and mother - hair in curlers - is shouting. The difference between Connie and Elsie is highlighted by Elsie's 'common' way of speaking, full of 'ain't' and 'got no'. The family are remarkably tolerant of Tommy's announcement that he wants to be a boxer and has already given up his job at the garage, perhaps because of the presence of Harry who - despite the ragging of the young people - is clearly a respected figure in the neighbourhood.

At the boxing hall, Harry and Tommy meet Sammy (it is interesting that almost everyone in this film has a diminutive name ending in 'y' or 'ie' perhaps indicating their working-class status), who they address with great respect, calling him Mr Sanders. This might indicate that they feel he is a class above them, but he is clearly working-class - though with bit of money and power - and despite his prattling on about 'the noble art', he is quick to get down to the essentials once he learns Tommy is short of money. He offers him a deal on his first fight: 5 shillings for a knockout, 10 shillings for going the distance, and 15 shillings if he wins. 'That's the cheapest pull-in we've had for a long time,' says Sammy's assistant once the visitors have left.

We only see two fights in this film: his first and his last, both of which *Motion Picture Herald* says were 'derided in the knowledgeable sections of the audience' at the previews.[125] There is no footage of Tommy training, so the first sight of him boxing is at his debut fight. While he waits in his corner, there is the usual charity appeal, but this has one has a particular poignancy and introduces a note of foreboding as to Tommy's future. In the ring stands Bill, a tall, well-built man who looks sightlessly across the hall: he went blind through fighting. He cannot see the money that is thrown into the ring for him by the audience - only hear the clatter of coins.

Connie (Jill Furse), pictured left, epitomises the 'good girl' of boxing films, with her dark hair, modest dress and her misgivings about the fight business. Mrs Frost (Sue Gawthorne), pictured below, is the typical femme fatale of the genre: blonde, clad in furs, sexually predatory - and good at following the money. When she sees Tommy is a winner, she actually licks her lips

With the confidence that comes with winning a few fights, Tommy - seen here with trainer Harry 'Punchdrunk' Dunn (Mike Johnson) - is reluctant to listen to advice

Tommy, tall and pale and wearing enormous baggy shorts that come down to his knees, swings wildly at his opponent, with more misses than punches. He is cut early, and blood cascades down his pale chest. But by Round Two he gains in confidence, taking advantage of his height and knocking out his opponent. From the stands, Connie reels as if she felt the blow herself. Pleased with his performance, Tommy gives little credence to the remarks of an experienced fighter, who tells him that getting ahead in the boxing game means losing as well as winning 'There's only one person on top…and that's Mister Manager,' he says. He is soon to learn the wisdom of these words.

After four more winning fights, Connie can't take it any more, but Tommy won't give up boxing. He's on a roll: at the gym, Tommy and Harry (now both wearing 'Tommy Mutch' sweaters) spar good-naturedly for Sammy and another promoter, who demonstrate that they have ways of making sure Tommy is brought to heel. The bait is Mrs Frost, who licks her lips like a predatory animal in anticipation of what's to come. Not just her name, with its connotations of cold calculation, but the fact that she is never referred to as anything other than 'Mrs Frost' - we never learn her first name - telegraphs her character effectively. Sammy is not just complicit in Mrs Frost's seduction of Tommy, but helps bring it about. At first, Tommy resists: like Joe Palooka, who'd rather have a cheese sandwich, Tommy would rather go home to his mother, but Mrs Frost is relentless and Tommy soon gives in. The two women - Mrs Frost and Connie - meet at his family party to celebrate the baby sister's second birthday, and the confrontation nearly comes to blows. Marcia Landy sees the portrayal of the two women as a polarisation between the domestic female who 'is identified with family and nurturing...pitted against the femme fatale who is in search of sexual gratification from young, virile fighters,' though Mrs Frost's motivation may be more about power and control than sex.[126]

A brief boxing sequence shows Tommy's next fight, at Putney Hall, against Frank Fox, the 'Hoxton Tiger' (Michael Hogarth) in a show billed as 'the fighters that really fight' - an ironic title as the match turns out to be fixed. We only see the fight in its final round, Round Eight, when Tommy delivers such a huge punch that the Hoxton Tiger sails clean out of the ring, landing squarely in his manager's arms, and pausing long enough to say 'nice faking'. Back in the dressing room, Tommy learns the truth about the fight and walks out. He is beginning to grow up, realising that the people around him are not as honest as he'd assumed them to be, but are corrupt (Sammy) and manipulative (Mrs Frost). He is to get a further lesson in character from Elsie's boyfriend Len.

Len (Michael Wilding) is a smooth and nattily dressed young man complete with pencil-thin moustache, chalk-stripe suit, and a keen eye on the till at the milkbar. This was an early part for Wilding, whose later screen persona was that of an eligible, wealthy and quintessentially English bachelor: in the 1940s he was to become one of the most popular actors in the country. Len perceives an easier way to get the £50 he desperately needs than stealing it out of the till, though clearly he's contemplated it on several occasions. He proposes to Elsie, knowing that he can rely on big brother Tommy to come up with a 'loan' if it's for something as noble as their wedding. But his plans go awry: Tommy quits the fight game and has no money to give them, so Len is forced to steal the money from the till. Tommy feels obliged to help out a distraught Elsie, so is forced to return to the fight game to repay the money, this time in no position to negotiate his own deal. 'You belong to me,' says Sammy. 'You win when I say so and lose when I say so.'

The first loss is lined up: in a 'Gala Night' rematch between Tommy and the Hoxton Fox, Tommy is to take a dive in the sixth round. This sustained fight sequence is extremely well-filmed, with lots of movement, hard punches, and sweat-spray arcing round the stadium. When Sammy realises that Tommy is fighting to win, he engineers a ruckus in the crowd and soon half the stadium are punching and wrestling. The two fighters carry on regardless, pausing only when the crowd spills into the ring itself, and resuming once the ring is cleared - not that anyone is watching any longer, as they are all too busy breaking chairs over each others' heads. Tommy wins the fight, is reunited with Connie, and vows he will never fight again. He's kept his integrity - and the girl.

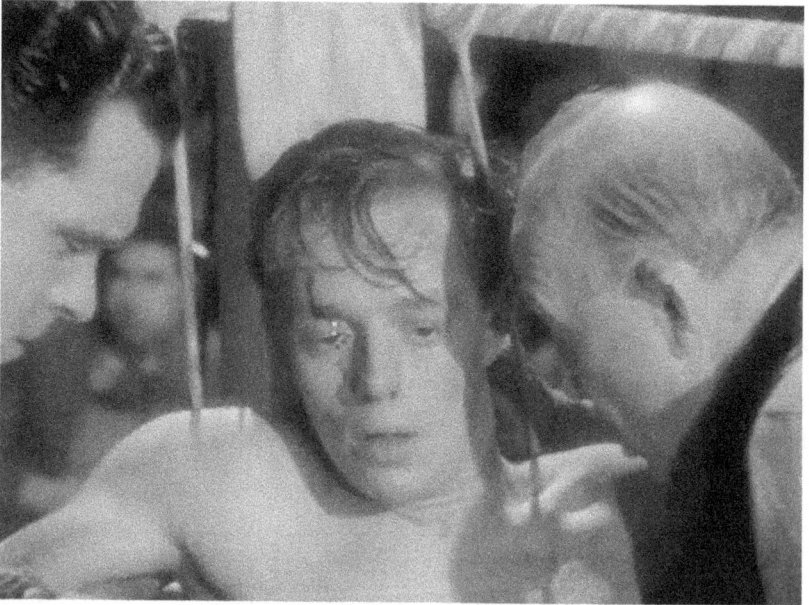

Tommy refuses to take a dive, even though Sammy tells him 'you win when I say so and lose when I say so'

Reviewing the film, Graham Greene wrote that *There Ain't No Justice* was 'intended to be an English tough film, but somebody's nerve failed...

The etceteras - setting of bar rooms and coffee stalls - are admirable, but the whole picture breathes timidity and refinement'.[127] Some 70 years later, critics were still making the same judgment: Matthew Sweet says that although it depicts the lives of the working-class 'we're still in the studio, still working under a rather patrician regime which prevents the real dirt of this world being impressed upon the screen perfectly.'[128] The unspoken comparison both Greene and Sweet are making here is with contemporary American films: he would have done better to judge *There Ain't No Justice* on its merits as a British film (and perhaps an interesting comment on real or wished-for working-class national identity). What is particularly well-observed in this film is the way it pinpoints gradations of the working class instead of seeing them as a homogenous unit. Despite the 'village' atmosphere given to London, distinct hierarchies are presented. At the bottom is Len, disapproved of by Elsie's family as a 'bad sort' and Mrs Frost, dismissed with one glance when she arrives with Tommy at the birthday party. The contempt with which these characters are treated is connected with money and the importance it is seen to play in their lives. Connie is shown, in her home, speech, dress and moral stance, to be a cut above Tommy's family, but Sammy Sanders - who Tommy initially treated with respect - is revealed to be in the same gutter as Len, prepared to cheat and thieve in order to get what he wants. The end of the film - Tommy's rejection of the corrupt world of boxing - represents, as Charles Barr points out, 'the rejection of a whole 'commercial' world in favour of...community values'.[129] In fact, the way Tommy channels his energies (his readiness to use his fists in street-fights) into something worthwhile; his modest ambitions; his loyalty to his family and his integrity essentially portray him as one of the 'deserving poor'. And perhaps that is what Graham Greene objects to. Certainly, the film was toned down from the novel: the abortion sub-plot (in which Elsie becomes pregnant by Len and Tommy arranges a back-street abortion, following which Elsie dies) was erased and the language toned down, changes which Martin Knight, in his Introduction to the re-issue of James Curtis' book, says Curtis would have fought against.[130] The book is uncompromising in its language: all women are 'janes' or 'tarts' (a neutral term) and race is prevalent (fighters are referred to as Jews, Yids or niggers). It is made clear that Tommy - who is an unpleasant person in the book - comes from the slums (he shares a bed in the front room of his parents' house with his brother Ernie), is quick to anger and wants to settle everything with his fists ('That's what janes wanted, a good left-hander every now and then to bring them to their senses').[131] In the novel, Tommy yearns for a proper girlfriend but does not have a Connie-figure to balance out his aggression, and it is made explicit that Dot (the Mrs Frost figure of the film) is a prostitute. When Tommy wins his final fight of the book after he was supposed to lose on a foul, he is not pleased and thinks only of the £17 that he would have gained by throwing the fight. There is no sign, even after his realisation that everyone is 'poncing' off everyone else, himself included as he pockets some of the money that he has forced Len to pay for Elsie's abortion, that he will quit the fight game.

The poster for the film has none of the impact of US film posters for boxing films. Instead of depicting fight scenes, or even a love-scene, the orange-and-black poster uses three smiling headshots - of Jimmy Hanley, Jill Furse and Phyllis Stanley - in a vertical orange strip down the side and the 'wanted' style typeface used for the film's title evokes a Western rather than a boxing film. A typographic border around the poster uses the slogan 'the film that begs to differ', which gives little clue as to genre. The tagline for the film is 'Real people - real problems. A human document - supercharged with action'. A much more genre-specific appeal is evident on the cover of James Curtis' book. The Ace Books paperback of 1960 shows a fighter lying on a couch, his hands taped, his chest naked. He is watched over by a cigar-smoking man in a sharp suit, and seated at the end of the couch is a glamorous woman. That these are not the fighter's friends or supporters is made clear by the caption: 'London's boxing underworld - the parasites who live on the exertions and agonies of the victims of the ring'.

Music and Fighting Just Don't Mix
Golden Boy (1939)

*G*olden Boy has had a longer life than probably any other boxing story, beginning as an influential Clifford Odets Depression-era play which opened on Broadway in 1937 and ran for 250 performances, becoming a Rouben Mamoulian film starring William Holden as Joe Bonaparte in 1939 (and re-released in 1947), then being reincarnated as a stage musical in 1964, with the latest version still going strong in 2003.[132] Along the way, the stage production has shed the central dilemma - the choice between fighting and musicianship - which made the film so powerful - and by the turn of the century had become a rather routine tale of a Harlem fighter corrupted by riches. Although the fighter/musician theme was to be explored a number of times in boxing movies over the next 15 or so years (including *Kid Nightingale* (1939), *Here Comes Mr Jordan* (1941) and *The Joe Louis Story* (1953)), *Golden Boy* was the first, causing *Monthly Film Bulletin* to remark on the combination as being 'to say the least, unexpected'.[133] It remains the only serious drama to tackle the subject, and to use the contrast between boxing and music as a metaphor for the contrast between masculinity (specifically, aggression and the attractions of the outside world) and femininity (sensitivity and the attractions of family life); or - as Leger Grindon points out - between body and soul. 'In order to cultivate his soul,' says Grindon, 'the boxer must take on attributes associated with the female' and, in the case of *Golden Boy*, that is exactly what he eventually does.[134]

Columbia made much of the film's literary origins, mentioning its Broadway success in all the advertising, partly to attract an audience already familiar with the stageplay, but also to associate the film with Clifford Odets' name and thus add status to the production, though in fact the screenplay was the work, not of Odets, but of four screenwriters

Exhibitors were told by the studio that Golden Boy was not a fight picture and should not be promoted as such. Hence the poster focuses on romance, with only a small illustration of a boxer in the top corner (newcomers Lewis Meltzer and Daniel Taradash, and veterans Sarah Mason and Victor Heerman).

The film is notable for its strong storyline and accomplished direction - Mamoulian had already made some critically acclaimed films including *Dr Jekyll and Mr Hyde* (1931), *Queen Christina* (1933) and *Becky Sharp* (1935) - as well as for the first film appearance of William Holden, as Italian-American boxer-violinist Joe Bonaparte. Clifford Odets had written his play with John Garfield in mind but in the event Luther Adler had taken the lead role on stage, with Garfield playing brother-in-law Siggie.[135] Garfield missed out once again in the film version, Columbia having been unable to borrow him from Warners. In the end the studio decided to cast an unknown, and its talent scouts interviewed thousands of aspirants over a period of a year: according to the pressbook, Holden was discovered living 'only 15 miles from the Columbia Studios.' Although Holden had bit-parts in two earlier films, this was his first credited role. Not only did he look the part (at 20 years old, here was an actor young enough - like Tommy Hanley in *There Ain't No Justice* - to be convincing as someone starting out on the boxing circuit), but he could play the violin too. *Today's Cinema* described him as a 'brilliant newcomer' and *Kinematograph Weekly* praised the 'complete and powerful conviction' of his performance.[136] Holden was supported by a first-class cast which included Barbara Stanwyck, Adolphe Menjou and Lee J Cobb, but managed to remain the focus of the audience's attention through his naturalistic acting style and fresh-faced good looks.

Joe Bonaparte gets into the fight game because he is desperate to 'be somebody'. His father (Lee J Cobb) - a stereotypical Italian with broad accent and flourishing moustaches - runs a neighbourhood grocery store in New York and dreams that one day his son will become a world-class violinist (he seems not to have the same aspirations for his daughter Anna (Beatrice Blinn), an accomplished pianist, presumably because she is a woman). Joe is very visibly of a different generation from his father, with every trace of Italian background eliminated apart from his name. Like Italian-Americans Paul Baroni in *Kid Monk Baroni* (1952) and Rocky Graziano in *Somebody Up There Likes Me* (1956), he has absorbed the American culture and that means he is impatient for success: 'everything goes by at 200 miles an hour and you want me to wait for the future,' he complains. He has already been playing the violin for 10 years, presumably with little public recognition, yet with boxing, he discovers the rewards are immediate. His opportunity comes when Lucky Nelson (as with the other characters in the film, it's clear a playwright chose the names) breaks his hand, leaving ageing promoter Tom Moody (Adolphe Menjou), without a good fighter on his books. Joe, pushy and aggressive, persuades Moody to take him on, despite Moody's misgivings ('he's got curls, too!'). Moody is finally convinced when he learns that it was Joe who broke Lucky's hand, in a sparring match at the local gym. The scene is all the more effective for the way the symbolism of the broken hand - clearly a portent of the future for Joe, and something that could wreck his violin playing forever - is understated.

Throughout the film, an effective use of contrast is made between the world of boxing (consumption, smart clothes, the city, modernity, glamorous women) and the world of Joe's home which is 'a shrine to traditional, bourgeois domestic comfort'[137] (thrift, Victorian furnishings, old-world values, religion, neighbourhood life, homely women). While Joe is winning his first fight, his father sits chatting with a neighbour outside the shop, cooling off after the hot day, a cat on his lap. Joe arrives home with his winnings - 100 dollars - and a report of the fight in the local paper (published remarkably quickly). This win and its instant reward has persuaded Joe that his future lies in boxing. 'But you're a musician,' protests his father. 'Tomorrow is my birthday. I change my life - just like that,' he replies. The scene is a particularly poignant one because, unknown to Joe, his father has bought him a 1,500-dollar violin as a birthday gift. In his rejection of musicianship, Joe is rejecting his father's vision of what his son might become, and also a concept of family unity. He has rejected the spiritual for the physical: in the boxing genre 'art, education, romance, the family and religion all serve as manifestations of the spiritual.'[138]

The picture of a close-knit home-life, though clearly indicated as the right goal for Joe, is not over-sentimentalised. The Holy Family is shown as an aspirational model for the Bonaparte family: when Joe leaves home to become a boxer, the confrontation with his father takes place in front of a painting of the Holy Family embracing and the same picture is in the background in the final scene of the film when Joe, his father, and his girlfriend Lorna mirror the embrace and are once again a united family. Less this be viewed as too much schmaltz, it is countered by the portrayal

The Holy Family is shown as an aspirational model for the Bonaparte family: when Joe receives his birthday violin, he is framed in the shot with his father by an image of the Virgin Mary

of Joe's sister Anna in her marriage to Siggie (Sam Levene), a lazy slob of a cab-driver, who spends his time slouching about the house and drinking too much: he is not above cuffing Anna around the head from time to time. *Kinematograph Weekly* felt that the film's opening stages were 'burdened with an excess of domestic sentiment' but that 'the pace appreciably quickens as the story develops'.[139]

The dilemma facing Joe is shown graphically through the shots of his first fight, and the shots of him trying out his new violin. In the ring, he looks unequivocally like a musician, with his slim figure and unruly curly hair; once he picks up the birthday violin, having made his life-changing decision (and slicked down his hair), he looks unmistakably like a boxer. Clearly, at this stage in his life, he fits into neither role comfortably and is thus caught between two worlds.

Joe is not the slow-witted, poorly educated, naive boxer portrayed in so many films (he reads books, goes to concerts) and he is therefore an unlikely victim for the familiar figure of the gold-digging woman. Instead, Joe makes a pass at Moody's smart, younger girlfriend, Lorna Moon (Barbara Stanwyck): although she rejects him, she is clearly impressed that here's a man who can woo with pretty words, not just with demonstrating his masculinity or desirability through punching it out in the ring. Like Joe, Lorna is also a more complex character than the typical 'love-interest' in the boxing movie. Throughout the film, she continues to switch back and forth between altruistic and selfish motivations, sometimes exerting a moral influence on Joe's life, sometimes doing anything to make good on her and Moody's 'investment'. Standing with Joe on the rooftop of a Manhattan skyscraper she tells him as they look down that he could 'make all that your carpet to walk on' in an echo of Satan tempting Christ. When, wracked by guilt over letting down his father, Joe declares he is finished with fighting, calling it 'an insult to a man's soul', Lorna sets out to make him continue: 'I know a dozen ways,' she tells Moody. She plays on the fact that Joe is obviously falling in love with her, seducing him with talk of the thrill of seeing him fight 'smooth as silk.' Joe makes it clear he sees

Lorna (Barbara Stanwyck) is a more nuanced character than the good/bad woman stereotype of the genre, switching back and forth between atruistic and selfish motivations and loyal to Moody (Adolphe Menjou) for reasons in her past that are not disclosed

straight through her ploy, but is goaded to carry on with boxing when she says: 'see you in 1960 - maybe you'll be somebody by then.'

Joe's rise through the rankings is told in the characteristic way, with six months of fighting being shown through a montage of headlines, train-tracks and winning punches.[140] Success brings Moody the money he so badly needs, but in its wake it also brings interest from sharp-suited gangster Eddie Fuseli (played by Joseph Calleia, who by this time was typecast as a mobster) who wants to buy a piece of the action. Moody advises Joe not to accept but in the time-honoured fashion of boxing movies, Joe insists that 'nobody tells me what to do.' In *The Pittsburgh Kid* (1941) and in countless other fight films, this decision ends in disaster: the outcome is exactly the same here. In fact audiences probably had a thrill of pleasure from hearing this line so often, knowing exactly what it foretold. Moody, reluctant to let go of his high-earning boxer, decides to use Lorna as leverage. Until now, he has seemed perfectly reasonable and fair, but when we learn that he is willing to pimp Lorna in order to get Joe back, the moral line between the gangster and 'honest' promoter begins to blur.

Lorna's motives in agreeing to the deal seem mixed. She is loyal to Moody, who she describes as having loved her 'in a world of enemies', hinting at a back story that is never revealed, but clearly she is also attracted to Joe. Invited to Joe's house for dinner (that quintessential Italian-American portrayal of the essence of 'family'), she listens to him play the violin and says she feels this is his rightful place. Joe believes that 'music and fighting just don't mix' but he won't quit the fight-game now - not even for Lorna. This incompatibility of the two worlds, masculine and feminine, is a theme which recurs throughout the boxing-movie genre, though the use of music to symbolise the feminine side (rather than using the more familiar symbol of the 'good woman') lends an interesting perspective to the film.

In line with Joe's impatience to 'be somebody', he challenges Fuseli to fix him a fight at Madison Square Garden, signing up with Fuseli when he fulfills his promise. 'I'm through with the small-time,' he tells Lorna, who promptly decides that, in that case, she is through with him. Under Fuseli's management, Joe undergoes a transformation, dressing in fancy suits in what Lorna calls 'a bad imitation of your gangster friend.' But he soon finds that Fuseli is just as controlling as Moody, even choosing his shirts for him. 'You use me like a gun,' he complains. 'You keep me oiled and polished.'

The climax of the film is Joe's fight at the Garden against the Chocolate Drop (James 'Cannonball' Green), a black fighter who is the pride of Harlem and thus draws a huge black crowd, the only scene in mainstream films of these decades where a large percentage of the ringside crowd is shown to be black, though in line with Hollywood's attitude to black actors at this time, not only is the Chocolate Drop's part a non-speaking one, he is not even credited in the on-screen cast-list. It is interesting that the scene went ahead at all: reputedly, when *Body and Soul* was being made in 1947, Joseph Breen rejected a similar black-versus-white fight-scene as being against the Production Code rules.

In the dressing-room before the fight, the light plays on Joe's bandaged hands, echoing the opening sequence of the film, where Moody talked about Lucky Nelson's broken hand and thus introducing a sense of foreboding. The stadium shots are impressive, with the huge arena packed to capacity, and misty light floating down onto the boxers: stock documentary footage is blended well with footage shot specifically for the film. The fight itself is brief (only two rounds) and is filmed in fairly conventional manner, though Graham Greene thought the sequence was 'among the finest in the talking film' because of the way Mamoulian used subjective shooting, 'with hate in the lens as well as in the gloves'.[141] This is partly achieved through the continued use of the close-up, both for the fighters and for the crowd, who are composed - says Greene - of 'febrile blondes with their moistened lips,...stout complacent backers at the ringside, and screaming Harlem in the gallery'.[142] In Round One, Joe is knocked to the floor; in Round Two he makes a comeback, with punches thrown at furious speed, the tension dispelled by the usual comic cutaways to the crowd whose excitement is now bordering on hysteria. Basil Wright felt the fight sequence to be 'painful to a degree in its tragic realism' but compared with other contemporary boxing films, (particularly *There Ain't No Justice*), this view is hard to endorse.[143] Joe knocks out the Chocolate Drop, who lies spread-eagled and unmoving on the floor. Joe clutches his own hand, which he has broken (fulfilling the prophecy), but the Chocolate Drop can do nothing: he's dead, killed by Joe's punch.

Joe initially seems quick to excuse himself for 'murdering' the Drop, but the bravado is only on the surface. In a touching scene, he goes to the

The fight at the climax of the film - just two rounds at the end of which the Chocolate Drop is dead on the floor and Joe's hand is broken - is shot in conventional manner though was praised by Graham Greene as 'among the finest in the talking film'

Drop's dressing-room, expecting a confrontation with the boxer's father but receiving forgiveness instead. Moved by this experience, and by the horror of having killed a man, Joe finally rejects Fuseli: 'I'm a cheap edition of you,' he says, 'but tonight's the end.' It is in this conversation that the only reference to Joe as 'golden boy' occurs, when Fuseli uses the name sarcastically as he dismisses him. The death of his rival, as Leger Grindon points out, 'provokes (Joe) to face his own vulnerability even at the moment of his triumph.' [144]

In the empty stadium, Lorna confesses her love for Joe, reassuring him that in time his hand will heal and that he will be able to play the violin again (a more optimistic future than would be on the cards for Stoker Thompson, whose hand is broken in *The Set-Up* (1949)). Marking Joe's commitment to life as a musician (and thus to family life), the final scene takes place in his family home, where he and Lorna enter a tearful embrace with his father - a very much more upbeat ending than that of Odet's play in which Lorna and Joe both die in his sports car.

What makes *Golden Boy* such a strong picture is the combination of musician/fighter and the implications of Joe's choice. Yet the posters and advertisements for the film concentrated on the romance almost exclusively, featuring illustrations of William Holden and Barbara Stanwyck embracing under a range of straplines that included 'an epic drama of heartbreak and romance!' and 'out of the heart of a great city beats a dramatic symphony of youthful romance'. Only in one advertisement did small inset images appear of Holden playing his violin, the caption reading 'with music I'm never alone' and striking a boxing pose, captioned 'I'll dazzle the eyes out of his head'. Although exhibitors were encouraged by the studio to run promotions that would attract fight fans, they were told that 'Golden Boy...is NOT a fight picture, and should not be identified as such to the general public'.[145] This positioning did not seem to be picked up by the trade press, particularly on the re-issue of the film in 1947, with *Motion Picture Herald* then describing it as a 'melodrama of the prize ring' that packs entertainment 'from bell to bell', thus reducing it to a plot indistinguishable from every other boxing movie (and which may indicate that boxing films were such sure-fire successes that there was no further need to 'sell' it).[146] Yet *Golden Boy* is different: certainly it is a more optimistic film than many of its contemporaries, because Joe is shown to have a future outside boxing (one that lies beyond

The Hispanic poster for Golden Boy - *'Sueño Dorado' means 'Golden Dreams' - has no indication that this is a boxing movie*

a mere domesticity) and therefore has a genuine choice to make - something that is just not available to boxers like Rocky Graziano in *Somebody Up There Likes Me*, where the only alternative is prison. Thus when Joe quits the ring, this does not signal the defeat that it represents in many films in the genre, but merely a crossroads in his life. Joe learns some valuable lessons through his contact with the fight game: that worthwhile achievements only come with time; and that family and community ties are more important - and more reliable - than those based on money. The film conveys other messages too, which perhaps sit less easily with a modern audience: that masculinity necessitates a rite of passage before it is acceptable to reveal a more sensitive side; that a woman's talents are of little significance compared with those of a man (there is no sense of Joe's sister Anna having made a life-changing choice in not pursuing a professional musical career); and that anything offered by modernity is inferior to the 'old ways', with their close affiliation to the 'home country'. The last line of the film sums up the moral message of the film: as Joe embraces his father, he says: 'Papa - I've come home.'

[52] Fisher died in 1955 and the strip was taken over by Tony DiPreta

[53] 'Joe Palooka' 1938 strip

[54] Hanson 1993 p1614

[55] Jeff Parker in *American Classic Screen* did, however, review the series (Jul/Aug 1983)

[56] *Variety* Mar 6 1934

[57] *Picturegoer* Nov 3 1934

[58] *Variety* Mar 6 1934

[59] Romano 2004 p144

[60] *The Great Schnozzle* pressbook

[61] Cagney, who bore a striking resemblance to his more famous brother, had a short film acting career, moving behind the camera to produce after 1950

[62] Armstrong had a prolific film career and had starred as Carl Denham in *King Kong* the year before

[63] Romano 2004 p144

[64] *Kine Weekly* Sept 9 1943. 'Industrial company' presumably meant the working classes

[65] *The Milky Way* pressbook

[66] Sarris 1998 p155

[67] *The Milky Way* pressbook

[68] A story, possible apocryphal, says that Sam Goldwyn was so keen for the remake to be successful that he bought and destroyed the negative of *The Milky Way*, together with as many prints as he could find. Lloyd's own original copy remained and was eventually used to make the transfer to digital

[69] *Film Weekly* Mar 7 1936

[70] *Monthly Film Bulletin* Mar 31 1936 p47; *Kine Weekly* Mar 5 1936 p25

[71] Romano 1994 p133. The delays may partly have been due to the illness of two cast members and the director. Norman McLeod was said to have stepped in while Leo McCarey was unwell

[72] As well as 'Burleigh' implying a burly stature, the 'Sullivan' alludes to the great fighter John L Sullivan

[73] Menjou was to reappear as a boxing manager three years' later in *Golden Boy*

[74] *The Milky Way* pressbook

[75] *The Milky Way* pressbook

[76] The inclusion of a pre-fight routine is interesting, as Lloyd was said to be a highly superstitious person with, for example, strict rituals of dressing

[77] The pressbook for the film reports that the lion was used when the studio were unable to hire a kangaroo, though as Sullivan is dubbed first a 'lion' and then a 'tiger' the kangaroo may just have been a publicity-writer's piece of creativity, particularly as the animal never appears in the ring with Sullivan - surely an unmissable opportunity

[78] Parkinson 1993 p84. Menjou was playing opposite his wife, Veree Teasdale

[79] *The Milky Way* pressbook

[80] *The Milky Way* pressbook

[81] Quoted in Cahn 1966 p161

[82] *Variety* Jun 2 1937

[83] Rode 2017

[84] *New York Times* May 27 1937 p21

[85] *Variety* Jun 2 1937

[86] Mushy Callaghan also appeard as the referee in the 1962 Elvis Presley remake of the film

[87] *Variety* June 2 1937

[88] Leger Grindon believes that Donati's ethnicity is crucial to his behaviour and ambition (and his temper), an outsider wanting to assimilate into Anglo society but reluctant to marry Fluff or to relinquish his overbearing hold on his family (Grindon 2011 p106)

[89] *Variety,* June 2 1937

[90] Swindell 1975 p136

[91] *They Made Me a Criminal* pressbook

[92] *They Made Me a Criminal* pressbook

[93] Christopher 1997 p101

[94] The film was a more sentimental, and arguably less realistic, remake of the 1933 Warner Brothers release, *The Life of Jimmy Dolan* which had starred Douglas Fairbanks Jnr and was based on the same play but with a script written by David Boehm and Erwin S Gelsey

[95] Millhouser and Dix 1948 p3

[96] *They Made Me a Criminal* pressbook. The pressbook also emphasises Garfield's boxing amateur boxing experience

[97] *They Made Me a Criminal* pressbook

[98] *Kinematograph Weekly* identified this scene as being plagiarised from a one-reeler called *Playing with Danger* (*Kine Weekly* Mar 9 1939 p39)

[99] Bergan 1982 p25

[100] The pressbook for the film claims that one of the fighters (it does not specify which) wore the gloves which James Jeffries had worn when he knocked out Jim Corbett in 1903

[101] Quoted in McGrath 1993 p25

[102] *Kinematograph Weekly* Mar 9 1939 p19; *Film Weekly* Apr 29 1939

[103] McGrath 1993 p25

[104] *Motion Picture Herald* Jan 7 1939 p38

[105] *Monthly Film Bulletin* v.6 1939 p118; *Film Weekly* Apr 29 1939

[106] Sklar 1992 p90

[107] *Kid Nightingale* pressbook

[108] *Today's Cinema* Jan 17 1940

[109] *Kid Nightingale* pressbook

[110] *Kid Nightingale* pressbook

[111] *Motion Picture Herald*, Sept 23 1939

[112] *Kinematograph Weekly* Jan 18 1940

[113] *Today's Cinema* Jan 17 1940

[114] *Film Weekly* Aug 5 1939

[115] *Kinematograph Weekly* Jun 8 1939

[116] *Monthly Film Bulletin* Nov 1939 p204

[117] *Variety*, Jun 28 1939

118 *Motion Picture Herald* Jun 24 1939 p42. The film was re-issued ten years after its first release and though *Today's Cinema* predicted it could still make 'a confident bid for the favours of the popular public', one wonders how it dated it must have seemed not just because the war had intervened and the world was a very different place, but because it was then being screened at the same time as *Champion* and *The Set-Up* (*Today's Cinema* May 13 1949 p9)

119 Landy 1991 p253

120 Perry 1985 p86

121 The novel had been largely forgotten until reissued in 2014 by London Books

122 *The Film Programme*, Radio 4, Oct 2 2009

123 Barr 1997 p19

124 *Variety* Jun 28 1939 p20

125 *Motion Picture Herald* Jun 24 1939 p42

126 Landy 1991 p252

127 Parkinson 1993 p323

128 Sweet, *The Film Programme*, Radio 4, Oct 2 2009

129 Barr 1997 p19

130 Knight in *There Ain't No Justice* by James Curtis, 2014 p11

131 Curtis 2014 p126

132 The 1964 version cast Joe as an African-American

133 *Monthly Film Bulletin* Nov 1939 p71

134 Grindon 1996 p1

135 Garfield did eventually play Joe Bonaparte on stage, in the 1952 revival by which time Garfield was 39, arguably rather too old to be credible as the young up-and-coming boxer

136 *Today's Cinema* Oct 25 1939 p7; *Kine Weekly* Oct 26 1939 p10

137 Boddy 2008 p266

138 Grindon 2014 p190

139 *Kine Weekly* Oct 26 1939 p10

140 Holden was coached by middleweight James 'Cannonball' Green for the boxing scenes: Green played the Chocolate Drop in the film. Later in life he appeared as Manuel Vega in *Rocky IV* (1985)

[141] Parkinson 1993 p350

[142] Parkinson 1993 p350

[143] Wright 1974 p78

[144] Grindon 2014 p190

[145] *Golden Boy* pressbook

[146] *Motion Picture Herald*, Aug 30 1947 p3806

SUCKER PUNCH - FILMS OF THE 1940s

JAMES
CAGNEY
ANN
SHERIDAN
A STORY WITH ALL THE
FIRE AND FURY OF ITS
TWO GREAT STARS!
CITY FOR
CONQUEST
FRANK CRAVEN
DONALD CRISP
GEORGE TOBIAS · JEROME COWAN
Presented by
WARNER BROS.
FRANK McHUGH
ARTHUR KENNEDY
An Anatole Litvak Production

A Heart Beating in the City
City for Conquest (1940)

New York is the city to be conquered in this James Cagney film and, as with other boxing films set in New York such as *Somebody Up There Likes Me*, it steals the show. Warner Brothers capitalised on this, with the film posters giving the city's skyline equal billing with Cagney and his co-star Ann Sheridan, and a tagline running above their faces that reads: 'New York's a pushover for us. We'll take what we want!', a line that encapsulates the American dream that anyone can rise to achieve their ambitions.

It's a sentimental melodrama with almost no boxing action until close to the end, and although ostensibly about 'conquering' New York, its protagonist - Danny Kenny (James Cagney) - is not an ambitious man. He's much more interested in helping family and friends and playing a part in his own neighbourhood, where he is accepting of everyone. While his girlfriend Peggy (Ann Sheridan) talks about seeing the world, Danny acknowledges that they maybe could move out as far as the Bronx. 'Everyone in New York wants to be somebody,' she tells him, 'except you.' Certainly, Peggy wants to be 'somebody' - in her case a professional dancer - and Danny's brother Eddie (Arthur Kennedy in his first screen role[147]) wants the symphony he is writing to be performed, but Danny is content to drive a truck for $27.50 a week and to leave his Golden Gloves boxing days behind him, visible only in a photograph taped to the wall in the rundown apartment he shares with his brother on the lower East Side. *City for Conquest* is no 'body versus soul' tug-of-war despite the boxing (body) and music (soul) underlying metaphors. Danny's soul remains intact throughout, as does his modesty, integrity and loyalty. He may not 'conquer' New York in the end, but he is genuinely content when his brother does.

The trade press picked up on the 'city as star' angle, with *Kinematograph Weekly* saying that the 'thronging, striving existence' of the East Side (where Cagney himself grew up) is 'brilliantly portrayed', and *Today's Cinema* praising the 'spectacular New York background' with its 'teeming millions of workers and players, each the victim or victor of ambition and desire'.[148] The pressbook emphasised the three weeks that the crew had spent filming around the city to ensure authenticity. Both the city and the plot of the film are given a mythical quality by the introduction of an on-screen narrator, listed in the credits as 'Old Timer' and played by Frank Craven, who had just performed a similar role in the film *Our Town* (also 1940). Fulfilling something akin to the role of a 'Greek chorus', he opens the film by talking to camera on the Williamsburg Bridge about the city, before being moved on by a policeman.[149] He leads the viewer to the corner of Forsythe and Delancey Streets where children are following a barrel organ and to a girl - Peggy - dancing to the music. On the way, he stops to reprimand a grubby urchin, who says his name is Googi, for stealing bread rolls from a stall. As he watches Peggy dance, Old Timer says 'What a town! Right out of the asphalt, flowers grow.' A boy pushes Peggy - and another young boy weighs in with his fists to defend her, calling Peggy his 'goil'. This, of course, is Danny. After he has punched his opponent to the ground, Danny runs back to the apartment where he lives. Sitting on the stoop is Eddie, his brother, playing the accordian and swearing that some day he'll get a piano to play. Old Timer then predicts a dancing career for Peggy, and that Danny will fight his way through life with his bare fists. Thus the whole story is prefigured for these three characters (and for Googi too), lending it not just a mythological quality but a fatalistic sense that there is nothing they can do to avoid their destiny. As an opening, it's also deeply sentimental, romanticising life on the poor streets of the lower East Side, so that when the next scene shifts to the present-day with Danny, Peggy and Eddie as adults, the viewer retains that sentimentality, something aided by the lush score, written by Max Steiner.

Danny turns to professional boxing, under the ring name 'Young Samson', but only for pragmatic reasons - to pay Eddie's music school fees, because Eddie is not getting by on giving local no-hopers piano lessons at 50 cents a time. Danny wins every fight because, as Old Timer says, 'he doesn't care whether he wins or not.' His career ends at the welterweight championship challenge when he is blinded in the ring by his opponent, Cannonball Wales (Joe Gray) who sticks his glove, coated with rosin dust, again and again into Danny's eyes. Danny's new job is running a street newspaper stand, but he has achieved what he wanted: Eddie plays his 'City For Conquest' symphony at Carnegie Hall and Danny is reunited with Peggy.

This was not the only time that boxing and musicianship occupied the same genre. In *Golden Boy* (1939) Joe Bonaparte (William Holden) tries to choose between fighting, which brings wealth, and being a violinist, which pleases his traditional Italian-American family, an Apollonian/Dionysian struggle. In other films the combination is treated lightly, more perhaps for the box-office appeal of such polar opposites: in *The Joe Louis Story* (1953) the young Joe (Coley Wallace) is quick to drop his violin lessons in favour of a chance to box; in *Here Comes Mr Jordan* (1941) Joe Pendleton (Robert Montgomery) is never without his 'lucky saxophone' propped on a corner-post of the ring (even though he plays it remarkably badly), and in *Kid Nightingale* (1939) Steve Nelson (John Payne) sings an aria or two to the crowd in between rounds. In *City for Conquest*, it is the two people that Danny cares most about - composer Eddie and dancer Peggy - and not Danny himself who represent the (notionally) opposite values to that of boxing.[150]

The film was based the best-selling novel of the same name by Aben Kandel, a screenwriter as well as a novelist who went on to write the screenplay for two more boxing films, *The Fighter*, and *Kid Monk Baroni* (both 1952). Kandel did not, however, adapt *City for Conquest* for the screen: this job was given by Warner Brothers to John Wexley, probably because he had just written the very successful *Angels With Dirty Faces* (1938) which had also starred James Cagney and Ann Sheridan in a gritty and realistic New York setting. Cagney had admired the novel - which, like the film, set the action in 1934 - and was pleased that some passages 'with genuinely poetic flavor' were being retained. 'Then I saw the final cut of the picture,' he said in his autobiography. 'The studio had edited out the best scenes ... leaving only the novel's skeleton. What remained was a trite melodrama.'[151] He had been uncomfortable with the original screenplay, telling his brother William (who was associate producer) that Wexley 'knows nothing ... of what went on during the period covered by the script and apparently knows less about the fight business.'[152] At the time, Cagney was Warner Bros' highest paid star, with a share of the profits - and *City For Conquest*, despite his misgivings and mixed reviews, was a profitable film. The director was Anatole Litvak, who was to spend the next five years making the 'Why We Fight' series of war films including *The Nazis Strike, Prelude to War* and *The Battle of Russia* (all 1943); *The Battle of China* (1944) and *War Comes to America* (1945).

Aben Kandel's book is much darker than than the film: New York is less a place of opportunity than a place that is 'deep, high and angry. Come in and you're swallowed. Leave and you're not missed.'[153] It may be a city ripe for 'conquest' but whether anyone actually does, and what that conquest might mean, is left open. The ethnic mix in New York - Italians, Jews, Irish, Germans - is ever-present in the book and unstated in the film (just as it will be in *The Set-Up*) even though the audience would have associated Cagney with Irishness through his previous films such as *The Pluck of the Irish* (1936) and *The Irish in Us* (1935).

As well as the comedy *The Irish in Us*, Cagney had already starred in another boxing film, *Winner Take All* (1932), which had some thematic parallels with *City for Conquest*, in that the motivation for Cagney's character to fight is not for glory, but to help raise money for someone else - in this case, a sick child.

Danny's professional boxing career begins with a fight in a small-time smoke-filled West Side gym where he is matched against a fighter called Kid Callahan (Larry Steers). Promoter Scotty MacPherson (Donald Crisp) is in the crowd, likes what he sees in 'Young Samson' and bets on him.[154] While he and his cronies are arguing about bets, there is a 'thump' off-screen and they turn to see that Callahan has been knocked out by 'a sock like Dempsey'. The audience would have to wait until more than 100 minutes into the film before seeing any sustained boxing action. Instead, the film focuses more on Peggy's dancing career: it is her ambition that will drive a wedge between her and Danny and persuade him to sign with Scotty to go all the way to the welterweight championship. Peggy - naive and eager to please - falls under the malign and controlling influence of professional dancer Murray Burns (an early role for Anthony Quinn), who constantly calls her 'babe' but does not allow her name on the bill and does not share the prize money with her. His total control of her is underlined in a scene where there is an implied rape after she struggles in his arms. The rise to fame of the dancers is told in the same way that a boxer's rise

Burns (Anthony Quinn) is a malign and controlling influence, not allowing Peggy's name on the bill or sharing the prize money with her, but her ambition drives a wedge between her and Danny

through the ranks is conventionally portrayed, this time in a montage of dancing feet and prize-cups as they go on tour. Danny's parallel career is also told through a montage of headlines, trains and knock-out punches as he travels around the country.[155]

Danny's loyalty to old friends is shown through the reappearance of his old childhood friend Googi (Elia Kazan who would later direct *On the Waterfront*), when Danny is still driving trucks for a living. Googi is a down-on-his-luck ex-con, who Danny gladly gives money to and buys him a steak dinner, despite Googi declaring that he's not given up his criminal ways but is 'not going to do it for peanuts' any more. When they next meet, Googi is dressed to the nines and is surrounded by a posse of young women: clearly crime is a paying business. He takes Danny to a ritzy club

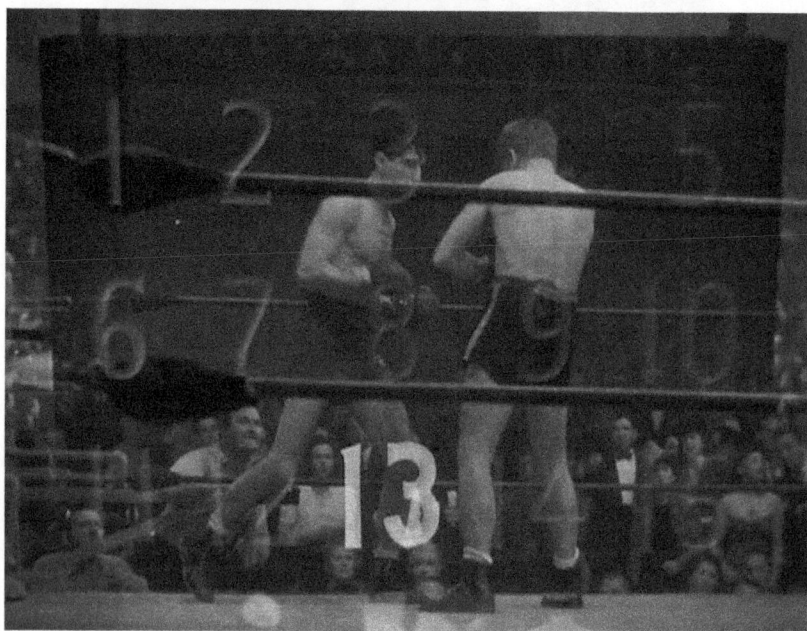

Although the Director of Photography was James Wong Howe, who would later break new ground in how fights were filmed, his request for a hand-held camera was turned down by studio boss Jack Warner, so the results are conventional

where Danny arranges for Eddie to get up on stage and play part of his symphony. The crowd ignore him and carry on partying, to Danny's disgust, yet when Eddie switches to ragtime, they all gather round. Danny walks out, into the nighttime streets, and spots a venue where Peggy is dancing. After a hostile encounter with Burns, Danny leaves and Peggy joins him in the street: they are reunited but although Danny promises they will be married in a fortnight when Peggy's tour ends, she does not tell him that Burns has signed for a further tour - and she won't be back. He only learns this later when, at his apartment, he opens a letter from Peggy.

The dramatic high-point of the film - and the only sustained boxing action - is Danny's championship challenge against Cannonball Wales (Joe Gray), at the beginning and end of which we cut away to Peggy, listening to the fight on the radio in her dressing-room while waiting to go on stage. Burns takes the opportunity to refer sneeringly to Danny as a 'palooka'. The director of photography for *City for Conquest* was James Wong Howe, who would later break new ground in the way fights were filmed, when he took to roller-skates to shoot *Body and Soul* (he would also go on to film *The Fighter*, a 1952 film based on the Jack London story 'The Mexican' and his fight scenes were the only element of the film praised by the critics at the time). He was keen to be innovative in *City For Conquest*, and asked to use a hand-held camera, but Jack Warner told him to forget it; 'the studio did not spend forty thousand dollars on a studio camera for Howe to use some 'hand-held toy'.[156] The film would have benefitted - using conventional methods resulted in what Rainsberger calls 'bland and unemotional' footage.[157] The action opens with overhead shots of the packed arena, with a slow zoom in to ringside for Round One, where 'Young Samson' is dodging Wales then slugging him. Wales drops to the floor but gets up at the count of seven. Round numbers are displayed; we see Danny's big punches, then cutaways to the crowd. By Round Seven, both men are tired. Danny knocks Wales down, but he is saved by the bell.[158]

From this point on, it's no longer a fair fight and 'unemotional' seems a strange way to describe it. At the round break, Wales' trainer puts rosin dust on his gloves, and Wales comes out with a flurry of blows to Danny's face. The camera is inside the ropes now, showing Danny wiping his eyes, unable to see properly. In Round Eight, furious punches all connect with Danny's face. The Round numbers are shown one after the other, until by

Round Thirteen, Danny's eyes are swollen shut. He misses a punch and falls into the ropes. He's not even defending himself now, and when the bells rings, he's unable to find his way back to his corner. 'It's a miracle of human courage' says the radio commentator, but Danny refuses to accept defeat, saying that he'll 'nail this round' and doesn't want the fight stopped despite Eddie rushing over to Scotty MacPherson to beg him to stop it. The final round - Round Fifteen - is not shown: the camera cuts away to Peggy listening on the radio, tears streaming down her face.

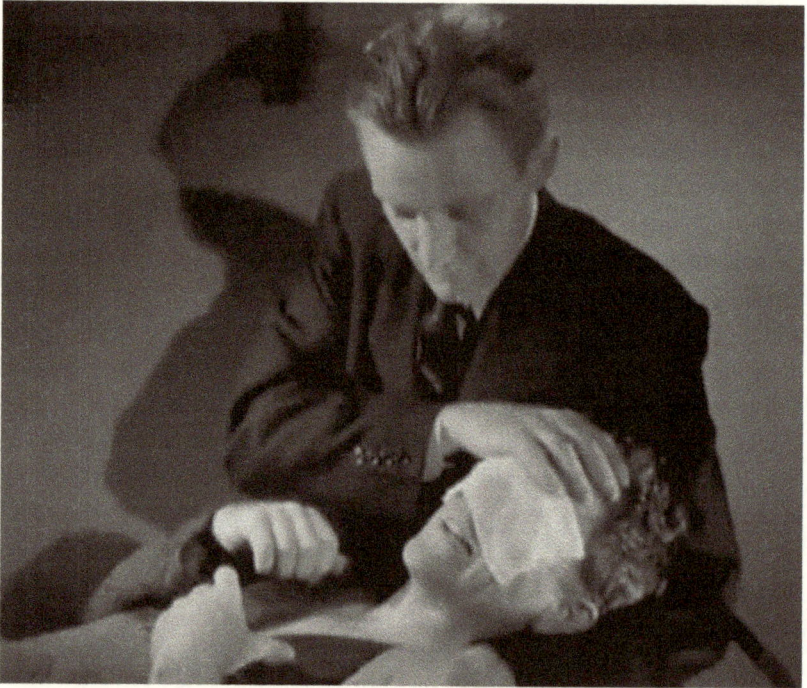

Eddie (Arthur Kennedy) tends to his brother after Danny has been blinded in the ring, in a pose suggesting a pieta

The next shot is of Danny lying on a bed having his eyes treated by a doctor, who notes the gritty substance in the eyes. 'This is my department,' says Googi and the film veers into gangster territory with Googi - still in full evening dress - abducting and then killing Wales' manager and dumping him in the river before being shot himself by Wales' trainer.

Danny is finished as a fighter and it will be a year before any eye operation is possible: for the time being, all he can see is shadows. As always, however, he is optimistic, assuring Eddie (in an echo of the Biblical Samson) that he can 'see things now that I never could before' and becoming lost in Eddie's music. Desperate for something to do, he asks Scotty for help, and the next time we see him, he's running a newsstand.[159] Throughout the film, Danny has been a natty dresser, always wearing a well-cut suit and tie, but on the newstand he wears a flat cap, open-necked shirt and a bomber-style jacket: neighbourhood clothes, rather than the aspirational clothes of the past.

The climax of the film is the premiere of Eddie's symphony of New York, a lengthy sequence with Eddie conducting the orchestra at Carnegie Hall - and with Peggy in the audience, visibly moved by the music. Danny refuses to go to the concert, preferring to listen to it on the radio while he tends the newstand and though he hears the tribute that Eddie gives to the audience at the end ('my brother made music with his fists so that I might make a gentler music') he pretends modestly to a newstand customer that he didn't hear that part.

On the newstand, Danny wears 'neighbourhood clothes' rather than the aspirational clothes of the past

The film ends with Peggy coming to the newstand: she is no longer with Burns and has been reduced to playing in the chorus-line of a Follies burlesque show. 'I always knew someday you'd pass by here and see me - because you're always my goil,' says Danny, and they embrace. This would be a perfect ending but for the fact that Old Timer appears again, talking about the fact that there's 'a heart beating in the city.' It's interesting to note that in DVD and TV versions of the film, the Old Timer sequences were deleted and were only restored in 2007.

Whereas many boxing films objectify the body of the boxer for the gaze of the viewer (in *Champion*, for example, quite literally putting the half-naked fighter played by Kirk Douglas on a pedestal), this is not done in *City for Conquest*. When we first see Danny in the gym, punching a speedball, he wears leggings, T shirt and leotard; he wears the same - plus a head guard - when sparring. It is not until the championship fight that we see him bare-chested and the fight scene appears on none of the posters. While Cagney doesn't have a boxer's physique - and was only 5 ft 5 ins tall (he fought as an amateur lightweight when young) - the lack of emphasis on his body may have been more due to his age: he was 40 when *City for Conquest* was filmed, implausibly late for his character's start of a boxing career. James Garfield was 25 when he made *They Made Me a Criminal* and 34 when he appeared in *Body and Soul*; William Holden was only 20 when he starred in *Golden Boy*. Robert Ryan was 40 at the time of *The Set-Up*, but he was playing a washed-up fighter, not someone just embarking on their professional rise through the ranks. Danny's opponent in the championship fight was played by Joe Gray, who was 6 ft tall, though the difference in their heights is elided by the camera angles and possibly by the use of stunt doubles. Cagney was said to have trained hard for the fight scenes, sparring with Harvey Perry (who had played his opponent in *Winner Take All*) and following a strict regime of running, shadow-boxing and wrestling.[160]

'It is a film', says Robert Sklar, 'filled with all the usual cliches and yet its touching power derives in part from their familiarity'.[161] In a sense, this might apply to all genre films: familiarity with the tropes being ironically a key part of their attraction. But although the press praised Cagney's restrained acting style, and the way the film 'plucks at the heart-strings fortissimo', they seemed unconvinced by the plot: 'the story does not make sense' said *Monthly Film Bulletin* and reviews were mixed. [162] Although the film did well at the box office, Cagney was so ashamed of it that he wrote a letter of apology to Aben Kandel, and vowed he would never view any of his own movies again in future.[163]

A Diddy Dame for a Manager
The Pittsburgh Kid (1941)

*T*he *Pittsburgh Kid*, a low-budget 'programmer' from Republic, one of the 'poverty row' studios, offers a twist in the rise-to-fame story of a boxing champion - a woman manager.[164] This plot device gives a fresh edge to the film, an edge which is underscored by the film's focus on a love triangle, rather than on the familiar theme of the corruption of the fight business. *The Pittsburgh Kid* also benefits from the presence of its star Billy Conn, 23-year-old former light-heavyweight world champion who was highly newsworthy at the time of the film's release, fresh from his June 18 match against Joe Louis where the fast-punching and fleet-footed Conn looked likely to win until he was knocked out in the 13th round. The film was shot on Conn's honeymoon in California - after the fight, he had eloped with 18-year-old Mary Louise Smith, marrying her in Philadelphia.[165]As might be expected Conn, an Irish working-class boxer who was reputedly signed to the picture for 25,000 dollars, brings to the film some authentic fight scenes, but he also has a surprisingly effective star presence.[166] Tall, loose-limbed and softly spoken, with a slightly stooped stance, he is highly credible as the boxer who vacillates between the need to assert his independence, and his increasing reliance on his manager's professional coaching. Reviewers at the time were not so complimentary about Conn's acting ability: *Kinematograph Weekly* said he was 'no great shakes' as an actor and *Variety* commented on his 'one continuous monotone', conceding grudgingly that 'he speaks clearly … looks okay and handles himself well, albeit a bit stiffly.'[167] Hindsight has not brought Billy Conn any acting plaudits either: Zucker and Babich, writing in 1987, say 'if you want to know why Billy Conn never made it big in the movies, all you have to do is watch him play himself in this film'.[168] Conn's wife Mary Louise claimed that he was subsequently offered the part of Jim Corbett in

Gentleman Jim 'but Billy turned it down ... He wanted nothing to do with Hollywood ever again'.[169] His feet did appear in *Gentleman Jim*, however, doubling for the star Errol Flynn in the fight scenes.

The film was directed by Jack Townley. A prolific screenwriter of comedies and westerns with more than 100 films to his credit, Townley only directed six films, this film being his last. The script was written by Earl Felton and Houston Branch and was based on 'Kid Tinsel' by playwright and short-story writer Octavus Roy Cohen. 'Kid Tinsel' was a hardboiled novel first published as a serial in Collier's magazine in 1940.

The Pittsburgh Kid is essentially about rules - not just the rules of boxing, but the rules of life, and the necessity of 'staying in your own corner'. In other words, it is about knowing your place and where your loyalties lie.

After the death of trainer Pop Mallory, his daughter Pat (Jean Parker) takes on the management of young fighter Billy Conn, her father having warded off an approach from city trainer Max Ellison (Jonathan Hale). Conn, however, is attracted by the glamorous Babs (Veda Ann Borg), Ellison's predatory daughter, and briefly signs up with Ellison before Pat snatches him back. Pat has to send him on a boxing tour in order to get him away from Babs' influence and to ready him for a championship bout. Conn gets into a scuffle with Babs' boyfriend, Joe Barton (Alan Baxter), at his city apartment and Barton is accidentally shot dead with his own gun.[170] The only witness flees and Conn is blamed for the killing. Pat embarks on a campaign to find the missing witness, but the only way she can raise money to hire an attorney is to sell Conn to the local gym at a rock-bottom price. Her campaign succeeds, but having sold Conn means that she will no longer be at the ringside in his championship fight. Conn looks set to lose, but at the last moment, Babs begs Pat to return and - with Pat shouting encouragement and instructions - Conn achieves a knockout in the fourteenth round.

One of the regular devices of the boxing film is to make a clear division between the city (which connotes corruption, greed and artificiality) and the country (which connotes wholesome exercise, friendly interaction and naturalness). This can be portrayed both by the locale itself and through the clothes, appearance and manner of the people that inhabit it. When the two environments collide, it is usually the catalyst for a character-change in the protagonist. In *The Pittsburgh Kid*, the visit of

Max Ellison and Babs to the training camp feels almost like an invasion of the country by the city - a declaration of hostilities. It also serves to point up a familiar contrast between two stereotypes: the gold-digger, who has artificial-looking blonde hair, high-fashion clothes, a predatory manner and a 'city' name ('Babs'), and the 'good woman' who has dark hair, neatly restrained clothes, an hospitable manner and a 'country' name ('Pat'). Babs is overdressed for the country, wearing a fur collar and muff, and it is notable that in every scene that the two women appear, they are wearing different outfits: clearly a device to appeal to women picturegoers. Pat's role, to be the moral force in the fighter's life, is clearly conveyed in this scene as she urges Conn to stay at the camp rather than go back to the city to fight: she makes him promise to 'work it out right, for Pop's sake as well as your own.'

At the training camp, the country is associated with wholesome exercise, friendly interraction and naturalness, an atmosphere 'invaded' by Max Ellison and Babs who represent city values

Pat was played by Jean Parker, who enjoyed a prominent stage career (she starred in *Born Yesterday* on Broadway, replacing Judy Holliday), as well as making nearly 100 appearances in film and on TV, notably in *Little Women* (1933) in which she played Beth opposite Joan Bennett and Katharine Hepburn. By 1937 she had moved to the smaller studios and made 70 films in nine years. She will be remembered, said Tom Vallance, as the 'shapely spirited heroine of a series of vigorous B-movies ... They usually had backgrounds that promised fast action, such as oil derricks, high explosives or airfields',[171] yet it was perhaps her 'wholesome' image as Beth that would have been best recollected by audiences viewing *The Pittsburgh Kid*. Veda Ann Borg, who played Babs, was frequently cast in sexy working-class roles: Lon Cross dubbed her the 'brassy queen of bit parts ... (who) 'had a snappy toughness that really clicked with audiences'.[172] She was the redhead who gives a 'sassy once-over'[173] to boxer Wayne Morris in *Kid Galahad* (1937) and was frequently cast as a bargirl, gum-chewing chorus girl or feisty Yellow Cab girl. These established screen personas brought a pre-existing 'layer' of meaning to the characters they were portraying, a form of 'shorthand' that helped audiences to immediately make a judgement about what they were seeing.

Although a contrast is made between Pat and Babs, it is done without over-emphasis. Pat's house at the training camp is elegant and well-furnished (not a piece of gingham in sight) and her clothes are smartly professional, not redolent of the country like the 'shepherdess' costume that Marie wears on the farm in *Kid Galahad* with its laced bodice and puff sleeves. She employs two black servants who call Pat 'Miss Patreesha' and with whom there is much humorous intereaction. Pat is no 'country fool' and is keenly aware of Conn's attraction to Babs. When Max asks again to manage Conn, Babs assures her: 'we'll take good care of him: I'll personally guarantee it', to which Pat replies (with an edge): 'yes, I'm sure you will.' Conn declares that 'from now on I'm gonna carve things out for myself,' which audiences would recognise as a harbinger of problems to come.

A female manager is big news in the boxing world, but Pat is afraid that *Tribune* reporter Cliff Halliday (Dick Purcell) will write about the 'gay young pug with a diddy dame for a manager.' In fact, Cliff becomes a valuable ally and lends a supportive ear to Pat: newspapermen are often portrayed sympathetically in boxing films, such as in *The Harder They*

Fall (1956) where the world-weary Eddie (Humphrey Bogart) gives his fee to fighter Toro Moreno who has been cheated out of his earnings, and in *The Joe Louis Story* (1953) where Tad McGeehan (Paul Stewart) - the moral centre of the film - is so miserable to see Joe Louis past his prime that he can't bear to watch his final fight. The portrayal subverts the perceived Hollywood stereotype of the reporter who will do anything to get the scoop (such as Kirk Douglas as reporter Chuck Tatum in *Ace in the Hole*, a Billy Wilder film of 1951, in which he prolongs the rescue of a trapped man in order to get more coverage for the story). Perhaps reporters get a more sympathetic portrayal in the boxing genre because of their symbiotic relationship to the fighter: they are right there at ringside, often throughout a fighter's career: the reporter needs a story but the boxer needs the coverage too. As Pat is increasingly alone in 'her corner', with Conn, Max and Babs all in the opposite corner, the character of Cliff is a useful device for allowing Pat to voice her plans - and her fears. For one thing, Conn is spending too much money and too much time with Babs: he's already got involved in fisticuffs at the Flamingo Club back in the city, when Joe Barton, Bab's boyfriend, warns him off and gets punched for his trouble. 'I can't control your life,' Pat tells Conn, 'but I've got something to say about the hours you keep,' reinforcing the notion that the city is a place of nighttime, of artificial light, whereas the country is a wholesome daylit place. Even Max is concerned about Conn. 'I don't like him waltzing around loose,' he says, 'out of hand', thus using a familiar child or animal analogy for a boxer.

Pat's solution is to send Conn on a tour - part of his build-up to the championship fight. The usual montage of headlines and punches charts Conn's success and, when he gets back to the training camp, the ringside is packed with interested parties (and the prosperous-looking camp is even charging a 25-cent entrance fee). Even Pat's coaching advice is being paid much more attention and it is clear the 'diddy dame' knows what she's doing. The boxing action scenes - sparring or skipping - often take place in the background of a dialogue shot, so that the plot moves on without seeming too static. One sparring scene is noteworthy for showing Conn's technique. He spars with black boxer Henry Armstrong, a world champion in welterweight and featherweight categories who had starred in the film *Keep Punching* in 1939, but here just playing a sparring partner. Pat tells Henry to 'keep throwing those straight lefts' while Conn holds his hands at

Billy Conn spars with Henry Armstrong, in a sequence showcasing Conn's fleet footwork

his sides. He is to 'slip everything' rather than blocking. Conn's footwork is fleet as he dodges the punches and pulls his head back (though despite Pat's instructions, Henry is jabbing with his right hand). The sparring is more mesmerising because there is no background music, just the soft contact noise of the gloves and of their feet moving on the canvas.

Back in the city, Conn breaks up with Babs: she has been pestering him and he's been ignoring her. After a confrontation, he throws her out, only for Barton to arrive and draw a gun. In the resulting struggle, Barton accidentally shoots himself with his own gun. Barton's sidekick flees, the police arrive, and Conn is the subject of very different newspaper headlines from the ones he is used to: 'Conn murder tangle makes fight doubtful' says the splash across the front page of the *Tribune*. He is arrested and detained in prison, the bars echoing the shadows in the early scene in Max Ellison's office. The only way now that the championship fight can go ahead is for the runaway witness to be found and Conn's name to be cleared. To raise money to hire an attorney, Pat sells Conn for a rock-bottom price to cigar-smoking Garvey (Dick Elliott), owner of Garvey's

The 'good woman' and the 'gold-digger' are clearly signalled by their choice of costume: the dark-haired Pat wears tailored suits and hats, often with a string of pearls; the blonde Babs is extravagantly dressed in furs

Gym. She's confident of his fighting ability: 'after all,' she says, 'Billy's gonna win that fight whether I'm in his corner or not.' (The audience, noting Conn's increasing reliance on Pat, might have had their doubts about this).

Pat pleads with Babs to help find the missing witness. After a night-time chase, and a shootout in a deserted factory, the missing witness is arrested and Conn is free. It is at Garvey's that Conn receives his new ring name: The Pittsburgh Kid.

The climax of the film is the championship fight against Grogan (Jack Roper, just listed as 'The Champ' in the credits), which is initially shown from high up above the ring, a dramatic shot from the radio commentators' box where Cliff (magically transformed from a newspaperman into a radio reporter) introduces the match. The fight is an interesting mix of loyalties: Max Ellison manages Grogan, but his daughter's heart clearly lies with Conn. It is, says Cliff, 'a blood fight with an Ellison in each corner.' Whereas it is common practice for the final fight in a boxing film to include the announcer's build-up and the referee's recitation of the rules, in *The Pittsburgh Kid* it is an important reinforcement of the film's theme - that there are rules in life which have to be observed. The fight begins and Conn is a disaster in the early rounds, slow-moving, defensive and forgetful of all his training, despite Garvey's earnest coaching. At one stage, he even walks back to the wrong corner, a neat symbolic touch. We know what's wrong: Pat is not at the fight and, without Pat, Conn has lost heart. At this stage, Babs redeems herself by persuading Pat she needs to be with Conn. It's not all altruism - as the rounds clock up, Babs has realised that Conn is unlikely to win. 'Girls are funny - we only like to ride with the winners,' she explains: in other words, as a loser, he is no longer of use to her. Pat comes to the fight, yells instructions from the stands and Conn is transformed, punching smarter and turning the fight around. He's left it so late - it's now Round 14 - that only a knockout can make him the champion, a knockout he delivers in fine style (and the camera moves inside the ropes for the first time to witness it). The film ends as Conn leaves the ring and takes Pat in his arms, the first time they have touched in the whole film.

The relationship between Pat and Conn is somewhat ambivalent throughout the film and until this embrace, it has been unclear whether their mutual dependence is professional or romantic. Though clearly jealous of Babs, Pat's behaviour remains strictly that of a manager. She is protective of Conn but never flirts with him, and her clothes (usually neatly tailored suits, sometimes teamed with smart hats and a pearl necklace) emphasise her professional attitude rather than her femininity. In fact, this is exactly what makes the film work so well - Pat is no 'diddy dame' and wins the respect of the fighting world through sheer talent and hard work. Only when she's achieved her goal does she reveal her true feelings. The underlying sexual tension is what the studio chose to depict on the film's posters, which show two head-and-shoulders illustrations of a smiling Conn in suit and tie, and a coy-looking Babs, each holding a telephone to their ear. In the background is Pat, unsmiling and looking across at Conn. There are no boxing scenes on this poster, though the background is a montage of newspaper clippings with headlines about Conn's fighting successes.

Variety pegged the film's appeal as being solely for 'action houses', where they predicted it would play to top billing, because of Conn's boxing fame, his clean-cut personable appearance and the advance publicity given to the film in newspaper sports pages. 'Its appeal to the non-sports fans is nil,' said the *Variety* reviewer; yet this disregards the appeal of the love-story which, with its fresh approach, constitutes the film's emotional focus.[174] As for Billy Conn, his own verdict on the film was that it was a 'real stinker'.[175]

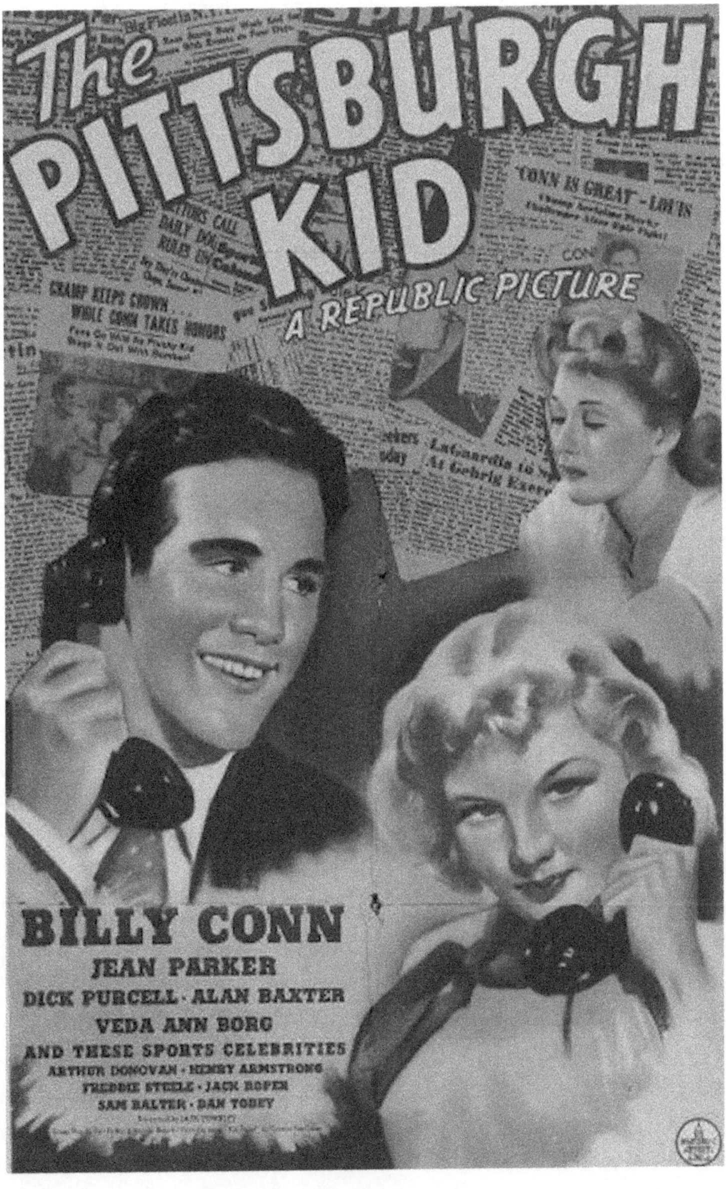
The PITTSBURGH KID
A REPUBLIC PICTURE
"CONN IS GREAT" - LOUIS
CHAMP KEEPS CROWN, WHILE CONN TAKES HONORS
BILLY CONN
JEAN PARKER
DICK PURCELL · ALAN BAXTER
VEDA ANN BORG
AND THESE SPORTS CELEBRITIES
ARTHUR DONOVAN · HENRY ARMSTRONG
FREDDIE STEELE · JACK ROPER
SAM BALTER · DAN TOBEY

That's My Baby!
Ringside Maisie (1941)

I n the 1940s the B-movie industry thrived on series, from Charlie Chan and Tarzan, to Sherlock Holmes and Boston Blackie, which pitted the same set of characters against different challenges in each low-budget, quickly produced film. Series were commercially attractive to studios because they built a loyal audience for each release and offered economies of production. The existing familiarity of the audience with the key characters, the type of narrative and the genre conventions of a particular series also meant that each film had the ability to be tightly plotted and sharply written, as screen-time did not have to be wasted in providing the 'backstory'. In its heyday, the boxing genre can claim only two series: *The Leatherpushers* set of 20-minute shorts in 1930-1931 made by Universal, and the 11 Joe Palooka films made between 1934 and 1951.[176] Other long-running series occasionally included a movie with a boxing theme - the Three Stooges, for example, made *Punch Drunks* in 1934 and *Fling in the Ring* in 1955; the East End Kids (later the Bowery Boys) appeared in *Bowery Blitzkreig* and *Pride of the Bowery* in 1941 and *Fighting Fools* in 1949; and of course Donald Duck (*Canvas Back Duck* (1953)) was never very far from a boxing ring in any of his films.

Another popular series - the ten Maisie films made between 1939 and 1947 - also took an excursion into the world of boxing with *Ringside Maisie* (1941), a light but entertaining picture directed by Edwin Marin and offering a refreshing perspective on the fight game and particularly on the role of the 'other woman'.[177] Like the rest of the films in the series, *Ringside Maisie* (called *Cash and Carry* in the UK) was made by M-G-M and starred Ann Sothern as the feisty 'Bonfire From Brooklyn' Maisie Ravier.[178] Ann Sothern had had only modest success as a B-movie actress at Columbia and then at RKO, but both studios had dropped her. When she transferred to M-G-M, she got the part that was said to have been intended for Jean Harlow and the series was a box-office success. Edwin Marin had directed Ann Sothern in two Maisie films before this one, *Gold Rush Maisie* (1940) and *Maisie Was a Lady* (1941). Attached to the B-movie unit at M-G-M, he also made a number of films in the Philo Vance series: after *Ringside Maisie*, Marin went freelance, specialising in westerns. 'The great appeal of Maisie is her frankness,' said Marin. 'That and the fact that she is constantly the underdog. Audiences unconsciously rally to her rescue, and they love her for it. She makes them all feel like heroes'.[179] Scriptwriter Mary McCall Jnr, whose sparkling one-liners gave Ann Sothern the ideal ammunition with which to build these aspects of Maisie's character, wrote eight of the 10 films in the Maisie series and was to become the first woman president of the Screen Writers Guild (1942-1944).

In *Ringside Maisie*, the character's brassy, hardboiled personality and sassy dialogue ensure that she - and not the male lead, boxing hero Young O'Hara - remains the focal point of the film. It is hard to think of another boxing film of the 1930s, 40s or 50s which does this, although arguably *The Pittsburgh Kid* (also released in 1941), with Jean Parker as the Kid's charismatic manager, comes close. A publicity photograph makes it clear who the audience should be cheering: it shows O'Hara, his manager Skeets Maguire, and Maisie in the ring, with Skeets holding up Maisie's arm in the traditional 'champion' pose. Maisie is also shown as a fighter in the poster for the film: alongside the tagline 'Maisie wins again in a knockout fun show!' is a head-and-shoulders shot of Ann Sothern, wearing boxing gloves and taking on the chin - with impassive expression - a giant blow from an unseen fighter. Even on the sheet-music for 'A Bird in a Gilded Cage', a song performed by Virginia O'Brien in the film - Maisie is portrayed as a boxer, adopting a crouched stance and wearing boxing gloves with a feminine dress and high heels.[180] From this it is clear that the action inside the ring is going to be less interesting than the action outside it.

Ringside Maisie tells the story of Maisie Revier who, after she is fired from her job as a taxi-dancer, secures a try-out partnering Ricky Duprez (Jack La Rue) at the upmarket Shady Lawn Hotel. Thrown off the train for not having the fare, she attempts to hike the rest of the way, meeting the

On the posters and even on the sheet-music cover, Maisie (Ann Sothern) is depicted as a boxer, despite the fact that she never goes into the ring

courteous and helpful Irish boxer Young O'Hara (Robert Sterling) on the road where he is training with his sparring partner Peaches (John Indrisano). When the engagement at the Shady Lawn does not work out, O'Hara takes Maisie under his wing, hiring her as a companion for his elderly mother (Margaret Moffat). O'Hara opens his heart to Maisie about his hatred of the boxing game and his longing to get enough money to open a grocery store and to marry his fiancee Cissy (Natalie Thompson). But manager Skeets Maguire (George Murphy), with whom Maisie is beginning a romance, refuses to let him out of his contract. O'Hara continues fighting and is blinded: on learning of what has happened, Cissie runs away, and Maisie falls out with Skeets. Full of remorse about making O'Hara continue in the ring, Skeets secretly pays for a specialist who restores O'Hara's sight. Maisie and Skeets are reunited at the end of the film, leaving O'Hara and his mother to realise their dream of opening a grocery store.

Maisie does not occupy the traditional role of the romantic lead, being neither the 'hometown sweetheart' of the fighter or the 'other woman'. Instead - and unusually for Hollywood - she becomes O'Hara's 'buddy' in an unambiguous relationship which allows the glamorous Maisie, seated alongside O'Hara's fiancee at the ringside, to shout out innocently 'that's my baby!' when O'Hara delivers a particularly good punch. Her cry is not misconstrued either by Cissy, or presumably by the film's audience: by now we have learned that Maisie is the exact opposite of the

Maisie with dancer Ricky Du Prez (Jack La Rue), who assumes that she will sleep with him, as her predecessor has done

traditional rival to the 'good woman'. She may be blonde, low-class and overdressed, but the resemblance is only superficial - Maisie is no gold-digger, but is a hard worker with a powerful sense of right and wrong, and a total indifference to riches.[181]

She is portrayed as being different to the other women in the film, and this is particularly apparent in her costume, which in its prevalence of bows and frills, suggests a type of 'fluffy' femininity that is at odds with Maisie's character as it is gradually revealed to the audience (though fans of the Maisie series, of course, would be familiar with this from previous instalments) and is therefore a source of comedy. Frequently her costume leads people to misjudge her: Skeets, O'Hara's manager, initially assumes she is the type of glamorous blonde gold-digger that often preys on up-and-coming boxers, and Ricky Duprez, the resident dancer at the Shady Lawn Hotel, assumes that because she 'fills out' her predecessor's dress nicely, that she, like her predecessor, will consent to sleep with him.[182]

Frills and bows characterise Maisie's costumes, a cheap and brassy look that is completely at odds with her feisty character

Maisie is differentiated right at the beginning of the film through a scene in the ironically named Elysian Fields dance-hall at which she is a taxi-dancer.[183] Other taxi-dancers wear floral day-dresses and a prolonged high-angled shot shows them dancing demurely around the floor with their partners. The camera pans down to a couple jitterbugging wildly and the first glimpse of Maisie is of her wiggling bottom. She is much more glamorously dressed than the other women and her bottom is emphasised by a large frill on the back of her floor-length, dark spangled dress. Costume continues to set her apart. When she has been fired from the dance-hall and is on the train heading for the Shady Lawn Hotel, she wears a suit with polka-dot trim, a flared skirt and a large bow at the neck. With this she wears a wide-brimmed hat with a big fake flower over each ear, and a plethora of jewellery including earrings, oversized rings and glittery bracelets that rattle when she shakes hands. Her costume is in high contrast to that of the other train passengers who are plain and dowdy. It marks her out as smart and careful of her appearance, but also as cheap and brassy. When she is thrown off the train for not having a ticket, this very urban attire is also shown to be completely impractical for hiking along country roads, just as, in *Congo Maisie* (1940), it was comically unsuitable for trekking through the jungle. Frills and bows characterise her dress throughout the film: at one of O'Hara's fights she wears a bow in her hair, a low-cut dress with flamenco-style frills around the hem and a bow on the front in a contrasting colour, drawing attention to her bosom. This outfit was, said *Variety*, 'cut much lower than kindly nature demands'.[184]

In part, these costumes serve - as they would with any leading lady - to draw attention to Maisie as the star, and the costumes of the other women in the film seem toned down accordingly in order for her to shine: O'Hara's girlfriend Cissy, for example, wears monotone tailored dresses and coats, usually teamed with a modest string of pearls, signalling not just her insipid nature but also a class status that is superior to Maisie's. Both O'Hara's mother and Maisie's landlady wear clothes that would have looked perfectly appropriate in the late nineteenth century: high collared blouses secured by cameo brooches, long skirts and shawls, and with their long hair drawn back in a bun. But the costumes go beyond establishing Maisie simply as the star, and the fact that Ann Sothern manages to look both comic and sexy in these outfits helps establish Maisie's unusual persona.

This persona sets Maisie apart from her contemporaries in two other important ways - in her behaviour and in her relationship with men. Plain-speaking, lack of artifice, feistiness and an instinct for survival are combined with an unexpected kindness and generosity in this Brooklyn girl who has learnt to live by her wits. She has high moral standards, subverting the stereotype of a showgirl - she does not drink alcohol, fights vigorously against injustice (even stopping to harangue the road-sign that still declares Cedar Lake to be 16 miles away despite her having walked at least a mile since the last 16-mile signpost), dislikes bad manners, makes no secret of her background and, although in pursuit of romance in every film, does not 'play around' with men.[185] Her only interest in money is that she never has any: when O'Hara asks her if she is vacationing at the country hotel, she says 'where I come from you spend your summers on the fire escape watching the El train'. Her sense of 'natural justice' allows her to attempt to cheat the railroad company of her fare ('the train was going there anyway') and to refuse to continue jitterbugging with the gum-chewing young man at the dance-hall even though he has paid for a whole string of dances. None of this conflicts with her assertion that 'I have never done a crooked thing or took one cent I didn't earn'.

The very first shot of Maisie demonstrates that she does not suffer fools gladly. Whereas the other taxi-dance women call out excitedly as a potential customer approaches, the women all gathered onto a fenced-off platform that makes a meat-market analogy inevitable, Maisie rolls her eyes as she is flung around the dance floor, assuming an outrageously bored expression while still going through the motions. In dealing with the manager afterwards, she has her hands on her hips, a pose she regularly adopts when sticking up for her rights.

If Maisie's outward appearance is that of the archetypal 'bad woman' of the boxing genre, and Cissy's that of the 'good girl', these preconceptions are quickly turned on their head. A cutaway from O'Hara's fight against Joe Gardia, the 'Bayonne Panther,' shows the two women seated alongside each other, Cissy - who might be expected to be either passionately engaged in her fiancé's battle for the title, or hiding her face unable to look at such brutality - is impassively watching and eating (she eats, snores or complains of feeling tired or sick throughout the entire film). It is Maisie who is excited, shouting out whenever O'Hara places a well-aimed punch. When the two women go to O'Hara's dressing-room after the match, Cissy demurely offers O'Hara her cheek to kiss, while Maisie kisses him enthusiastically on the lips, yet Maisie is no sexual predator and has no designs on O'Hara. Their relationship remains a 'buddy' one, with Maisie taking the symbolic place that Hollywood would more often have assigned to another man. It is in Maisie, not Cissy, that O'Hara confides his hatred of the boxing game, and when he is blinded in his final match, Cissy simply deserts him. Being 'buddies' means that Maisie can visit O'Hara late at night, alone in his bedroom, calling him 'honey' and hugging him without any suggestion of improper behaviour.[186] The bed remains visible in the background of the shot, but its connotations are innocent, unlike the bed in the background of the scene in *Champion* where the outcome of Midge Kelly's secret meeting with Emma is a shotgun wedding, instigated by her father. At the end of *Ringside Maisie*, with O'Hara's sight restored and his relationship with Cissy finished, it might be expected that Maisie and O'Hara would become a couple, but instead Maisie leaves with Skeets. Their romance has been largely built on verbal sparring, echoing the fighting in the ring. Director Edwin Marin said that the days of 'love-sick sighs and proposals on bended knee' were gone and now 'the more humour in a love scene the better'.[187]

If the film excels in its humour and its portrayal of Maisie as 'America's Girlfriend',[188] then it falls short in terms of boxing action. The narrative is told sequentially and it is a long time before we see any fighting in the ring other than a brief scene of O'Hara and Peaches sparring at the outdoor training camp. *Kine Weekly* noted that the first half of the film 'with its wisecracking, tiffs and flirtations, is characteristic Maisie comedy, while the second leans towards more conventional boxing melodrama'.[189] Even in O'Hara's fight, against Hank Johnson (played by Eddie Hogan who had also appeared as a heavyweight in *The Champ* in 1940) there is frustratingly little boxing shown, with repeated cutaways to the crowd and to Maisie listening at home to the radio commentary, returning to the fight only to see the seventh-round knockout. It is not until 36 minutes into this 92-minute film that there is a sustained fight scene. O'Hara is facing Joe Gardia, a dark-haired, olive-skinned fighter who contrasts with O'Hara's pale skin and lightly muscled body.[190] The entire fight is not shown, being ellipsed between rounds, but there is enough to get a sense of O'Hara's fighting style: the boxers' punches, however, despite the sound-effects and snapping-back of heads, seem without power and sometimes look as if they do not connect. When O'Hara wins on a knockout, the announcer's summing-up of him as 'a shadow with a pile-driver's punch' also seems not to connect with what we have seen on screen.

Only in the final fight, against Jackie-Boy Duffy (played by heavyweight Eddie Simms who went on to appear in *Sunday Punch* (1942) as well as two of the Palooka series) is the boxing given a more serious treatment. Duffy is huge and muscled, a heavy hitter who makes O'Hara look leaden. Round after round goes by, with O'Hara constantly backing away, unable (or unwilling) to land a punch. The fight is more imaginatively filmed than the previous bouts, with a highly effective montage of punches, crowd faces, the clanging of the round bell, and the slow movement of the clock hands.[191] By Round Six, O'Hara's face is agonised: cut and battered, he sways under a fusillade of punches from Duffy until at last he is knocked out.

If the audience had to wait a long time for an authentic-looking fight, then at least the atmosphere of the business is well-created and sustained

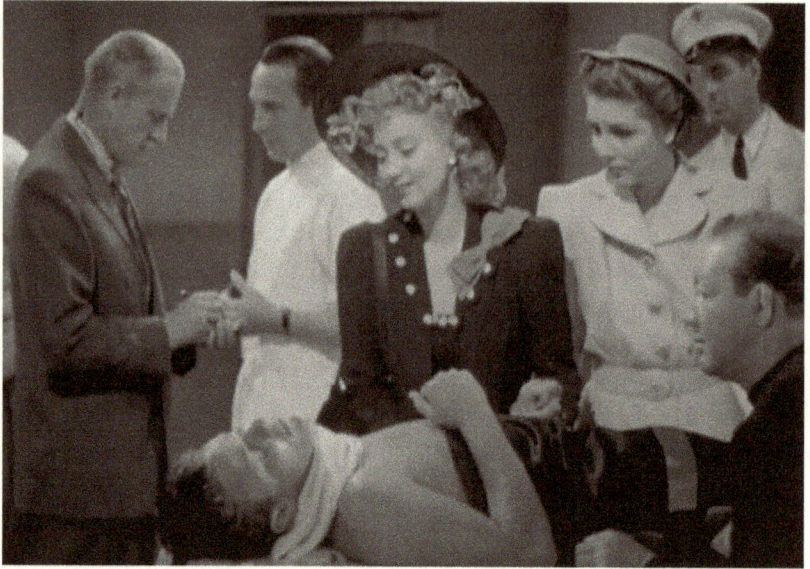

When O'Hara is knocked out by Jackie-Boy Duffy, it is Maisie who takes pole position in the dressing room, with Cissy - her insipid clothes mirroring her insipid nature - hovering alongside

throughout, due principally to the presence of O'Hara's team which includes three professional boxers: John Indrisano as Peaches (Indrisano also choreographed the fights), Maxie Rosenbloom as Chotsie and Rags Ragland as Vic, whose battered noses and cauliflower ears contrast with Robert Sterling's undamaged, chiselled features. The fight scenes are hampered, perhaps, by the fact that it is Ann Sothern who is the star of the film rather than Sterling and, given her character as Maisie, she cannot help but outshine him. Sterling never really looks like a boxer: described as 'a nifty newcomer' in the theatrical trailer, he worked mainly as a lead in B-movies, but war service interrupted his career which never really gained its momentum.[192]

The world of hoxing portrayed in *Ringside Maisie* is very different from that shown in many other fight films of the 1940s: what distinguishes it is its lack of corruption. Fight-fixing and gangsters are absent. Skeets may threaten O'Hara when the boxer wants to tear up his contract, but he supported the young fighter for four years with no financial return (he is someone who, as the theatrical trailer says, 'plays tough....but who's really as soft as a two-minute egg'); when Jacky-Boy Duffy learns that his punch has blinded O'Hara, he comes to the hospital; and even the ringside crowd are shown as well-dressed and respectable. O'Hara himself is uninterested in money, women or fame. He got into the fight game by accident, when - then known as Terry Doland - he was arrested for punching the men who had taken his mother's grocery store away from her. The punch-up was witnessed by Skeets, then a total stranger, who testified on Dolan's behalf and subsequently signed him up as a boxer under the fighting name of Young O'Hara. This is a virtually identical scenario to the ones used to explain how Knobby Walsh signs up Joe Palooka (*Palooka* (1934)), and how Skip Davies signs up Steve Nelson (*Kid Nightingale* (1939)). Like Joe and the Kid, O'Hara's fighting ambitions are modest and all he really wants is enough money to get married and buy another grocery store for his mother (unlike Joe Bonaparte in *Golden Boy* (1939) who cannot wait to escape from everything that his parents' store represents).[193] The high moral standards of O'Hara and Skeets reflect those of Maisie and also offer an understated comment on Irishness: both men come from Irish families and Mrs Dolan, O'Hara's kindly mother, has a noticeable Irish accent. When she first meets O'Hara on the way to Cedar Lake, Maisie confesses that although 'I fight under the name of Maisie Revier' that her real name is Mary O'Connor, revealing her own Irish roots.

The film was well-received on its release. *Today's Cinema* remarked on the 'happily inconsequential atmosphere' of the film with its well-knit story and pert wise-cracks and said it 'contrives to appeal powerfully on a smooth blend of sophisticated comedy and beserk fistic action'.[194] *Variety*, however, felt that its only box-office 'pull' was the fact that it was part of a series, without which it was merely an 'an exhibition filler'.[195] Maisie was to go on to further exploits in tales of showbiz, undercover police work, divorce and blackmail. She never returned to the ringside, but the boxing genre is undoubtedly the richer for her contribution.

A Tinhorn Shanty Irishman
Gentleman Jim (1942)

T he biopic is a staple of the sports-film genre and with *Gentleman Jim* - a Warner Brothers film based on the life of world heavyweight champion Jim Corbett - it gains additional interest through its nineteenth century setting. This allows for some elaborate costumes and lavish interiors, thus positioning the film as period drama and broadening its box-office appeal beyond the traditional male fight-film audience.[196] *Gentleman Jim* gives an insight into the history of boxing in the US at a key stage in its legalisation, the introduction of the Queensberry Rules; yet like all 'period' films, it tends to reveal just as much about society in the 1940s as it does about that of the 1880s. This is part of its fascination: it falls, as Romano says, 'comfortably short of creating a historical chronicle...nonwithstanding this, and perhaps due in part to it, the picture captures the spirit and personality of the...champion'.[197]

Gentleman Jim tells the story of Jim Corbett's rise from an Irish immigrant family to his defeat of John L Sullivan to become the heavyweight champion of the world. Corbett is a brash, ambitious but penniless young man from a boisterous but close-knit family who lives by his wits and triumphs in the ring through quick thinking and fancy footwork. The film stars Errol Flynn and, given his good looks, energy and athleticism, this alone makes it worth watching, even if, as the trade press said, 'he is always Errol Flynn' and makes 'a rather unconvincing bruiser'.[198] The quality of his acting may be debatable, but he does bring considerable dynamism to the smallest scene. Flynn claimed to be Irish, but was actually born in Tasmania, Australia, getting his first Hollywood break as Fletcher Christian in *In the Wake of Bounty* in 1933, before establishing an athletic, swashbuckling screen persona with starring roles in films that included *Captain Blood* (1935), *The Charge of the Light Brigade* (1936) and *The Adventures of Robin Hood* (1938). His star persona was matched by an equally swashbuckling private life of drunken debauchery and womanising and he was rarely out of the headlines. Apart from the box-office draw of Flynn, several other factors contribute to making *Gentleman Jim* an enjoyable film, including the direction of the experienced Raoul Walsh (who had been directing for 30 years when he made this), a sharply written script by Vincent Lawrence and Horace McCoy based on Jim Corbett's autobiography *The Roar of the Crowd*, and the presence of Ward Bond in a memorable portrayal of John L Sullivan. This is a light-hearted, lavishly staged film which nevertheless has some serious points to make about the class-ridden society of so-called 'classless America' and about attitudes to the Irish in particular. Zucker and Babich rate it as 'the most thoroughly enjoying boxing biography ever put on screen' and the *New York Times* praised its 'warm, earthy spirit'.[199]

Jim Corbett became world heavyweight champion on March 17 1892 after a 21-round fight against John L Sullivan (who is also the subject of a biopic, *The Great John L* (1945)). It marked the entry into a new age, moving from bare-knuckled strength into an era 'where even prize-fighters wore evening dress and sipped cocktails'.[200] Corbett's nickname came, according to the *American Film Institute Catalog,* 'from his good looks and scientific method of boxing'.[201] For the former, Errol Flynn was ideal casting; for the latter, Flynn had veteran boxer Mushy Callahan as trainer.[202] Callahan had been crowned light welterweight champion in 1926 when he beat Pinky Mitchell, but retired from the ring in 1932 to work as a referee and to choreograph fights for the Hollywood studios. He had already appeared on screen as a boxer in *Kid Galahad* (1937) and *They Made Me a Criminal* (1939), and had been technical adviser on *Golden Gloves* (1940). His interventions on *Gentleman Jim* ensured that the fights looked seamless and authentic. Good looks and good boxing were more screenable than what *Variety* noted as Corbett's quiet and self-effacing personality, so in the interests of good entertainment, Hollywood did what it always had done - showed Corbett as being loud, pushy, witty and arrogant or, as *Today's Cinema* rather more politely phrased it, 'a lovable opportunist'.[203]

The film starts with Corbett as a young Irish bank clerk in San Francisco in 1887. With his parents, two brothers and sister, he lives at

'Corbett's Livery Stables', a South Side house and farmyard - complete with goats and chickens - on the 'wrong side of the tracks'. They are the stereotypical Irish family, fond of drinking, singing and religion, but fond of fighting most of all. In the late nineteenth century, says Kasia Boddy, 'Irishness was almost synonymous with pugnacity, and pugnacity was almost synonymous with Americanness; ergo, the Irish were the 'real' Americans, the immigrants who best performed the accepted version of national identity'.[204] No excuse is too small for the Corbett family to leave the dinner table and rush outside for a fight, a fact which is well-known to the locals. As the cry goes up: 'the Corbetts are at it again!' a stream of neighbours - usually headed by the priest - rush towards the farmyard to see the action. This is something of a contrast to Jim's public persona. At the bank, he is immaculately dressed, in fact something of a dandy, and always keen to pass himself off as a gentleman, a pretension which is roundly mocked by his brothers whose strong accents, coarse facial features and country clothes contrast strongly with Jim and mark them out as lower class. While his brothers work in the livery stables, and later in a bar, Jim has a white-collar job and this is reflected in his behaviour at home: in a scene outside the house, the rest of the family sweep the yard or clean their boots, but Jim relaxes on the banister of the porch helping his sister to wind a skein of wool, a scene that would feminise a leading man if his screen persona were not so overtly masculine. In common with the protagonists of other boxing films which feature young men who want to leave the restrictions of their ethnic background behind (including Joe Bonaparte in *Golden Boy* (1939) and Paul Baroni in *Kid Monk Baroni* (1952)) Jim has no trace of an accent to betray his origins: in his mind, he is already the person he wants to become.

Boxing action opens the film, with a bare-knuckle fight between two barrel-chested bruisers. Despite the fact that boxing is illegal in California, most of the great-and-good of San Francisco seems to be at the open-air contest, including Judge Geary (Wallis Clark) who just happens to be a director of the bank where Jim works. Never one to miss an opportunity, Corbett makes sure he is stationed next to Geary, where he watches the fight from a grassy knoll. In a high-angled shot from Jim's perspective, we see the the crowds running along the ropes from one end of the ring to the other in their keenness to follow the action. The fight is stopped short by a police raid. Corbett, along with the Judge, ends up in the cells, where the judge makes a plea for the legalisation of the sport: his plan is to stage matches in a private club, the exclusive and upmarket Olympic, and to take on 'a few clean-cut boys from good families' to train as fighters, the implication being that the current problem is one of class or character. He has even hired an English trainer, Harry Watson, fresh from teaching the Prince of Wales to box. The acquisition of Harry, and the respect that greets this announcement, is an interesting comment on America's warmer relationship with Britain at the time the film was made, 1942 being the year that the US joined the war.

Corbett is eager to see what the Olympic Club is all about but, having no hope of being accepted for membership, he has to find an excuse for getting inside. Victoria Ware (Alexis Smith), a customer of the bank, provides the entrée, with Corbett accompanying her to the club to deliver gambling money to her father at the poker tables. Corbett gasps at the splendour of the building, all marble floors and chandeliers ('this is only the foyer,' remarks Miss Ware); mistakes a classical statue for a monument to a 'member who has passed away'; and graciously allows Miss Ware to buy him lunch whilst dodging out of leaving a tip.[205] He makes the natural assumption that everyone at the Olympic Club is from the upper classes, but Miss Ware puts him right: her father was a silver-mine grubstaker who just happened to make his fortune. This does not put Jim on the same footing as Mr Ware however: when Jim delivers the cash, he is dismissed immediately - the difference is that Mr Ware has 'made it', and therefore become 'society', and Corbett has yet to make it, and is therefore of no consequence.

This was only the second leading-lady role for Alexis Smith, having played uncredited minor parts in a dozen films in 1940 and 1941, before taking the romantic lead in *Steel Against the Sky*, a unremarkable picture about bridge-builders despite Warner Brothers billing her as 'The Dynamite Girl'. Director Raoul Walsh had apparently suggested Ann Sheridan (who had recently starred in boxing film *They Made Me a Criminal* (1939)) or Rita Hayworth for the role of Victoria Ware, but Smith's combination of beauty and dry delivery brings an edge to her performance as the 'belle of Nob Hill'.[206]

In the gym, Corbett meets Londoner Harry Watson (Rhys Williams), whose unrewarding task is to try to turn a group of elderly and overweight Club members who can barely touch their toes into something resembling athletes. The camera shoots the line-up of men in semi-profile, so that their bulging stomachs and scrawny limbs are emphasised, and this serves as an (anticipatory) contrast with Flynn's body as it will be revealed in the ring. Watson welcomes Corbett's invitation to a bit of instant sparring, even if Corbett is still wearing his waistcoat and fob-watch. Harry and the members are so impressed with Corbett's fighting skills - shown in only two or three well-delivered punches - that he is immediately put up for athletic membership. Corbett is delighted, having realised that boxing might provide, as Aaron Baker puts it, a remedy to the limitations of a white collar career that requires 'long years of study and apprenticeship'.[207] The Olympic members soon regret their decision, tiring quickly of Corbett's pretensions, which include having himself paged throughout the club, a ploy that fools no-one. They'd like him taken down a peg or two and a visiting former heavyweight from England, Jack Burke (Art Foster) is just the man to give him 'a good drubbing'. This is Corbett's first 'exhibition' fight, taking place in the grand surroundings of the club complete with gentlemen in evening dress and crinolined society ladies applauding politely with gloved hands. The Stars and Stripes and the Union Jack hang prominently around the walls of the room (the combination providing a special contemporary resonance for 1942 audiences), and smaller versions of the two flags are attached to one of the cornerposts of the ring itself. Up above, on a mezzanine, stands Corbett's father, still in his cabman's clothes, and flanked by the chefs and porters of the club marking a class divide not just in terms of space, but in behaviour too, with the workers shouting, pointing and gesturing excitedly while the seated audience below sits demurely.

In keeping with the refined atmosphere of the Olympic, the fight itself is gentlemanly, an impression reinforced by Corbett's arrival at the match in top hat and tails (all rented, of course). It is the first fight to be conducted under the new Marquis of Queensberry rules, which regulated the size of the ring and the duration of the rounds/breaks, made the use of gloves compulsory, and outlawed any wrestling. The men fight bare-chested, in full-length leggings: in this fight, and in all Corbett's subsequent bouts in the film, his opponents are shown as larger and more burly than him, with hairy chests, in contrast to Flynn's smooth athletic body. This contrast also points up the 'gentlemanly' qualities of Corbett and the 'animal' qualities of the other fighters. At the sight of Corbett in

At Corbett's first exhibition fight, at the Olympic Club, the Stars and Stripes and the Union Jack hang prominently on the walls

the ring, a small boy in the audience points to him and asks his mother: 'why doesn't daddy look like that in HIS underwear?', it is another overt reminder that one of the purposes of this film is the display of Errol Flynn's body, arguably of sexual interest to both male and female fans.

The fight against Burke is over in two rounds, with Jim literally running rings around the former champ, his dancing feet (which are constantly shown in close-up) ensuring that his opponent never gets chance to land a substantial punch. Such punches as are shown are lightweight, with no sense of impact or hurt - in fact, Corbett's hair is barely even ruffled by the end of the fight. It's not quite the outcome the members had anticipated. The message that this 'society' fight conveys, argues Joan Mellon, is that 'the working-class male is far more virile than his effete, wealthier counterparts. The athletic club members who are his antagonists are stuffy and arrogant. Flynn, brash and self-confident, is much more the man'.[208] This would be true if it had been a wealthy club-member rather than a working-class fighter facing Corbett in the ring. But

Burke is only a stooge for these 'effete' members whose own antagonism is restricted to verbal battling. and the fight is much more about the power of the 'new spirit' of America, quick-thinking and fleet of foot, over the old reliance on brute strength. This idea is repeated in the climax of the film when John L Sullivan, swinging huge punches that meet only empty air, is literally baffled as to where Corbett has gone, and is even shown to be an everyday urban skill in a scene where Corbett negotiates a crowded sidewalk by nimbly dodging and weaving.

The presence of 'society' women at the fight, the subsequent foregrounding of the burgeoning romance between Corbett and Miss Ware, and the period-costume setting were all, as *Motion Picture Herald* noted, 'smoothly contrived to overcome any latent objection on the part of women to a film in which prize fighting is a dominant factor'.[209] This positioning is reflected in the theatrical trailer for the film, which describes *Gentleman Jim* as 'the grandest story of the naughty nineties...(which) becomes the gayest picture of the fighting forties', thus hinting at titillating content with the word 'naughty', but appealing to women with the notion of 'grand' and 'gay'.[210] Costume design was a key part of any period drama with the fashions worn by the stars promoted through the pressbooks. *Gentleman Jim* steers a careful course between giving a general sense of the nineteenth century while allowing the two romantic leads to appear contemporary. This is achieved through dressing secondary characters, such as the male members of the Olympic Club, in overtly period costume while Corbett's own dress would not look out of place in the 1940s. The men wear morning coats, cravats, high-buttoned waistcoats and sport elaborate hairstyles and side-whiskers, whereas Corbett wears smoothly tailored suits, a straw boater and slicked-back hair. Similarly, female secondary characters wear fussy Victorian crinolines, while Miss Ware is seen in tailored figure-hugging dresses with fur-trimmed jackets - a style very fashionable in the 1940s.

At the dance after the fight against Burke, Miss Ware again stresses the illusion of the Club's 'aristocracy', telling Corbett that there is no right or wrong 'side of the tracks', but simply 'those that happened to grab the right moment and those who didn't.' Corbett's only sin seems to be that he is too overt or pushy in his eagerness - and has too high an opinion of himself. Miss Ware's reassurance is not enough, however, to stop Corbett and his friend (Jack Carson) getting thrown out of the party through drunkenness. When the men wake up next morning, and several bars later, at a cheap hotel in Salt Lake City (another excuse to show Flynn in his underwear), Corbett finds he's agreed to a 10-dollar fight against local pug Miller. This is no society fight, but takes place in a rowdy, male-only, smoke-filled stadium against a hard-hitting opponent - a marked contrast to the Olympic club match. Corbett is cut, dazed and confused, but still wins. The mention of the 10-dollar purse is important in helping to chart

A different class of fight, for a 10 dollar purse

Corbett's rise to fame: the more he fights, the larger the purse until, when he meets John L Sullivan in the championship challenge, he needs a sidebet of 10,000 dollars simply to ensure the fight will go ahead.

Society-fights are still a long way off, however. Back in San Francisco, Corbett meets his next challenger, Joe Choynski (Sammy Stein), in a spectacularly staged scene, with the fight taking place in the San Francisco docks at night - 'offshore' to avoid any legal problems. On a floating wharf, with the crowd packed onto the decks and even the rigging of a nearby schooner, the ever-confident Corbett slugs it out with Choynski, who 'accidentally' loses his gloves and has to fight in thin leather gloves, the equivalent of bare-knuckle fighting.[211] Clearly, the Queensberry Rules were applied only selectively, with this fight taking place under the old Prize Ring Rules, which at least outlawed head-butting and throttling. The fight sequence is a prolonged one but again, though the men move and fight authentically, the punches look to be without power. The tension of the fight, conveyed by alternating high-angled shots looking down on the ring with close-ups of the fighters and of Corbett's dancing feet, is dispelled by constant cutaways to his family on the dockside, his brothers making comic feint-punches and Pop (Alan Hale) taking his hat on and off in a routine that looks to be straight out of music-hall comedy.[212] In the Miller fight in Salt Lake City, where no-one knew Corbett, he emerged bruised and dishevelled: back on his home territory, he quickly complains when his 'second' pours water over him during a break: 'don't mess my hair up,' he says, smoothing it back into position. Both fighters are knocked to the ground again and again, until a powerful punch sends Corbett flying clean out of the ring, through the ropes and into the water.....allowing him to climb back, soaking wet (more titillation for the audience) to continue the fight. The police raid comes hot on the heels of the knockout by Corbett and there is plenty of action as the spectators jump into the water to avoid being arrested.

It is time for Corbett to move up the rankings, the narration of which is handled in conventional style through a montage of newspaper headlines, train wheels, and knockout punches. The fight purse is now reaching 2,500 dollars and something of the true challenge of the business is indicated in a headline that reports Corbett going 61 rounds with his latest opponent, an endurance-test that is not even hinted at in the brief fights shown on screen. The fact that this fight, against black contender Peter Jackson, is not shown on screen is indicative of Hollywood's continuing nervousness about featuring black fighters. Jim Corbett is now a celebrity, and the film casts some interesting sidelights on just what that means, showing him appearing on stage as an actor - he has aspirations to play Shakespeare - and in a box at the opening of a play, being ogled by the society ladies who bicker over the right to look through the opera glasses at him. Jim has now earned enough money to move his family (and their goats) to Nob Hill and buy his brothers a saloon. When he wears top hat and tails now, he doesn't have to rent the outfit.

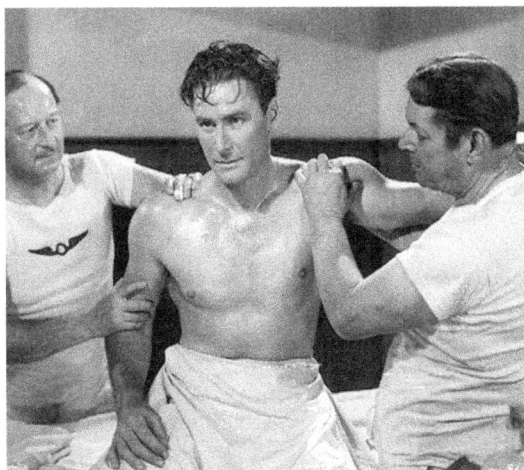

Sullivan (Ward Bond) boasts that he can 'lick any man in the world' but his talent is positioned as brute strength, whereas Corbett possesses a 'gentleman's' more refined talents, which leave Sullivan looking flat-footed and foolish

His final challenge is for the heavyweight championship of the world, a title that is held by the legendary John L Sullivan, whose celebrity status far outranks that of Jim Corbett. Wherever Sullivan (Ward Bond) goes, he is surrounded by adoring fans and his name is spoken in awed tones. When Pop shakes hands with his idol, he vows never to wash his hand again, and even the sceptical Miss Ware is a fan, rushing over to Sullivan to feel the strength of his arm. His boast is that he can 'lick any man in the world' and his imposing presence - tall and stately with a handlebar moustache and as fancy a line in clothes as Jim - makes him seem proud rather than arrogant. Sullivan's talent, however, is positioned as being brute strength, whereas Corbett possesses a 'gentleman's' rather more refined talents: whereas Corbett aspires to Shakespeare, Sullivan appears on stage as a lumberjack in The Honest Woodsman, hacking at a giant tree-trunk with an axe.

Sullivan accepts the championship challenge, which is to take place in 1892 in New Orleans, where boxing is legal and where the pre-fight parade rivals the Mardi Gras. The only condition is that Corbett raise 10,000 dollars for a side-bet, a sum that Miss Ware anonymously donates, despite ridiculing Corbett as a 'tinhorn shanty Irishman'. Vast crowds pour into the stadium to watch the match. Corbett is now in shorts, not leggings - another opportunity for display - and listens seriously to the referee as the Queensberry Rules are once again recited ('he thinks he's playing Hamlet,' says Miss Ware). During the fight itself, he makes Sullivan look flatfooted and foolish, his punches swinging wide as Jim dances and dodges around him, with Sullivan often looking around in bewilderment at where his opponent has gone. Flynn was coached by former welterweight champion Mushy Callahan, and for the first time in the film the fight looks authentic: the *New York Times* said that 'if the original battle (between Corbett and Sullivan) was as good as that served up by Warner's, then it surely must have been a corker'.[213] The first two rounds are shown in full, followed by a montage of match reports and telegraph poles symbolising the news travelling across the country. Suddenly, it's Round 19: the punches are harder now and a dead silence follows Corbett's winning knockout blow.

Corbett has won more than the championship. The men and women who were so contemptuous of him when he was working his way up the ladder, are now all anxious to claim him as their own discovery: he's finally made it into what he perceives as the upper echelons of society. Thus it is shown that being Irish, or being from the 'wrong side of the tracks' had little to do with his initial rejection by the hierarchy: instead, acceptance is shown to relate to merit, which on the one hand can be viewed as a clear egalitarian message, or on the other as a 'pseudo-democratic mystique'.[214] Those doing the judging are revealed as being no better than Corbett - in this apparently class-ridden society, class is actually an illusion. All through the film, Corbett is eager to demonstrate that he is a gentleman, when he clearly is not. Now, having made it, he can say happily to Miss Ware as they finally embrace (after spending the entire film in verbal sparring that parallels the sparring in the ring): 'I'm no gentleman,' to which she replies: 'I'm no lady.'

At the very time that audiences in cinemas were hearing these closing lines, Errol Flynn was in court facing four counts of statutory rape. One of his accusers, Peggy Larue Satterlee, told the court that she had said to Flynn that it 'was not very nice for a gentleman to enter a lady's bedroom' and, as Flynn recalled in his autobiography, audiences were quick to notice the similarity between this and the film dialogue. 'A lot of merriment went around,' he said. 'The wartime public was thrown into mild hysterics over this. In some parts of the country they even had to throw out the last line so as to prevent anything too raucous happening in the theatres'.[215] The trial was big news throughout the US media, with Flynn claiming that it even pushed 'the war against Nazism' onto the inside pages. He was cleared of all charges, and his autobiography - which contains much supposedly verbatim dialogue between Flynn and the police, even though his account was not written until 16 years later - veered between claiming that it was his 'personality...and way of life' that was on trial, and accusing the whole case of being cooked up as an act of vengeance against the big studios who had not paid enough protection money to a local political administration. Whereas a rape scandal had ruined Fatty Arbuckle's film career some 22 years earlier, Flynn's box-office appeal seemed undiminished and, like other leading Hollywood men, he was cast in patriotic roles in war films in the years that immediately followed, including *Edge of Darkness* (1943), *Northern Pursuit* (1943), *Uncertain Glory* (1944) and *Operation Burma* (1945) before returning to swashbuckling roles in the 1950s.

Three years after the release of *Gentleman Jim*, another period costume boxing film dealing with the late nineteenth century, this time focusing on John Sullivan, was released by Bing Crosby Productions, the singer's first venture into independent film-making. *The Great John L* (also known as *A Man Called Sullivan*) was directed by Frank Tuttle and starred the unknown Greg McClure as Sullivan in a tale strongly marketed as appealing to 'students of the gay nineties'.[216] It charts the fighter's rise from Boston Strong Boy to world champion, through his years of 'drunken disillusionment' and finally to the 'mature man...who becomes the exponent of clean living'.[217] Greg McClure was touted as a future star - he had only played as an extra in films prior to this - but he never fulfilled this early promise and his career petered out within a few years, marked only by his appearance in two of the low-budget Palooka series, in 1949 and 1950. Contemporary reviews, disappointingly, did not compare *The Great John L* with *Gentleman Jim*, or Greg McClure with Errol Flynn, though *Motion Picture Herald* felt that 'it would be better off in less than 96 minutes' and that when there was no ring-action, 'the pace inclines to saunter'.[218] The pressbook for the film stresses the arduous nature of the filming of the fight between Sullivan and the Bull's Head Terror (George Mathews) on board a barge in the Hudson (actually shot in the General Service studio tank). It took one day to film the long shots, another to film the fight itself, and a third to do close-ups, with the fighters being coached by Johnny Indrisano. But the real enthusiasm of the pressbook editorials is saved for the way the personalities of the era - including the Prince of Wales and Diamond Jim Brady - are depicted in the film, and in the 'familiar' locales, such as Delmonico's and the Waldorf. Along with the posters, that show Sullivan raising his top hat to ladies in crinolines carrying parasols, this makes clear that *The Great John L*, like *Gentleman Jim*, was seeking to expand its audience beyond the fight-fan, in its appeal to nostalgia and to women.

The presence of the Union Jack alongside the Stars and Stripes in the inset photograph would have had special resonance for 1942 audiences, as the USA had just entered the war

Everybody Dies
Body and Soul (1947)

I f critics felt John Garfield's first appearance as a boxer, in *They Made Me a Criminal*, was somewhat run-of-the-mill, they were unanimous in their praise of his portrayal of anti-hero Charley Davis in *Body and Soul*, for which Garfield received an Oscar nomination for best actor.[219] Directed by Robert Rossen and produced by Garfield's independent company Enteprise Productions, *Body and Soul* is an altogether darker film which reflects the pessimistic, postwar/coldwar mood that would be picked up in other boxing films such as *The Set-Up* (1949) and *The Harder They Fall* (1956), both of which deal with organised crime and corruption. Like these other two films, *Body and Soul* has since been 'appropriated' for the film noir genre and it is perhaps this categorisation that accounts for much of its ongoing critical attention.

This was Rossen's second film as director, following a 13-year screenwriting career for Warner Brothers: his credits include *The Treasure of the Sierra Madre* (1948). He came from what Walter Bernstein describes as 'the school of bang-bang storytelling where what counted was what happened next and the sooner the better. He acknowledged the primacy of content but his heart was in the action'.[220] Rossen's work in Hollywood was to be put on hold immediately after *Body and Soul* when he came under the scrutiny of HUAC, the House Committee on Un-American Activities in 1947, as did the film's screenwriter Abraham Polonsky, and its stars John Garfield, Canada Lee, Lloyd Gough and Anne Revere.[221] Rossen was blacklisted for refusing to admit his alleged Communist sympathies: he held out for two years, then named names in order to be able to work again.

Comparisons are often made between the fight scenes in *Body and Soul* and those of *Raging Bull* (1980) - the film is said to have influenced director Martin Scorsese. Cinematographer James Wong Howe achieved a new mobility and realism when he stepped through the ropes to film the final fight sequence: fight scenes had traditionally been filmed from outside the ring itself, distancing the spectator and thus making for a certain detachment from the action. As part of an eight-camera set-up, Howe used two handheld cameras, gliding around the fighters on roller-skates. 'The camera moved as a fighter would move,' says Todd Rainsberger in his book on Howe, 'stalking the opponent, moving in and out, from side to side, never steady.'[222] However, the fight scenes in *Body and Soul* may expand in the memory - in fact, the sustained boxing action is saved until the climax of the film, the championship challenge fight between Charley Davis and Jack Marlowe (Artie Dorrell). Until then, the audience has to make do with a few shots of Charley at his open-air training camp, and a montage of punches showing his rise to championship status. It is intriguing, then, to read of Rossen despatching three film crews to film stock footage at fights in 26 cities across the country: presumably much of this ended up on the cutting-room floor.[223]

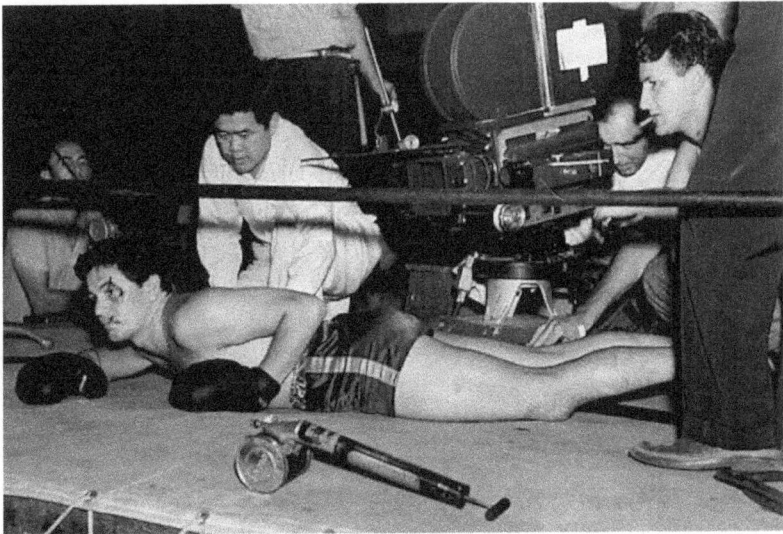

On set, with Director of Photography James Wong Howe coordinating eight cameras, two of which were handheld so the cameramen could glide around the fighters on rollerskates

All the stylistic devices of film noir are present in *Body and Soul*: claustrophobic framing such as in the scene where Charley and his estranged mother talk in the kitchen of her East Side apartment, the one light-bulb barely fending off the surrounding darkness; the prevalence of night-time or interior scenes, such as in Charley's late-night drive back into New York where the neon signs and street-lights are filmed from inside the car itself; the use of shadows and extreme high-angle shots, as in the scene where Roberts tells Charley he must defend his title, the shadows of the venetian blind suggesting imprisonment; and the use of flashback. So too are the thematic devices: the doomed hero's struggle against his demons, the fatalistic attitude ('everybody dies' is an oft-repeated line), the money-chasing femme fatale, and the tone of the narrative, which Maureen Turim has called 'pervasively remorseful', though it stops short of being a confessional narrative due to the absence of a voiceover.[224]

The idea for the film - whose working title was The Burning Journey - stemmed from an original story by Barney Ross. Ross was a Jewish-American whose rabbi father was shot in his grocery store in Chicago in a robbery: after that, Ross turned to street-fighting and then to boxing. He became a triple-champion in lightweight, junior welterweight, and welterweight classes and was never knocked out in his 81 fights. He went on to have a glittering military career in the Second World War but his reputation was blighted by drug addiction. Garfield bought the rights to the story in 1945 but little of its structure, and little of its Jewish flavour, survives in the finished film. The latter is surprising given that the screenwriter was also Jewish: Abraham Polonsky's upbringing echoed that of Ross, growing up in a poor but educated Jewish family in the Bronx surrounded by, but separated from, the 'mainstream' American working-class. In Polonsky's case, this resulted in a strong social conscience: he joined the Communist Party in 1936, married an activist, and was intent on portraying what he termed 'social reality' in his work. Tony Williams describes *Body and Soul* as being a reworking by Polonsky of 'Golden Boy', the Clifford Odets play, 'combining the boxing movie genre with thirties' Warner Bros social consciousness.'[225] The film, however, may have been too controversial for a major studio like Warner Brothers: it is significant that it was made by a new independent company after the anti-trust legislation had broken up some of the majors.

The timing for *Body and Soul* was opportune for two reasons: firstly because this social consciousness took on a new topical relevance with the sense of disillusionment brought by the aftermath of the war, and secondly because, as John Garfield's biographer, Patrick McGrath, points out, the film was released at a time when boxing and gambling were under investigation, especially in Manhattan where the film is set. This makes the opening scene of the film - the aftermath of the death of Charley's 'second', black boxer Ben Chaplin (Canada Lee), especially poignant.[226]

The film begins and ends in the present, with the bulk of the 104 minutes consisting of a flashback that charts Charley's life from his beginnings as a poor boy on the East Side, helping his parents run their candy store, to his victory as champion. The opening scene uses the high-angle shots characteristic of film noir: from high in the trees the camera looks down on the training camp at night, the ropes of the ring casting deep shadows on its wooden floor, and the shadow of the punch-bag swinging gently in the breeze. The connotation of this particular image, as John Schultheiss observes in his critical commentary to the *Body and Soul* screenplay, is of lynching - it is a shot that will be repeated later in the film, though by then the audience can make the direct link between the punchbag's shadow and Ben, the fighter who dies in this same ring.[227] The camera tracks through the trees to look down through the window of a bedroom where Charley is lying on his back fully clothed and calling out in his restless sleep. Sweat beads his face and the moonlight falls on his facial scars and cuts. This is an image of the fighter that Paul Buhle and John Wagner say is 'shriven of its 1930s optimism and possessed now of a postwar familiarity with death,'[228] though - as with the metaphor of the punchbag - this change in Charley can only be perceived when the same sequence is repeated near the end of the film and the audience understands what has happened to him. Awakening, he rushes out to the car and drives back into the neon-lit city. There is a pervading sense of doom throughout these opening sequences: in the tense and unfulfilling reunions with his mother and his former girlfriend, Peg (Lilli Palmer); in his visit to the nightclub where his follow-the-money current girlfriend, Alice (Hazel Brooks), is singing; but most of all in the contrast between the way Charley behaves like a defeated man while all around him - from the bartender and the hat-check girl, to children in the street - are enthusiastically calling him 'champ'. It is a term, says Joan Mellon, of 'bitter irony'.[229] The emotional mood is complemented by the cinematography: Todd Rainsberger remarks on the 'dirty, dark gray quality' of the images which provide a 'sombre, depressing atmosphere.'[230] The scene therefore sets the tenor before revealing its cause: that, as part of a 'business deal' Charley has agreed to lose his upcoming fight. The cinematography technique that opened the sequence closes it in the same way, with another high-angle shot of Charley lying on his back, this time on the dressing-room couch as he awaits his fight. As he closes his eyes, the flashback begins.

The store that Charley's parents run is portrayed as an oasis of innocence, trying to hold out against the encroaching tide of pool halls and speakeasies that surround it.[231] His parents - the way they live and the traditional values they uphold - are positioned as the moral centre of Charley's world, though it is a lifestyle and a morality that he is already rejecting. The neighbourhood children are described by Charley's mother Anna (Anne Revere) as being like wolves and she blames the environment for her son's wish to become a fighter: 'we live in a jungle,' she says, 'so he can only be a wild animal'. The animal/primitivism metaphor, often used in the boxing genre to describe fighters, is repeated when Charley has his first date with his future wife Peg, a painter. When he asks why she finds him attractive, she quotes from the poem 'Tiger Tiger' by William Blake:

> Tiger tiger burning bright
> In the forests of the night .
> What immortal hand or eye
> Can frame thy fearful symmetry?

Through his questions - Charley asks what 'symmetry' means, and what a sculptor does - the narrowness of his world is revealed, a narrowness pointed up by the contrast between Charley's local accent (he has barely ever left the neighbourhood) and Peg's educated but hard-to-place accent (she has travelled around the world). The impetus for Charley's fighting career comes with the destruction of the candy store by mobsters bombing the speakeasy next door and the death of his father, crushed under the rubble - events that mark the end of 'old world' values and the freeing-up of Charley to take control of his own life.

The film is essentially about money and its morality - or lack of it - and offers a strong criticism of rampant capitalism. Charley's parents are poor: they point out that the only shop they could afford to buy was on the East Side; and Charley's neighbourhood friends are penniless. Shorty (Joseph Pevney) has seven brothers and sisters all out of work, and Charley himself has no job: this is the time of the Depression. Charley's mother cautions him to 'fight for something, not for money,' but it is not until the end of the film, when he defies the mobsters and refuses to take a dive, that his motivation becomes something other than cash: in this case, his soul. Charley's seduction by money is effortless. Like Eddie Willis (Humphrey Bogart) in *The Harder They Fall* (1956), he believes that it is 'only money' and that where it comes from is unimportant. 'It's money,' he cries. 'It doesn't think. It doesn't care who spends it. Take it while you can.' Charley keeps on taking the money, even though it is tainted by corruption. In his rise to the championship, he surrounds himself increasingly with people to whom money is the driving force: the sinister mobster Roberts (Lloyd Gough) who will risk an injured fighter's life because it's simply a 'business' deal and paying for the hospital treatment is surely enough; and femme fatale Alice who attaches herself to Charley, saying 'I don't care where his heart is - just the money.'

The people who represent Charley's moral conscience - his mother, who believes that getting an education is better than fighting; Peg who is well-travelled and cultured; Shorty, who holds out against Roberts; Ben, who supports Charley despite his injury - are swept away one by one, to be replaced by cold-hearted schemers. Charley stops listening to his mother, rejects Peg in favour of Alice, and sees both Shorty and Ben die. The only morality that remains in his life is that of money. 'After mink,' says Roberts, admiring the fur coat that Charley has bought for Peg, 'comes sable.'

Slugging it out around the country (his progress conveyed by that familiar montage of posters, punches, train wheels, dates and newspaper headlines), Charley builds his reputation until he's ready to fight in New York. When he is told he cannot get a fight in the city without cutting in Roberts, he sees this as only reasonable, as a natural part of the pecking-order of the boxing world. 'When I'm the champ,' he says, 'I'll say what and when.' Until then, he seems childishly content with the luxuries of his new world, parading in front of the mirror in his new overcoat, and - in a scene reminiscent of Tony Camonte (Paul Muni) bouncing on the bed in

Scarface (1932) - expressing a delight at the built-in bar in his apartment. The decor and furnishings of this apartment are lavish and ostentatious with gilded mirrors, chandeliers, blackamoors and French-style furniture, and it is significant that the revolving panel that reveals the fully stocked bar has, on its reverse, the self-portrait that Peg once gave Charley, together with a pair of small classical figures. For much of the film, the painting and sculptures - and thus the sensitive, cultured side of his personality that both his mother and Peg thought he should develop - lies hidden behind the flashy sign of shallow wealth. Charley's childlike attitude towards what money can buy is contrasted with that of Roberts, whose apartment is masculine and restrained, with dark furniture, low lights, leather-bound books, wing chairs and a case of good cigars. There are no liquor bottles: Roberts never drinks. It is the room of a businessman for whom fighters are simply another piece of collateral. Whereas Roberts is not given a first name - and is often referred to as Mr Roberts - Charley is known by his first name throughout: the fact that it is a diminutive makes the contrast between him and Roberts even more striking. Baker notes that 'Roberts' name, conservative suits, and public avoidance of alcohol and sex...make him look and act less like a gangster than the stereotype of a WASP businessman'[232] or, as Leger Grindon says, 'a respectable member of the established order'.[233]

Roberts is colder than the smalltime hoods like Quinn (William Conrad) that Charley is used to: this is corruption on a major scale. When discussing whether Ben, who has a blood-clot on the brain, should go back into the ring to fight Charley, Roberts thinks only of the gate money and conveniently forgets to tell Charley to go easy on Ben because he is injured. Boxers are not human beings to him, but money machines: when Roberts says 'I like fighters better than horses', the unconscious analogy with animals is revealing of his attitude. If the death of Charley's father marked the first turning-point of Charley's path to self-destruction, shaking hands with Roberts on a deal which will give the gangster a 50 percent cut is the second, a Faustian bargain that will result in the near-eclipse of Charley's soul. Clinching his alliance with Roberts is also the impetus for Charley to postpone his wedding to Peg and take up instead with Alice, one of those glamorous but hard-edged women who are a fixture of every boxing film, even comedies like *Palooka* (1934).

The filming of Charley's fight against Ben is horrifying in its ferocity,

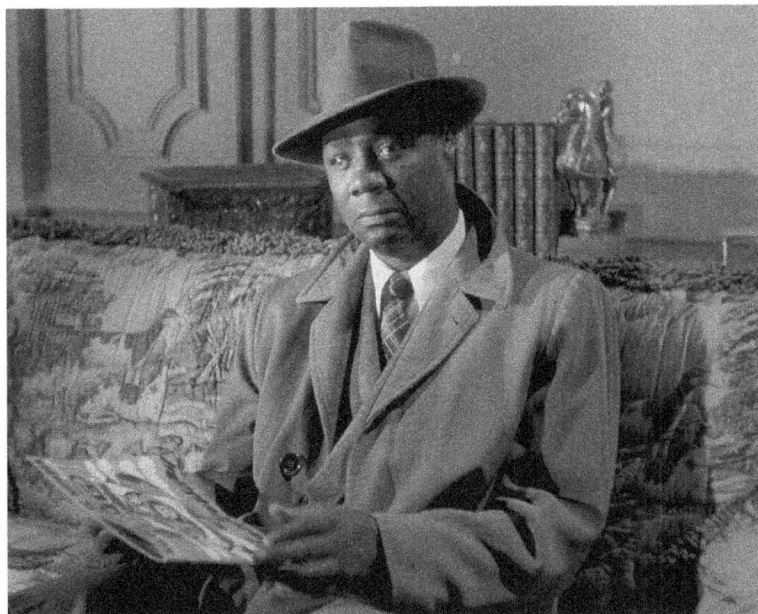

One by one, the people who represent Charley's conscience are swept away. Charley hires Ben (Canada Lee) as his second, perhaps to assuage his guilt at fighting him when he was already injured, but Ben dies one day at the training camp

not least for the cutaway to Alice sitting eagerly in the crowd and shouting 'kill him, Charley', while Peg cowers in her seat. Yet only the final few seconds of the fight are shown, as Ben collapses under a torrent of punches and lies face-down in the ring, one arm outstretched above his head. When Ben's trainer says that the fighter might die from his injuries, Roberts remarks laconically 'everybody dies'. The cut from Ben's unconscious body to the champion's party, all champagne and greedy feasting, shows how far Charley has strayed from the moral values of his parents. His life has become a endless round of betting, money, sex, nightclubs and liquor - and haunting every scene is the sinister figure of Roberts. 'You're not the champ, Roberts is,' says Peg, trying to force Charley to quit. But he can't quit: he's addicted to the lifestyle, spending every cent he earns and more. His only spark of humanity is in his hiring of Ben as his second, perhaps an attempt to assuage guilt from discovering that Ben was already injured when they met in the ring. But Ben's career on Charley's team is short-lived: he dies one day at the training camp, after Charley tells him the championship title fight is fixed; Roberts fires him and in the argument Ben trips over the ringside ropes, falls and dies. It is a beautifully handled and poignant scene which sees him sprawled on the ground in exactly the same pose as when Charley knocked him out in the fight - a 'fearful symmetry' indeed.

The scene of Ben's death marks the end of the flashback and the film returns to the present, repeating the opening scene of Charley lying on his bed at training camp, but imbuing it now with a new significance in which the empty ring has become a place of death, and the scars on Charley's face are marks acquired not by 'fighting for something' as his mother had urged him to do, but merely 'fighting for money'.

The climax of the film is the championship challenge, when Charley faces young contender Jack Marlowe. As agreed with Roberts, Charley is to lose, but to make it look realistic, fighting for 15 rounds, to give the crowd value for money, and then losing on a decision. Roberts even gives Charley 60,000 dollars to place a bet with: against himself. 'Nobody backs out now,' he says. When Charley tells his mother and Peg that the fight is fixed, they accuse him of betraying the neighbourhood and it is perhaps in this moment that critics see Charley as representing or symbolising Jewishness, a view that is undermined by the fact that it was only by turning his back on his own neighbourhood, its people and its values, that Charley has risen to fame and fortune. Larry Swindell says argues that Davis is constructed as 'specifically Jewish' but the references to race are, in fact, very muted and none relate directly to Charley.[234] The first time it is mentioned is when a charity worker comes to Charley's family home shortly after his father's death, to arrange a loan. In filling in the application form, she checks with Anna Davis the entry against her religion: 'Jewish'. Anna nods. The only other reference occurs right before the big fight when Anna's friend and neighbour, grocery man Shimen (the only character in the film to have an overtly Jewish name) says that 'over in Europe, Nazis are killing people like us just because of their religion, but here Charley is a champion.'[235] Stuart Hands feels that in addition to these 'occasional Yiddish inflections' that audiences would easily have read *Body and Soul* as a Jewish film, just as they did with Garfield's other vehicles (*Humoresque* (1946), *Gentleman's Agreement* (1947) and *Force of Evil* (1948)) 'by the nature of the characters' family relations...predilection

By Round 14, Charley realises that Jack Marlowe is fighting for a knockout. The camera begins swooping and diving around the fighters, building a sense of documentary realism

towards social collectivity...and locales such as the Lower East Side'.[236]

The fight itself is all the more effective for the restraint shown in the rest of the film, where any boxing sequences serve as mere 'teasers' for the finale. Fight adviser on *Body and Soul* was former welterweight Johnny Indrisano, whose boxing career lasted from 1924 to 1934, after which he worked as a referee before moving full-time into technical advisor to the studios. Before coaching John Garfield in *Body and Soul* he had previously worked on *The Crowd Roars* (1938) and *Golden Gloves* (1940), and went on to appear in, or choreograph fights, in nearly 200 films including *The Set-Up* (1949), *Right Cross* (1950), *The Harder They Fall* (1956), *Somebody Up There Likes Me* (1956) and much of the Palooka series. He reputedly spent six weeks training Garfield in advance of shooting and is visible in this final fight as the referee. Garfield was said to have vowed to do all his own fight scenes without using a double.[237] The opening rounds are traditionally filmed, with low angles but a fairly static camera which stays outside the ropes, highlighting the slow pace of the fight and the emotionally unengaged fighters. The fighters spend most of their time clinching, rather than fighting, to the boos and slow-handclapping of the crowd. Suddenly, at Round 13, the camera moves inside the ropes, building the sense of documentary realism and, with it, the tension. As the bell sounds for Round 14, Charley realises that Marlowe is no longer fighting for a technical victory, but for a knockout. He decides to do the same: his motivation is left unspoken, whether it is from racial pride as some critics have interpreted it, guilt for causing Ben's death, or simply to win back his integrity.[238] The match is now transformed: point-of-view shots, the screams of the crowd baying for blood and an unending series of punches (*To-day's Cinema* called it 'beserk fistic action'[239]) underscore Charley's determination to win more than the fight. In the last round, Round 15, the crowd is suddenly silent and we hear the hushed voice of the radio commentator, comparing Charley to a tiger (echoing the 'Tiger Tiger' poem with which Peg sought to describe Charley when she first met him). James Wong Howe's lightweight handheld camera tips and weaves, swoops and dives, up close to the fighters so the audience can almost feel the blows, in a dizzying sequence that is sometimes deliberately out of focus. Charley delivers the knockout blow and retains his title. Howe 'employed the camera in a way never before attempted,' says Rainsberger. With a grip pushing him around the ring on roller-skates, Howe sought to put the audience in the fighter's place: so when Charley is hit and falls to the floor, the camera does not follow him but rocks upwards, towards the lights - exactly the view that Charley would have.

Stepping from the ring, having retained his title and won back his integrity, Charley makes a symbolic rejection of Alice, who he passes by waiting at the ringside. Roberts has also been sidelined. 'What makes you think you can get away with this?' he asks Charley, who replies: 'What you gonna do - kill me? Everybody dies.' Ronald Bergan, in his book *Sports in the Movies*, is uneasy about this ending, feeling it to be a cop-out and an avoidance of the social issues raised. We are left,' says Bergan, 'with the impression that the gangsters are going to let him get away with his betrayal of them as if his new morality somehow conferred on him a defence against them.[240] This is, as Mellon argues, 'a myth as fantastic as the exploits of Fairbanks Senior sailing through the air on his magic carpet at the close of The Thief of Baghdad'.[241] But the real point is that Charley is no longer willing to pay the price for the money and power that Roberts has to offer; only when these things were important to him was he in

*Point-of-view shots mean that the audience can almost
feel the blows*

Roberts' grip. As to any punishment they might inflict on him, the
'everybody dies' line gives it away: Charley is simply not afraid any more.
There were, in fact, two endings shot for the film: according to Brian
Neve, one was advocated by Rossen 'in which the boxer dies a squalid
death at the hands of Roberts's minions', and the other, advocated by
Polonsky in which 'the couple (were) swallowed up by the
neighbourhood'. Polonsky's view prevailed, providing an ending that 'was
most in keeping with the tone of the story as a Depression fable of the
streets.'[242]

In her book on flashback in film, Turim notes that biopics that use
flashback 'display the conviction that wealth and power necessitate a loss
of humanity, honesty and happiness', though it is hard, even at the start of
Charley's career, to glimpse much of these qualities.[243] He remains an anti-
hero throughout and, as such, Charley is compelling. Like Jake La Motta
in *Raging Bull*, Charley is as quick with his fists out of the ring as he is in
it, settling scores with a punch or two. 'He is never shown as a noble
figure, but always a forceful man,' said William Weaver in *Motion Picture
Herald*.[244] It is a difficult line to tread: to be at once repugnant, but to

retain the audience's faith in your eventual redemption. *Theatre Arts* said that Garfield played the role 'with a combination of cocky grace and the humorlessness of the self-made man, which is more disarming than repugnant'.[245] Apart from the reversal of the rags-to-riches theme, it is essentially the same character he portrayed in *They Made Me a Criminal*. The studio publicity of the time sought to conflate character and actor: in a bylined article in *Opportunity Magazine* in 1948, Garfield draws parallels between his own boyhood and that of Charley Davis. 'I grew up on New York's Lower East Side,' he said, 'where a fellow had two choices if he wanted to survive: fight or run. I became pretty handy with my fists'.[246]

It is not until Charley has retained his title and regained his integrity that he is able to reject Alice (Hazel Brooks)

It is interesting that although categorised at the time as a man's picture, women are far more than a cipher in this film: Peg continues her independent career as an artist and designer throughout Charley's rise to fame, and her own rise in status parallels that of Charley's. It is her moral stance (more forceful than that of Eddie's wife in *The Harder They Fall*) that eventually wins through and convinces Charley that he has to take a stand against the corruption that is consuming him. Mike Wayne points out

All for you....
BODY
and
SOUL

The ENTERPRISE STUDIOS present

JOHN GARFIELD · LILLI PALMER

in

"Body and Soul"

NOT SUITABLE FOR GENERAL EXHIBITION

and introducing

HAZEL BROOKS as "ALICE" with ANNE REVERE

WILLIAM CONRAD · JOSEPH PEVNEY · LLOYD GOFF · CANADA LEE

Directed by ROBERT ROSSEN · Produced by BOB ROBERTS

A Metro Goldwyn-Mayer RELEASE

Offset Printing Coy. Pty. Ltd. Sydney

The poster gives no indication that this is a boxing film, the 'body and soul' opposition being characterised as a choice between two women that Abraham Polonsky was known, both in his pulp fiction books and his screenplays, for including a 'proto-feminist lead'.'[247] *Kinematograph Weekly*, reviewing *Body and Soul* on its release, felt that 'it should make history by being the first fight film to thrill the women', though maybe this was accounted for by the limited amount of onscreen fighting, rather than the strong portrayal of women characters.[248] Certainly, the love story and the boxing angle were given equal weight in the film's promotion: indeed, the film's posters promote only the love story, leaving the lobby cards to portray the fight scenes. Part of the film's appeal to women is revealed by the poster straplines, which emphasised toughness: 'he could kill an guy with his hands...he's the kind of guy that women go for!'

Body and Soul ushered in a new era of boxing movie - or, more accurately, an alternative strand of boxing movie that would coexist with the comedies and light dramas that would continue to represent the mainstay of the genre over the next decade. Zucker and Babich, writing in the book *Sports Movies*, believe the freshness of the film's approach - coming as it did in the wake of so many well-worn 'formula' boxing films - represented the beginning of a 'Golden Gloves decade'. Diversity would still be the genre's hallmark, however, and it is hard to substantiate some of the claims made for the film, such as Carmen Ficarra's assertion that, with *Body and Soul*, 'out went the tender pathos of Keaton, the indomitable smile of Cagney. In came the greedy fighters, crooked managers and malicious syndicate bosses'.[249] Leaving aside the strange timeframe (Keaton hadn't made a boxing film for 20 years), the underbelly of boxing was hardly a new phenomenon. These corrupt figures were always there, even in the lightest of comedies, but only now had they moved out of the shadows, to occupy centre-stage and to look like serious moral threats.

You'll Always Be Just One Punch Away
The Set-Up (1949)

I f there is one film that can be called the quintessential boxing film, the one against which all the others are judged, it is *The Set-Up*. Not particularly successful from a commercial point of view, being eclipsed at the box office by Kirk Douglas in *Champion*, released in the same month, it has gained an enviable critical reputation and continues to be invoke fresh comment and insight. In fact, more column inches have been (and continue to be) expended on analysis of *The Set-Up* than any other boxing film. This is undoubtedly due in part to its inclusion - along with *Body and Soul* - in the film noir canon, but also more recently because of the rise in academic interest of gender studies and in representations of masculinity. At the time of its release, critical interest largely stemmed from the fact that the film was so bleak and uncompromising. It carried off the Critic's Prize at the Cannes Film Festival, but there was some unease expressed about its level of violence: *Monthly Film Bulletin*, for example, praised the fact that none of the brutality was gratuitous, but Dilys Powell worried that presenting it in 'such intimate detail must tend to debase rather than deter'.[250]

The Set-Up, directed by Robert Wise for RKO, has an unusual origin, being based on a book-length narrative poem by James Moncure March, now-forgotten chronicler of the jazz age. March was born in New York in 1899 and came from a privileged background; after writing poems for *The New Yorker*, and a brief spell as its managing editor, in 1928 he published his first long narrative poem, 'The Wild Party', to great acclaim. 'The Set-Up' followed later that year: Jefferson Hunter believes that March was inspired by Jack Johnson, the notorious heavyweight champion whose life had been the subject of 'Black Boy', a Broadway play starring Paul Robeson; by Hemingway's short story 'Fifty Grand' which had been published in the *Atlantic Monthly* the year before; and the painting 'Negro Boxer' by James Chapin, whose studio March visited.[251] Though the film retains a poetic quality in its rhythm and staging, March's narrative underwent a number of changes in its route to the screen: Hunter describes these as relating to the 'domestication' of the fighter.[252] March's boxer was a black man called Pansy Jones, who had just served five years in prison for bigamy:

> He looked like something
> To catch and cage:
> Like something that belonged
> In a Jungle Age.[253]

In the film he is a white married man called Stoker Thompson, and whereas Pansy dies at the end of the poem, hounded to his death under an express train, Stoker lives, his crushed hand a constant reminder that he will never fight again. In addition to avoiding the controversy of casting a black leading man, the film also tones down other portrayals of race: Hunter points out that 'no one in the film is as Jewish or Italian or German as the characters of the poem; no one even says 'dem' or 'dese' or 'dose' and that by this homogenisation, the film lacks the edge of the black-versus-white rivalry in the ring that characterised the sport at this time.[254] Romano calls it a 'neutering' of the poem but acknowledges that RKO replaced the ethnic diversity with 'equally unsavoury' characters and perhaps avoided stereotypes in the process.[255] The sense of bleak poetry, however, in the cinematography and the editing, remains intact and it is perhaps this quality which appealed to poet Nicholas Christopher who describes the film as 'less a morality tale than a nihilistic sprint that skirts the abyss'.[256]

Given a level of bleakness that is uncharacteristic of the Hollywood studio system at this time, what exactly is it that makes *The Set-Up* so memorable? The story itself is a modest one: aging fighter Stoker Thompson (Robert Ryan) who has never quite made the big-time, is due to fight at Paradise City, a seedy 'tank town' on the road to nowhere. He believes that winning one more fight will enable him to leave the business and set up a cigar-stand: a modest enough ambition, but it's a line he's been spinning for 20 years. His dream - as his wife Julie (Audrey Totter) reminds him - will always be 'just one punch away.' It is not as if he is much of a fighter: in fact, he has been losing so often that his manager doesn't even bother to tell him that a deal has been done with local gangster Little Boy (Alan Baxter) to fix the fight to allow his opponent Tiger Nelson (Hal Baylor) to win. But the scheme comes unstuck when Stoker reveals a dogged determination to win, even in the face of a hastily whispered instruction in Round Three to take a dive. Little Boy and his cronies are not pleased: 'I paid for something tonight and I didn't get it,' he explains, reasonably, as if he has been cheated of his change in the local grocery store. Stoker is chased and beaten, his hand crushed so that he will never fight again.

If the storyline of the boxer who puts his life on the line by refusing to take a dive is familiar enough, the difference here stems from the fact that we get no sense of the trajectory of Stoker's career as we do in films like *Body and Soul* (1947) or *Champion* (1949). 'There's no saga of a rise and fall here,' says Christopher. 'For this boxer, we see only the tail end of a downward spiral'.[257] Film noir often uses flashback or voiceover as a means of positioning the events of the film in the context of the boxer's life - and of lending a confessional tone to the narrative. *The Set-Up*, however, adheres to a complete unity of time, with the action taking place over 72 minutes of a single evening, its progress charted by a shot of a clock at the beginning and end of the film.

The timing, in addition to its emphasis lending a fatalistic quality to the narrative (Stoker is a man whose time is running out, as J M Welsh points out in an appraisal of the film for *American Classic Screen*) also has an implication for the way the fights are shown: while we see very little of the matches taking place earlier on the bill, the camera instead concentrating on Stoker in the dressing-room as he prepares for his fight, we do see the entire length of his four-round battle against Tiger Nelson, which takes up a quarter of the film.[258] Boxing film audiences would have been accustomed to constant cut-aways from the fighting - often, in otherwise serious films, to comic action - therefore this complete concentration on the fight itself increases its impact and was perhaps one of the reasons why reviewers felt the film to be unusually brutal.[259] This brutality is not signalled to the audience in the opening sequence of the film, which runs over the credits, and which shows in close-up the feet of two boxers in the ring as they move and dance lightly around each other. As the name of the director, Robert Wise, appears on screen, the fight is won with a knockout. Only the complete absence of music indicates that this might not be an 'average' boxing drama: instead of a music soundtrack there is the ring of the bell and the yells of the crowd.

The Set-Up *adheres to a complete unity of time, with the action taking place over 72 minutes of a single evening, its progress charted by a shot of a clock at the beginning and end of the film*

The aura of violence and brutality in *The Set-Up* stems not just from the fighting, but from the unrelieved drab seediness of the surroundings, ironically known as Paradise City; the two-bit gangsters; the hand-to-mouth existence of Stoker's scruffy manager Tiny (George Tobias), who'd fix a fight for just 50 dollars; the paucity of the fighters' ambitions; and the desperate and futile search for enjoyment of everyone in the town: on the sidewalks, in the cafes and amusement arcades, and in the boxing arena itself. There is no glitter here, no wild dreams, no glamorous women: even Stoker - the choice of name is significant - has the attitude of just doing a job, with the 'demeanor of a weary plumber or handyman'.[260] From the first post-credits shot of the film, in which a boy selling newspapers deliberately encroaches on the pitch of an ex-boxer selling fight programmes, the attitude is one of dog-eat-dog. In the Ringside Café, thick with noise and smoke, a punter operates a coin-slot crane machine to win a prize. It cheats him, just like Stoker's manager cheats his handler, passing on only 30 dollars of his payoff, and giving none at all to Stoker. Martin Scorsese, an admirer of the film, sees the crane-machine as a metaphor for Paradise City, an unsentimental place in which life is dependant on the notion of chaos or fate. The cranes would pick up an item and 'just at the last minute it'd go down - and that's fate', he said.[261] Yet the film's emphasis on the way that each layer of society preys on the layer beneath it is surely indicative less of the randomness of fate and more of a deliberate crushing of hope.

This hope - of deriving a spark of excitement, of elation, of winning - remains absurdly alive, however. The boxing crowd is the epitome of this attitude, eager for blood, their mouths in close-up (the same technique would be used later in the British film *The Square Ring* (1953)) urging Tiger Nelson to 'kill him.' They appear 'demented in the excess of their blood-lust' said *Today's Cinema*.[262] Even watching the bloody battle in the ring is not quite enough for many of the spectators: one man holds a radio to his ear throughout the entire fight, alternately watching what's happening in front of him and listening to live baseball commentary; another eats gluttonously, cramming his mouth with food as if he is devouring the very boxers themselves; another, blind, his eyes fierce and animalistic, listens intently to the sounds of pain. This is the crowd of March's poem:

> They looked like jail-birds
> Out for a bat.
> They looked nasty:
> They looked vicious:
> Sullen-faced;
> Hard;
> Suspicious.

Against this atmosphere of the predatory is set Julie, Stoker's wife, who waits alone in the cheap room at the Hotel Cozy (another ironic name) just across the street, until she is able to bear the tension no more.

Approaching the boxing arena with her ticket, she hears a great roar from the crowd, and backs away, repelled, to walk instead through the neon-lit, jazz-music-saturated streets, past amusement arcades, bars and tattoo parlours, cigar stands, street salesmen and laughing couples, the night-time heat almost palpable. Against the sooty brick walls and dark clothes of the passers-by, Julie in her pale suit and with her blonde hair stands out, ghost-like, unbelonging. Julie has reached the end of the line: for 20 years she has watched Stoker fight in no-count towns with forgettable names. For 20 years she has had the same conversation with him, where she pleads with him to give up the business, and he - not listening - goes on about his next win and how good it's going to be. At Paradise City, she tries again to get through to him: 'don't you see,' she says, 'you'll always be just one punch away?' But Stoker can think only of that next punch and, Julie, even when poised on the bridge high above the tramcar tracks, cannot really consider abandoning him. In the end, it is only her ticket that she shreds and throws over the parapet.

Despite Stoker's refusal to give Julie what she wants, his dependence on her is absolute. In his dressing room, he looks repeatedly through the window to catch a glimpse of her in the hotel room window; in the ring, his first glance is to her empty seat in Section C; and at the end, broken and lying in the gutter, he repeats her name over and over like an incantation. Mild-mannered and quiet in the pre-fight sequence, he is nevertheless quick to react when a trainer says; 'I never seen a dame yet that's still around when you hit the skids,' sensing a slur on Julie, or perhaps wanting to crush any sense of this being his future if he loses.[263]

We learn little of Stoker's life from the man himself, but everything about his character. He has few lines of dialogue and, in the first half of the film - up to the start of his fight - little action to perform, but Robert Ryan's restrained acting allows us to read his reactions and chart his anxieties through the subtlest of facial expressions and movements. Unlike the other boxers, who boast about the damage they've done to their opponents, Stoker sits quietly in his corner of the dressing room, introspective and detached from (though accepting of) the rackets of the fight game: 'everyone makes book on something,' he says, calmly. Even entering the ring for his fight, he continues to look somewhat bemused and lost in thought, even when someone in the crowd yells 'where's your wheelchair?' at him. Joan Mellon argues that the way Ryan portrays Stoker

Robert Ryan (left) has few lines of dialogue but his reactions and anxieties can be read through the subtlest of facial expressions

makes him more of a real person: 'he is neither heroic nor vicious. His physical attributes are unexceptionable and workmanlike...If he is like most fighters in reality, he is also like most men'.[264]

As with other boxing-film climaxes, we hear the fighters announced, and listen to the referee recite the rules - though this time they are delivered at high speed, the words run together in a meaningless monotone which brings home the message that this is just one more fight - tomorrow there'll be another, and another. As J M Welsh observes, the fact that the fight takes place in 'real time' drives home the realisation of 'just how long three minutes can be for a fighter who is taking a beating in the ring'.[265] The sequence is bloody, visceral and unrelenting, the furious hitting causing each fighter's head to snap back alarmingly with every punch, sweat and water spraying out to be caught in the glare of the lights. Stoker's face is screwed up with determination: 'I'm gonna take this guy,' he keeps saying in between rounds, even though one eye is already cut and Nelson is being entreated by the crowd to 'close the other eye.' By Round Three, Nelson's moving head is a blur, the lights blazing over the two men as they fight on and on at a seemingly unsustainable pace; by Round Four both men are unstoppable. Stoker has been told he must throw the fight, but he's having none of it - he's fighting for his life, his pride, for Julie.

When Stoker finally wins with a knockout punch, he almost topples onto the prone body of Nelson and can barely stagger out of the ring and back down the litter-strewn corridor to his dressing-room.

A chilling confrontation with Little Boy, played with icy calm by Alan Baxter, ensues.[266] Despite the crush of the crowd, the heat and the sweat, Little Boy's suit is immaculately pressed, his tie still neatly knotted, his

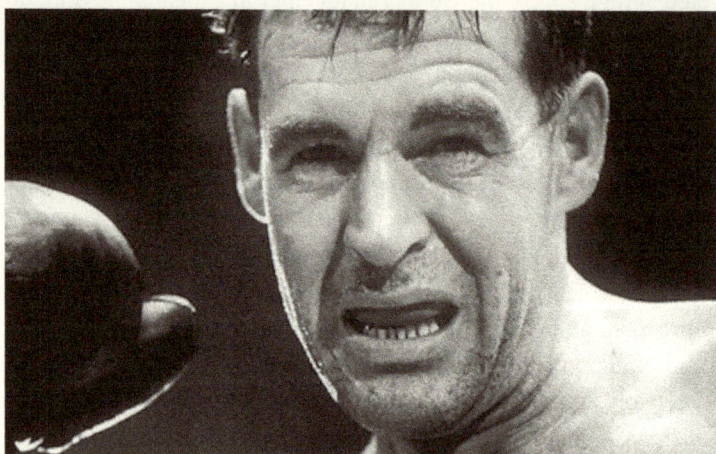

The fight against Tiger Nelson is bloody, visceral and unrelenting

wide-brimmed hat perfectly angled on his head. In addition to the irony of the name 'Little Boy', a diminutive for someone who in fact wields such power, it is surely no coincidence he shares his name with that of the nickname for the first atom-bomb, which inflicted such damage on Hiroshima. Stoker is left to get dressed in a scene that in other films, may have been accompanied by tense, dramatic music, but here is conducted in complete silence. His haste is contrasted with a similar scene in Hotel Cozy at the beginning of the film, when he was so careful to knot his tie exactly right, to straighten his jacket. Here, in fear of his life, he throws on his clothes, putting his trousers on over his boxing shorts, his shirt unbuttoned, his shoe-laces hanging loose, and goes out into the deep-shadowed corridor where every tiny sound constitutes a threat. Spotting Little Boy and his henchmen outside, he runs instead into the echoing and empty stadium, down the tiered seating to the ring, the camera - high above - pinning him there with a sense of inevitability: there will be no escape. For the first time, we look down on the ring, small and insignificant, the spectacle over and the crowd all vanished, gone in search of the next source of excitement.[267] Furiously, he rattles the fire-exit doors one by one until he finds a door that opens into a blind alleyway. The sound of the jazz band, heard in all the scenes on Main Street, resumes, forming an eerily celebratory soundtrack to a brutal scene. Little Boy and his three cronies are waiting and, as they walk threateningly down the alleyway towards Stoker, the fighter rattles the doors in the alley one by one, almost in a repeat of the previous sequence except this time the aim is to find his way back into the safety of the arena. While Little Boy stands aside, with evident disdain for physical contact, the men beat Stoker, with Tiger Nelson landing the punches he probably wishes he had inflicted on Stoker in the ring. Held prone on the ground, Stoker still manages to punch Little Boy in the face as he leans over the fighter. This punch seems to decide his fate. Dabbing delicately at the trickle of blood, Little Boy says 'you'll never hit anyone with that hand again'. The camera moves away so that the crushing of Stoker's hand (and whether it is Little Boy himself who inflicts the damage) happens off-screen: instead the shot is of the wall of the alley on which can be seen the shadows of the jazz musicians silhouetted against the brickwork, instruments lifted in joyful exuberance. There is a sense that the brutality in the ring could be shown unflinchingly because the fight was a performance or spectacle, part of Paradise City's endless search for excitement, but that this is an altogether darker, more private moment and so cannot be shown. In the fight, the camera positioned the viewer as a member of the blood-hungry crowd; in the crushing of Stoker's hand, we are the passer-by who hurries away.

The Set-Up ends with Stoker in the gutter outside the neon lights of 'Dreamland', his head cradled in Julie's arms. 'I can't fight no more,' he laments in a double-edged statement that to him means failure, but to Julie means victory. He still wants to make the point, however, in a gesture of futile pride, that he won tonight. 'We both won tonight,' is her reply.

Julie cradles Stoker in her arms, his hand broken, their future together unimaginable

In addition to the Critics' Prize, the film won Best Cinematography at the Cannes Film Festival in 1949 for Milton Krasner. Krasner started working in films in when he was just 14 years old, as assistant cameraman for Vitagraph and Bioscope. Through the 1930s and 1940s he worked on a vast number of productions: no single genre seems to have dominated, but his film noir sensibilities can be seen in *The Ghost of Frankenstein* (1942), *The Woman in the Window* (1944), *Scarlet Street* (1945) and *The Dark Mirror* (1946). Three aspects of the film highlight what makes Krasner's technique so successful, in terms of camera movement, in using the camera to convey emotion and in the choreography of the fight.

In the opening scene, as people pass by on the sidewalks of Paradise City, he uses a very fluid technique that Robert Wise said allowed audiences to be drawn into the picture.[268] The camera is initially positioned high above the street, perhaps from the point of view of the bedroom at Hotel Cozy, with the clock prominent in the foreground. As a newsvendor walks into shot, crossing the road, the camera gradually descends to street-level, following him as he walks up to the boxing arena entrance. The cameos that follow - the spat with the fight-programme seller, the women who say they look away during a fight, the blind man being led in, the man who strikes his match on the fight poster, putting a scratch through Stoker's name - give the impression that the viewer is right there on the sidewalk, overhearing the crowd. This impression is retained even when the camera begins to follow Tiny into the Ringside Cafe, past a man working the crane machine, a drunk asleep in a booth, a couple necking, and a woman laughing raucously. Tiny sits down at a small table opposite Danny (Edwin Max), Little Boy's 'fixer', the men shown in profile facing each other in a tight midshot, their hands on the table, hammering out a deal nose-to-nose, just as if they were fighting the ring. The camera remains in the position of the third seat at the table, the point of view of the crowd at the ringside and thus their confrontation foreshadows the one that will take place between Stoker and Tiger Nelson.

In terms of using camera angles to convey emotion, Krasner employs a simple series of shots in Julie's scene on the bridge, which switch between low-angled shots of her leaning over the parapet, and point-of-view shots looking down at the trolley-buses and cars moving swiftly below her. As Julie walks to the bridge, the noise of the street with its jazz music, sidewalk hustlers and amusement arcades dies away. She descends the steps, the sky very black behind her and the lights of the suburbs twinkling in the distance. The stone balustrade of the bridge is elegantly carved: this could almost be a scene in Rome or Paris instead of a US tank-town, and a romance instead of a tragedy. The camera is positioned behind her as she leans on the parapet and looks out at the lights of the highway below. Krasner cuts to a track-level shot with a trolley-bus and cars streaming out of the tunnels towards the viewer. Before we can gauge Julie's thoughts, the scene is broken by a brief return to the boxing-arena dressing room where Stoker is having his hands bound, holding out the very hand that is soon to be crushed. The camera returns to similar tunnel-shot, then to a low-angle looking up at Julie, a globe-shaped street lamp glowing in the background. The shot is changed to her point-of-view, the roof of the trolley-bus visible as it enters the tunnel, then back, an even lower angle this time with her face strongly underlit and the light catching her wedding ring. The sequence of shot/reverse shot is repeated three times, heightening tension and leading the viewer to believe that she is considering jumping to her death. In the end, she simply tears up her fight-ticket, and the last shot down onto the tracks shows the little pieces fluttering down like confetti.

Krasner's filming of the fight between Stoker and Tiger Nelson is the most memorable demonstration of the quality of his cinematography. Martin Scorsese remarked on the scene's shocking and 'primal' nature. When planning *Raging Bull* (1980), Scorsese said 'I could not come close to (it), so I had to do it differently'.[269] Krasner used three cameras: one to film the entire ring, one filming just the two fighters, and one handheld for close-ups. A fight scene may be thought to be about camera movement, but this essentially an illusion of the finished, edited film: it is actually much more about careful choreography, which in this instance was provided by Johnny Indrisano. It was filmed in a series of 20-second bursts. 'This takes a lot of rehearsals,' said Wise, though the result is a seamless action sequence of startling documentary realism. For much of the time, the camera remains just outside the ropes of the ring, locating us, as Hunter points out, 'uncomfortably in that screaming crowd', a crowd of hoarse voices, sweat, prurience and blood-lust.[270]

Joseph Moncure March was not invited to write the screenplay, though he did work in the film industry - for Paramount - throughout the 1930s. Instead it was written by first-timer Art Cohn, though Hunter believes it could best be termed a collaborative effort with contributions from a number of RKO personnel included director Robert Wise, producer Richard Goldstone and production head Dore Schary. The poorer sections of dialogue, however, he attributes solely to Cohn, saying that they are 'ordinary, occasionally mawkish' and that Julie's lines in particular render her 'one-note and little-womanly'. Audrey Totter, however, transcends any inadequacies of the script in her acting: familiar to audiences through her recent roles in *The Postman Always Rings Twice* (1946), *The Lady in the Lake* (1947) and *The Unsuspected* (1947) Totter was fast establishing a screen persona as a classic film noir 'bad girl', so any 'little-womanly' lines in *The Set-Up* gave this persona a different dimension. As she spends much of the film alone, a number of her scenes are without any dialogue at all: her walk along Main Street is an example of this. She laughs at the young couple posing as lifeguard and bathing belle, is amused and then repelled by a mechanical boxing game, and falls into despair, and eventually an acceptance of fate, as she stands on the bridge looking down at the highway below. Through her acting, the direction and the cinematography, the narration of Julie's emotional journey in this scene is perfectly conveyed without the need for dialogue. Despite his criticism of the script, Hunter acknowledges that *The Set-Up* is such a visually powerful film that it 'tells its stories best in images'.[271] Cohn is most effective, Romano points out, in the way he develops the characters of the boxers through scenes in the dressing-room, the 'modern-day equivalent of a gladiator holding pen', where we see not the fights themselves, but the boxer's preparation - the revealing of their fears or dreams - and the harsh reality as they return in 'exultation or heartbreak.'[272]

The film was a low-budget one, described by Robert Wise as a 'A- or B+' shot in nineteen days, mainly on the studio's back lots in Culver City.[273] Wise was an editor as well as a director (he had, most notably, edited *Citizen Kane* (1941)) and though he is perhaps best known for his professionalism rather than for an 'auteur' stamp on his work, he drew attention for the unity of time that *The Set-Up* portrays and for its realism.[274] *Variety* said that even though the film was 'obviously made on a programmer budget, the picture rates classification in a higher bracket, for it's certain to please in the twin-bill situations and may even be strong enough to solo in some spots'. The paper particularly liked the depiction of the crowd at the arena which they said Wise portrayed with 'scalpel-like scrutiny'.[275] This aspect also appealed to the *New York Times* who praised the 'harsh realistic terms' in which the 'ringside types' had been put on screen, though it was more critical of the cutaways while the fight was in progress, comparing this unfavourably to *Body and Soul*.[276] The film's posters bill *The Set-Up* as 'the sensational picture you've been hearing and reading about', capitalising on its controversy. The title, hand-drawn and in red (with that colour's connotations of violence) dominates the poster, positioned across the image of the back of a fighter who stands with his hands to his sides and his feet planted firmly apart. Through the gap between his legs we see Robert Ryan as Stoker sprawled on the floor of

The viewpoint of Stoker sprawled on the floor of the ring suggests we are seeing him from the position of the victor and thus suggests our complicity in his downfall the ring: the viewpoint suggests that we are seeing Stoker from the position of the victor and thus suggests our complicity in his downfall. The seediness of the deal is spelt out in stills from three key scenes from the film which run along the bottom of the poster: Little Boy giving the order to lose the fight, Stoker hunted in the alleyway ('for $30', says the caption), and finally Stoker lying in Julie's arms ('for every scar on his face...two in her heart').

Trapped at the end of the alley, Stoker can only await his fate.
Little Boy and his cronies will walk away, unpunished, in an ending
that shows the weakening of the Production Code

Frank Krutnik, in his study of masculinity in film noir, *In a Lonely Street*, says that *The Set-Up* suggests 'there is no honour, security or real achievement to be derived from the sport'.[277] In other films, this absence may be disguised, through glamour, money or sex, but in *The Set-Up*, the fight game is stripped bare. Even the fight itself, site of a traditional demonstration of masculinity, is not the proud arena portrayed in films like *The Pittsburgh Kid* (1941) or *Gentleman Jim* (1942). In fact, as Krutnik points out, it is less about the fulfilment of masculine ambition and more about impairment.[278] This was very much a characteristic of the post-war period. In his study of consensus in Hollywood, Richard Maltby identifies the latter half of the 1940s as the period when 'the individualist hero lost his innocence....and found himself engaged in an ever more perilous struggle to secure the once-guaranteed happy ending.' It was the era,' he says, 'when mythic perfection gave way to human frailty'.[279] In other words, given the exposure to the realities of war, audiences were no longer receptive to the fairy-tales that had served classical Hollywood well for decades: they were likely to find stories about flawed individuals facing a hostile society more akin to their own experience. Constrained by the Production Code, Hollywood was slow to respond, but examples of this shift, outside the boxing genre, include *The Lost Weekend* (1945) where the struggle is against alcoholism, and *The Snakepit* (1948) about insanity. Even in *The Set-Up*, the weakening of the grip of the Production Code on the industry can be seen in the fact that Little Boy and his cronies walk away at the end of the film, something which *Motion Picture Herald* saw as its one weakness: 'justice never catches up with the wrongdoers'.[280]

J M Welsh interprets *The Set-Up* as allegorical, with Stoker a symbol first of Adam, then of Christ, falling from Paradise and being reborn into a higher existence through the love of a good woman.[281] Aside from the somewhat hectic mix of symbolism here, the truth is probably much simpler: the struggle of the post-war male to find a new definition of masculinity, one compatible with masculine pride as well as the demands of the modern-day 'companiate' marriage.

I'm Not Going to be a "Hey You!" All My Life
Champion (1949)

Considering the downbeat nature of many boxing-film titles - from *They Made Me a Criminal* and *There Ain't No Justice* (both 1939), to *The Set-Up* (1949) and *The Harder They Fall* (1956) - the name 'Champion' strikes a celebratory note, but the only person doing the celebrating in this film is its anti-hero Midge Kelly. Midge is a thoroughly nasty piece of work whose only redeeming quality, apart from his superficial charm which easily turned on to get what he wants, then turned off at will, is the care he seems to take of Connie, his brother. But in the end, this proves to be an illusion and Midge cannot resist betraying him too. From the point of view of the audience or, more accurately, the 'female gaze', as Tony Williams identifies it, Midge's other redeeming quality is the fact that he is played by Kirk Douglas: to a large extent the film is a hymn to the beauty of Douglas' muscled and honed body which is given every plot-related opportunity (and a few more unnecessary ones) to show itself off.[282] Steve Cohan says *Champion* 'clearly exceeds whatever narrative motivation the sport setting supplies for putting the actor's physique on display' and even Douglas joked that he was 'probably the only *man* in Hollywood who's had to strip to get a part'.[283] Douglas is shown stripped to the waist in the foreground of the posters and advertisements for the film, which show a montage of three photographs, each of Douglas standing behind a different woman and embracing her. In the first, he wears a check shirt, to indicate his humble beginnings; in the second he wears a suit, and in the third his boxing trunks. 'Every woman goes for a champion' reads the tagline, a clear appeal to the female audience particularly as the posters do not include a boxing 'action' shot. With each photograph, and charting his trajectory to championship status, the woman being embraced becomes more blonde, more glamorous, and

Every woman goes for a

CHAMPION

Screen Plays Corp. presents

KIRK DOUGLAS

in Ring Lardner's

"CHAMPION"

featuring

MARILYN MAXWELL
ARTHUR KENNEDY

with

PAUL STEWART · RUTH ROMAN · LOLA ALBRIGHT

Produced by STANLEY KRAMER

Associate Producer Robert Stillman

Directed by Mark Robson

Screenplay by Carl Foreman

Released thru United Artists

her dress more revealing. In the first two photographs, the woman faces the camera, and Douglas looks down at her, his mouth touching her forehead, but in the third Douglas looks away cold-eyed, out perhaps towards a potential audience or towards the 'next new thing'. In this shot, the woman has turned to Douglas and her face is buried in his naked chest: a signal to the potential audience for the film that the focus will be on the display of Douglas' body.

Despite the overt marketing emphasis on sex, *Champion* is actually a full-bloodied melodrama in the school of gritty realism for which director Mark Robson was becoming known. Robson had worked as an editor at RKO, where his credits include assisting Robert Wise on *Citizen Kane* (1940) and editing the ground-breaking horror films *Cat People* (1942) and *I Walked With a Zombie* (1943). He continued to work with producer Val Lewton when he moved into the director's chair and prior to *Champion* he had worked on *The Ghost Ship* (1945), the teenage delinquency film *Youth Runs Wild* (1944) and the Boris Karloff thriller *Bedlam* (1946). After *Champion*, which was made by independent company Screen Plays Corp, he was to direct another boxing film, *The Harder They Fall*, for Columbia in 1956. *Champion* is sometimes talked about in the context of film noir, but although some of the cinematographic techniques of noir are present, such as the use of deep shadows, low-key lighting, tilted camera-angles and a prevalence of night-time/indoor shots, the familiar thematic devices of noir are absent.[284] Midge Kelly does not seem to embody widespread post-war anxieties about masculinity, merely his own angst; there is no confessional tone to the narrative; and his ruthlessness ensures that he is never trapped either by the gangsters that threaten him or the femmes fatales who attempt to lure him.

Champion was made on a tight budget of less than 600,000 dollars and a 24-day production schedule. Douglas says that he turned down the offer to play opposite Gregory Peck and Ava Gardner in the big-budget film *The Great Sinner* in order to play in *Champion* because the story reflected so much of his own life.[285] It tells the rags-to-riches story of Midge Kelly, a young man with a chip on his shoulder: his father left the family when Midge was young, he grew up in an orphanage and now he has been cheated out of his war service savings. He burns with resentment at the world and particularly at having to take on menial, low-paid jobs. 'I don't want to be a 'hey you' all my life', he says, 'I wanna hear people call me 'mister", driving a wedge between himself and his more sensitive brother Connie. He sees fighting not just as a way of making money, but of becoming 'top of the heap' and dedicates himself to it with an iron will. He achieves his ambition but, corrupted by money and an addiction to 'winning' in every aspect of his life, he mistreats and betrays his friends, family and colleagues. The film ends with Midge dying of a brain haemorrhage in the dressing-room after successfully defending his title against Johnnie Dunne.

Champion is based on a short story of the same name by Ring Lardner and was adapted by Carl Foreman, one of Hollywood's top screen writers who was nominated for an Academy Award for his script.[286] Despite the 'backstory' about the probable causes of Midge's resentment, this is no 'social problem' film but a tale of naked ambition featuring a protagonist who is unusually unsympathetic for a Hollywood film. *Monthly Film Bulletin* felt that there were 'constant attempts to excuse his brutality on account of his early poverty and his desire to provide for his mother', but in reality these attempts are few and far between and the only person who seems to spending time (rather than just money) caring for his mother is Connie.[287] Midge Kelly had been considerably 'softened' in bringing the character to the screen: Lardner's short story, which focuses on the discrepancy between the fighter's public persona as a generous-hearted, teetotal, family-man, and the altogether more brutish reality, begins with Midge stealing money from his crippled brother before kicking him in the leg and pushing his mother to the floor.[288]

The film is shot in flashback, a technique conventionally associated with a confessional tone, but there is no indication anywhere in the film that Midge has a sense of remorse about how he has treated people. Indeed, the opening sequence, shown over the credits, has an unambiguously celebratory feel. Against martial music, Midge and his handlers walk like gladiators along the darkened corridor towards the light and noise of the boxing arena. The camera follows the backs of the men, each of whom wears a robe with Midge's name written in large white letters. There are shots of the crowd on their feet, pointing and jostling to get a better view. In one swoop, the movie cameramen, there to record the fight, swivel their cameras around to focus on the entrance to the arena. A radio commentator, standing ringside and holding a microphone, tells his listeners that the champion has just entered: 'this is the most popular champion in the history of this division', he says. As he relates Midge's rise from poverty, the camera cuts to another rear view of the champion, standing in the corner of the ring, still wearing his robe. At the words 'champion of the world', Midge turns and we see his face for the first time, in a very low-angle shot which immediately dissolves into the bright lights and loud whistle of the freight train that signal the start of the flashback sequence. For the match itself, we have to wait until the end of the film when the fight and its aftermath form the emotional climax, one which *The Cinema,* reviewing the film on its release, felt was 'unexcelled for portraiture, brutality and cumulative power'.

The flashback starts with Midge and Connie (Arthur Kennedy, playing another virtuous brother role as he had in *City for Conquest* (1940)) riding a freight car, being fleeced by robbers and having to jump off the train to safety. As they walk through a dusty landscape hoping to hitch a ride, Connie is revealed as lame and though the reason is not explained, the assumption is that this is a war injury. He is immediately positioned as the weaker of the two men in physical terms, the man in need of protection, yet will turn out to be stronger in terms of morality. In many ways the film is about the impaired body versus the 'body beautiful': Connie's damaged body (but virtuous soul) is constantly compared with Midge's magnificent body (but heartless character). The portrayal serves to heighten the contrast between the two, but is unusual in that the 'moral force' of fight films is usually a role assigned to a wife or hometown sweetheart, rather than a man. It is made possible by the fact that Midge's wife Emma, who would be expected to occupy this position, is absent for much of the film. Christine Gledhill, commenting on the way female audiences 'read' the portrayal of males on

Initially, the only person Midge (Kirk Douglas) seems to care about is his brother, Connie (Arthur Kennedy), but in the end he will betray him too

screen, could be talking about Connie when she says that 'at one extreme the Romantic Hero promises to become the Soul-Mate who recognises from the outset the worth of the heroine, because he is in many ways like her - he is feminised'.[289] It could be argued that Connie, rather than Midge, is the Romantic Hero of this film, and his subsequent attachment to Emma moves him into 'Soul Mate' category.

The feminisation of Connie goes beyond his physical weakness (even his name connotes that of a girl): when the owner of a Kansas City bar calls Connie a 'gimp', it is Midge who socks him in the jaw, and when the brothers become hired hands in the Step Inn, Connie seems content to do the washing-up without complaint while Midge is resentful and bitter. It is the fight with the bar-owner that gets Midge into the boxing game: unable to pay for the bottles broken in the scuffle, he is offered a deal: his debt will be wiped off if he will go four rounds in a boxing bout, with a 35-dollar cash prize into the bargain. Midge enters the fight with easy confidence but his wild swings and evident lack of technique make the match a comic one. He lasts the four rounds and learns a valuable lesson about the boxing racket: a fighter never gets what he was promised. After various deductions for management and dressing-room fees, he is left with just 10 dollars.

His early ineptitude is made much of in the film: when he begins to train at Bradey's gym in Los Angeles, the soundtrack features comic music to punctuate the montage of Midge punching the bag, tripping over his skipping rope, doing sit-ups and sparring. For these scenes he is clad in T-shirt and shorts, his torso only being revealed when he has become a 'real fighter'. Three years of bouts as a professional are conveyed in a well-established genre style, as a fast-paced sequence of cities and knockout punches, the camera showing the final punch from a very low angle, designed to show off Douglas' body. The predatory nature of the business is made clear from the beginning, the early comic element sitting uneasily with the promise of Midge's manager Tommy Haley (Paul Stewart) to teach him 'every dirty trick in the book': there is no talk of sportsmanship or athleticism here.[290] Connie does not like the transformation he sees in his brother: 'I didn't know you up in that ring,' he says, 'I kept thinking you were hitting every guy that ever hurt you…there's something wrong about that.' His comment is both the key to the film and the key to their relationship - Connie sees the hatred and bitterness, Midge sees only the crowd and the money.

Midge confides his ambitions to Emma (Ruth Roman), daughter of the owner of the Step Inn diner. Emma is a neatly dressed, dark-haired girl in the classic mould of the 'good girl' familiar from the boxing genre. Emma is the first girl pictured on the film's poster and, as in many films of the genre, she will be replaced by a gold-digging blonde as Midge rises to boxing fame. In this case it is Grace (Marilyn Maxwell), the hard-nosed girlfriend of his opponent Johnnie Dunne, a woman who only backs winners, and then Palmer (Lola Albright), wife of his manager Jerome Harris (Luis van Rooten). His covert romance with Emma is treated in the conventional screen manner, their relationship coy and teasing, providing a contrast with his later conquests. Midge takes Emma swimming at dusk, and there are shots of their silhouetted bodies running along the shoreline, focusing on shots of Midge's naked torso and legs), and an exchange of aspirations - Midge's first declaration of not wanting to be a 'hey you' all his life. By their next meeting, with a double bed framed ominously in the background, Emma is talking about marriage and Midge is saying he is not ready. The camera captures their embrace, then pans slowly across the room and over the bed to the doorway where Emma's father stands with a shotgun. Emma's dreams are becoming reality, though not quite in the way she had expected. At the conclusion of the marriage ceremony. Midge turns off his charm like turning off a switch: he walks out on Emma and immediately dismisses her from his mind.

Through the portrayal of Midge's relationships with these women, the importance of the act of winning is made clear: it does not seem to matter what particular prize is being fought over, as long as he wins it. When Grace says he can only afford her if he sacks his manager, Tommy Haley, and signs up with Jerome Harris, Midge does not need much persuading, even though it is his soul he is signing away. 'The capital of the whole world,' says Harris, gesturing to the view that Midge is admiring through the window of his high-rise office. 'It's all yours if you want it.' If Midge recognises the Biblical allusion, it doesn't give him much pause for thought. The exact position that love occupies in Midge's life is shown in a scene where Palmer tells her husband that she wants to marry Midge. Harris volunteers to show her just how worthless Midge is. Hiding her in a side room, he calls Midge to the office and offers to write off Midge's debt to him, plus give him all 65,000 dollars of the Dunne fight-fee, if only he willll give up Palmer. He agrees without a pause for breath.

His relationship with Palmer exposes a less self-assured side of his personality and, as with Charley and Peg in *Body and Soul* (1947), the initial encounter between boxer and sculptor is a somewhat awkward one, with the men revealing their ignorance of art and their self-consciousness at posing. So suave and sophisticated while dancing with Palmer in the nightclub, Midge is clearly out of place in the sculptor's studio. His pose, standing on a plinth, clad only in boxing shorts and strongly lit, is an overt opportunity for the audience to gaze on his body and, perhaps resenting this objectification (body as display, rather than body as a weapon), Midge reacts by twisting the head off the clay sculpture. His violence towards women at this stage is either a displaced one, as in this scene, or consists

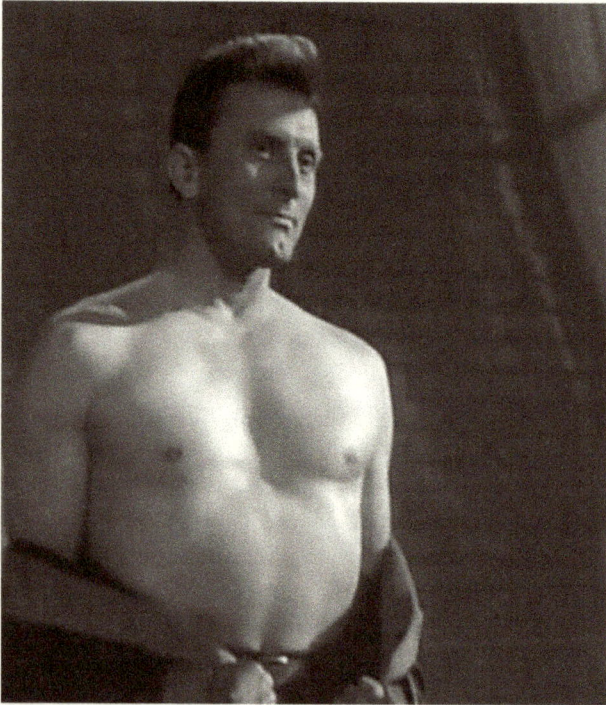

Kirk Douglas' body is quite literally put on a pedestal when he poses for Palmer (Lola Albright), as she sculpts him

196

merely of verbal threats, as in telling Grace 'I'll put you in the hospital for a long time'. When he finally meets Emma again, the violence becomes real: he is indifferent to her until he learns that she and Connie are in love and it is then that he decides to claim his 'rights' as a husband in a chilling (implied) rape. What would otherwise be an upbeat series of scenes at Midge's outdoor training camp - in which Midge's body looks almost superhuman and the 'healing' quality of the countryside imbues the camp with a genuine community feeling - is marred by Midge's constant manipulation of Emma's feelings. 'You're my wife,' he tells her finally, as his body eclipses hers in the shot and the screen fades to black. Hearing about the incident, Connie tells him: 'you stink from corruption. You couldn't let her live and be happy.' It is characteristic of the contrast between them that Connie does not mention himself and his own happiness in this accusation - only Emma's.

This obsession with winning may get him back the 25 dollars of which he was cheated in his first fight, but it also gets him into trouble with the local gangsters when he refuses to take a dive. 'They' (who are unnamed) want him to lose the fight against Dunne because it is Dunne's 'turn' to win and go on to claim the title. When Midge challenges this, protesting that 'they don't own us', Tommy laconically replies: 'that's open to question.' Unlike *The Set-Up*, where Little Boy expects to get the result he has paid for, or *Body and Soul*, where Roberts treats fighters simply as business collateral, 'they' in *Champion* are unnamed and unseen, just 'the fat fellows with the cigar' as Midge terms it. In a sequence that bears strong narrative similarities to the climax of *The Set-Up*, Midge renegs on the deal and beats Dunne, delivering blistering blows from the outset with no pretence of going easy on his opponent. The knockout is swift to come. Leaving the dressing-room after the fight, Tommy and Midge look fearfully down the dimly lit, long corridor that represents the exit from the building and where 'they' are undoubtedly lurking. The scene is a stark contrast to the triumphal, heroic march into the stadium shown at the beginning of the film.[291] Tommy is caught and beaten, but Midge makes it back into the stadium, instinctively heading for the protection of the ring. His fight with the gangster's thugs is the antithesis of a disciplined boxing match, ungainly and brutal, the men using not just their fists but any weapon that comes to hand, including the stools and buckets. A stark contrast is also made by the rows of empty seats, the utter silence other than the grunts of the fighters (even Tiomkin's over-busy score is absent at this point) and the fact that all the men wear suits and ties. Midge is knocked to the floor and left battered and bruised.

The scene caused some controversy at the time because of its similarity to the climax of *The Set-Up*. Richard Keenan, writing in *American Classic Screen*, reports that RKO boss Howard Hughes demanded an injunction against the release of *Champion*, along with a claim for 500,000 dollars in damages should the relevant 'borrowed' scenes not be cut. The basis of the accusation was that director Mark Robson had previously been employed at RKO at a time when *The Set-Up* was in production, and was well acquainted with the script. Despite protestations from Screen Plays Corp, the production company for *Champion*, the judge in the case ruled that cuts would have to be made: thus the version released omitted a small number of sequences, most notably one where Midge runs around the darkened arena, trying to escape through locked doors.[292]

In *The Set-Up*, this may have been the scene that destroyed Stoker Thompson; in *Champion*, Midge just bounces back from his beating, lauded by the press for his bravery, and unwilling to acknowledge a problem. 'You know what a golem is?' asks Tommy, when Midge fires him. 'I think I knew all the time I was building one.' The 'golem', as in Jewish folklore, was a creature built to defend its maker or community, but has turned on it instead, its violence wreaking havoc on the very people who had created and nurtured it.

By the climax of the film, Midge has run out of women and managers, and is forced to hire back Tommy and Connie to get him ready for the title-fight against Johnnie Dunne. Thus the film returns to its opening sequence. Punishing punches and extreme close-ups give the fight a dynamic quality (Mushy Callahan was the fight adviser) and though the whole of the match is not shown, the technique of showing the round-numbers flick by, one by one, is enough to convey the toughness of the battle, though not perhaps to warrant Zucker and Babich's commendation as being 'one of the best fights ever put on celluloid'.[293] The camera switches between low-angled shots from just outside the ropes, to close-ups and point-of-view shots that put the audience right into the ring. Midge is dominant from the outset but by Round 6 his face is cut and bloodied, the camera moving into unfocussed, blurry close-ups so that we see the fight through Midge's eyes, the bright lights dazzling overhead. By Round 9 he appears to be

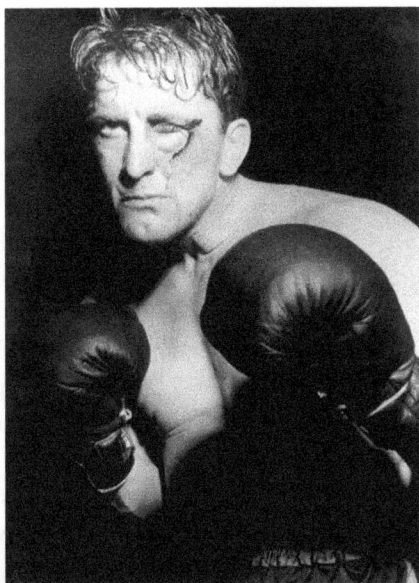

Close-ups and point-of-view shots of the title-fight against Johnnie Dunne put the audience right into the ring

unconscious but is still on his feet, rocking with Dunne's punches. Tommy tells him he is going to throw in the towel, but Midge says 'I'll kill you' and the fight goes on. By Round 11, he is battered and dizzy. As he falls to the floor, he hears a commentator say 'he's wholly washed up, he's finished' and a reaction close-up of his face shows him grimacing, teeth bared, one eye raging and the other punched shut. When he gets to his feet for Round 12, snarling and unrecognisable like some primeval beast, he goes into overdrive to finish off Dunne, knocking him to the floor and retaining his title.

Back in the dressing room with Tommy, delirious with what seems to be victory ('people were cheering for ME,' he says triumphantly, thumping his chest), Midge lurches about the room, rambling incoherently. Suddenly it becomes clear that this is not a celebration of victory, but the approach of death. Midge dies in Tommy's arms. Even at the last, and despite the betrayals and beatings, Connie is loyal to his brother. When asked for a press statement, he says simply: 'he was a champion; he went out like a champion.' Baker calls this 'Connie's tacked-on happy ending' and argues that it serves to parody other boxing films in which a facade of sports stardom masks a greedy and violent reality.[294] Equally, it could be argued that Connie's statement actually does nothing to temper the darkness of the ending: in choosing to perpetuate, rather than explode, the myth of Midge Kelly, Connie demonstrates his understanding and forgiveness and therefore his moral superiority. The impaired body has finally eclipsed the magnificent body and Connie walks off with Emma on his arm.

This is a powerful film, due mainly to Kirk Douglas' tour de force performance, which *Today's Cinema* described as 'magnificent'.[295] For an actor relatively early in his career - he had by then only appeared in seven films, all made between 1946 and 1949 - it was surely a risky decision to take on the portrayal of quite such an anti-hero, but *Champion* catapulted Douglas to stardom. It is a hard film to like: Ronald Bergan feels that this is principally because, as with Jake La Motta in *Raging Bull* (1980), Midge 'is basically such a nasty character' and it's true that without the 'balance' that Connie offers, it would be hard to care too much about what happens to Midge.[296]

The film treads a well-used path through the boxing racket, the ambitions of fighters, the gold-digging women and the sweethearts left at home, but all it seems to offer that is new is a particularly overt attention to

The emphasis on the display of Douglas' body was not even commented on by contemporary critics

the box-office. In this way, sensationalism seems to take over, from Tiomkin's over-busy melodramatic score which 'tells' the audience what to think (a contrast with the subtlety of the ambient jazz music used in *The Set-Up*) and the 'risqué' themes (the rape of Midge's estranged wife), to the emphasis on the display of Douglas' body. None of these issues, it has to be said, were raised either by *Motion Picture Herald* which argued that 'the dramatic sequences are never sacrificed for any axe-grinding and everything is told in perspective and held in its place', or by *The Cinema*, which saw the direction as 'in the documentary manner...without recourse to emotion or sentiment' and felt that the romantic interludes were 'utilised more as indications of character than to introduce sex appeal'.[297] Evidently, the reviewer, hearing Palmer's immortal line while dancing with Midge ('I suppose you know you've got a beautiful body') felt immediately appeased when it was revealed she was a sculptor.

[147] Arthur Kennedy would go on to play Midge Kelly's gentle brother Connie, who is the moral centre of the film *Champion* (1949)

[148] *Kinematograph Weekly* Feb 27 1941 p19; *Today's Cinema* Feb 26 1941 p12

[149] The policeman was played by Ward Bond, who would appear two years later as John L Sullivan in *Gentleman Jim*

[150] The love between a boxer and a dancer is also the theme of *Glory Alley* (1952)

[151] Cagney 1976 p96

[152] McCabe 1997 p191

[153] Kandel 2017 p4

[154] Donald Crisp's long career in the silents included a memorable performance opposite Lillian Gish in D W Griffith's film *Broken Blossoms* (1919), in which he played boxer Battling Burrows, the abusive father from whose beatings Gish flees, locking herself in a cupboard

[155] It is ironic that in the only scene where Danny and Peggy dance together - at a neighbourhood dance - he lets her take to the floor alone, protesting that he can't dance: Cagney was, in fact, an accomplished hoofer, a talent that would be demonstrated in his performance in *Yankee Doodle Dandy* (1942)

[156] Rainsberger 1981 p190

[157] Rainsberger 1981 p194

[158] The referee for the fight was played by John Indrisano

[159] When Young O'Hara is blinded in the ring, in *Ringside Maisie* (1941) he ends up in a similar 'neighbourhood' occupation: running a grocery store

[160] McCabe 1997 p193

[161] Sklar 1992 p100

[162] *Monthly Film Bulletin* Mar 1941 p9

[163] Cagney 1976 p96

[164] Oscar Micheaux's all-black film *The Notorious Elinor Lee* (1940) also featured a woman manager, as did *The Big Timer* (1932), *The Personality Kid* (1934) and *Kelly the Second* (1936)

[165] *Pittsburgh Post-Gazette*, Mar 30 2012

[166] Kennedy 2007 p165

[167] *Kinematograph Weekly* Dec 4 1941; *Variety* Sept 3 1941

[168] Zucker and Babich 1987 p120

[169] Kennedy 2007 pp165-166

[170] Alan Baxter was later to appear in *The Set-Up* (1949) as the chillingly detached gangster Little Boy

[171] Obituary in *Independent* Feb 6 2006

[172] *Classic Images* Apr 16 2010

[173] imdb.co.uk

[174] *Variety* Sept 3 1941

[175] Kennedy 2007 p166

[176] It was not until the 1970s that a boxing genre series was to assume A-feature status with the advent of the blockbusting Rocky films featuring Sylvester Stallone

[177] Marin directed three of the Maisie series: *Gold Rush Maisie* (1940), *Maisie Was a Lady* (1941) and *Ringside Maisie* (1941). The running-time of the Maisie series was uncharacteristically long for a B-movie: *Ringslde Maisie*, for example, is 92 minutes whereas a B-movie usually did not exceed 70 minutes, indicating that perhaps in some cinemas it may have been shown as the main feature

[178] Maisie is referred to as the 'Bonfire From Brooklyn' in the theatrical trailer

[179] *Cash and Carry* UK pressbook

[180] O'Brien is the singer at the Shady Lawn, the country hotel where Maisie is hired as a dancer. The nightclub scene that is a customary interlude in boxing films is given a new twist here with O'Brien's high-comedy, deadpan manner of singing that earned her the nickname 'Frozen Face'. She appeared in comedy roles in many M-G-M films in the 1940s, including the Marx Brothers' *The Big Store* (1940), *Lady Be Good* (1941), *Panama Hattie* (1942), *Ship Ahoy* (1942) and *Thousands Cheer* (1943)

[181] *Variety* Jul 30 1941

[182] These situations give scriptwriter Mary McCall Jr plenty of scope to use an inventive range of insults all based on animal metaphors: Skeets refers to women like Maisie as being 'yellow-haired mice', while Maisie accuses him of being a 'big mongrel dog.' Cissy is a 'nasty slug' for deserting O'Hara, and dancer Ricky Duprez is 'a skunk doing the adagio'. These metaphors parallel the way that boxing films often code the fighters as animals, suggesting that they are primitive or untamed: even in *Ringside Maisie*, O'Hara's opponent is nicknamed the Bayonne Panther and O'Hara says the reason he has never told his mother that his is a fighter is because 'they're animals to her'

[183] For this scene, the studio built a 300 square foot dance-hall set, employed 200 dancers and according to the pressbook, spent a week filming it - a considerable investment considering that B-movies usually only had around 15 days' of shooting in total - including building a circular camera-track that allowed for shots of the entire floor as well as close-ups of individual couples

[184] *Variety* Jul 30 1941

[185] Trying to avoid the guard on the train, she hides behind a copy of *True Love Story* magazine, giving an insight into her character and aspirations

[186] The relationship perhaps gains an added edge from the real attraction between Ann Sothern and Robert Sterling on the set: they were to marry two years later.

[187] *Cash and Carry* UK pressbook

[188] She is billed as this in the theatrical trailer

[189] *Kine Weekly* Oct 2 1941 p20

[190] Joe Gardia was played by Italian-American boxer Frank Riggi who also appeared in *They Made Me a Criminal* (1939), *Knockout* (1941), *The Kid From Brooklyn* (1946) and *Body and Soul* (1947)

[191] This shot is echoed in a later scene, when O'Hara undergoes a risky operation to restore his sight and we see the hands on the operating-theatre clock crawl by, just as they had done in the ring

[192] Sterling did a screen test in 1938 for the part of Joe Bonaparte in *Golden Boy* (1939), a role that eventually went to William Holden. Sterling can be seen briefly in that film, however, uncredited as the elevator boy

[193] O'Hara is so ashamed of fighting that he has not told his mother that he's a boxer. She believes her son to be a razor-blade salesman, an interesting choice of bogus profession as boxers were well-known for endorsing razor-blade brands (point-of-sale cards featuring boxers are visible in both *Somebody Up There Likes Me* and *The Set-Up*)

[194] *Today's Cinema* Sept 26 1941 p6

[195] *Variety* Jul 30 1941 p18

[196] Boxing references are absent from the main US posters for *Gentleman Jim*, which feature only the disembodied heads of the two romantic leads

[197] Romano 2004 p63

[198] *Motion Picture Herald* Oct 31 1942 p981; *Monthly Film Bulletin* Sept 30 1943 p101

[199] Zucker and Babich 1987 p86; *New York Times* Nov 26 1942

[200] Boddy 2008 p113

[201] Hanson 1993 p873

[202] Some accounts say that the shots of Corbett's fast-moving feet in the ring were of Callahan, others claim that they were of Billy Conn

[203] *Variety* Nov 4 1943; *Today's Cinema* Sept 15 1943 p12

[204] Boddy 2008 p169

[205] The Olympic Club, the oldest athletic club in the US, was founded in 1860. Its building was destroyed in the 1906 earthquake

[206] Theatrical trailer

[207] Baker 2006 p63

[208] Mellon 1977 p163

[209] *Motion Picture Herald* Oct 31 1942 p981

[210] Given the display of Flynn's body having sexual appeal for men as well as women, hindsight lends the word 'gayest' a double meaning it did not have to contemporary audiences. In the trailer, he is seen running through the streets wearing a suit-jacket and derby hat over his boxing tights, while the voiceover says 'his adventures made all of San Francisco gayer'

[211] The scene was filmed in the Warner Brothers' water-tank, where *The Sea Wolf* and *Captain Blood* were also shot. Romano notes that former middleweight champion Freddie Steele doubled for Flynn in the fight sequences, despite studio claims that Flynn did his own boxing sequences, while footwork close-ups were doubled by Billy Conn (Romano 2004 p64)

[212] Hale was a well-established character actor with over 200 films to his credit by 1942: he had appeared with Errol Flynn in *The Adventures of Robin Hood* (1938)

[213] *New York Times* Nov 26 1942

[214] Mellon 1977 p163

[215] Atwan and Forer 1986 pp.125-6. How audiences interpreted it at the time may have depended on what they thought of Franklin D Roosevelt's Democrat administration, which came to power in 1932 but by 1940 was facing strong opposition both from Republicans and from the conservative wing of his own party

[216] Pressbook for *A Man Called Sullivan*

[217] *Variety* Jun 6 1945

[218] *Motion Picture Herald* Jun 9 1945 p2485

[219] Garfield's character begins life as 'Charlie' but fights under the name of 'Charley'

[220] Bernstein 1996 p6

[221] Garfield, who Bernstein describes as a product of the New York streets, was never a Communist but would not 'snitch' on his friends. He did, however, lend his name to a ghostwritten article called 'I Was a Sucker for a Left Hook' (Bernstein 1996 p198)

[222] Rainsberger 1981 p218

[223] Hanson 1993 p.268.. Rossen was a keen fight-fan: Bernstein recalls that in the office, while talking about a script, he would 'bounce around in front of me, throwing stiff jabs and vicious hooks from a discreet distance'. (Bernstein 1996 p7)

[224] Turim 1989 p121

[225] Williams 2006 p188. Odets had written the play with Garfield in mind, but he was not to play the lead role on stage until 1952, in its first production having to be content with playing Siggie, Joe Bonaparte's cab-driving brother-in-law

[226] McGrath 1993 p38

[227] Schultheiss 2002 pp188-189

[228] Buhle and Wagner 2001 p113

[229] Mellon 1977 p164

[230] Rainsberger 1981 p216

[231] It is the presence of speakeasies that indicates that the portrayal of Charley's teenage years is set in the early 1930s (prohibition was revoked in 1933). Even though Charley's career ostensibly spans the war years, the war is never mentioned except in a single reference by the neighbourhood grocer, Shimen

[232] Baker 2006 p116

[233] Grindon 2011 p200

[234] Swindell 1975 p209

[235] Interestingly, though Charley's career begins in the Depression, and presumably spans the war years, this is the only mention of the war: nor is there mention of any other external event that might anchor the temporal setting more firmly

[236] Hands in *Cineaction* Dec 2010

[237] Swindell 1975 p210

[238] Mellon argues that Charley 'regains his manhood not so much by returning to an honest course, as through the prowess of his body - what the male in American films has always relied upon (Mellon 1977 p166)

[239] *Today's Cinema* May 21 1948

[240] Bergan 1982 p26

[241] Mellon 1977 p166

[242] Neve 2005 p62

[243] Turim 1989 p122

[244] *Motion Picture Herald* Aug 16 1947

[245] Quoted in McGrath 1993 p93

[246] McGrath 1993 p103

[247] Wayne in *Labour* magazine 2004 p314

[248] *Kine Weekly* May 27 1948

[249] Ficarra, www.moviemaker.com published Feb 3 1999

[250] *Monthly Film Bulletin* Aug 1949 p145; Cook 1991 p386

[251] Hunter in *The Hudson Review*, summer 2008

[252] Hunter in *The Hudson Review*, summer 2008

[253] March 1929 p78

[254] Hunter in *The Hudson Review*, summer 2008

[255] Romano 2004 p180

[256] Christopher 1997 p178

[257] Christopher 1997 p178

[258] *American Classic Screen* Jul/Aug 1978 p15

[259] *New York Times* begged to differ, saying that 'the director cuts away too frequently from the action to provide ringside comment and this switching to and from the fighters gives a conventional quality to these episodes' (*New York Times* Mar 30 1949 p31)

[260] Christopher 1977 p178. The *New York Times* recognised this workaday quality in Stoker, calling him a 'wheelhorse heavyweight' in their review of the film (*New York Times* Mar 30 1949 p31)

[261] In audio commentary, with Robert Wise, on *The Set-Up* DVD

262 *Today's Cinema* Jul 1 1949 p10

263 Robert Wise as apparently unhappy with the casting of Audrey Totter as Julie: he had wanted Joan Blondell. Leger Grindon feels Totter was 'adequate but fails to project the interiority with the eloquence that would have made the performance glow (Grindon 2011 p142)

264 Mellon 1977 p167

265 *American Classic Screen,* Jul/Aug 1978 p15

266 Baxter had appeared in another boxing film, *The Pittsburgh Kid* (1941) as hoodlum Joe Barton

267 The scene was shot at the Ocean Parkway Arena in Brooklyn

268 Robert Wise on audio commentary, *The Set-Up* DVD

269 Martin Scorsese on audio commentary *The Set-Up* DVD

270 Hunter in *The Hudson Review,* summer 2008

271 Hunter in *The Hudson Review,* summer 2008

272 Romano 2004 p181

273 The bridge scene and the empty stadium were filmed on location

274 He was also to direct *Somebody Up There Likes Me* (1956)

275 *Variety* Mar 23 1949

276 *New York Times* Mar 30 1949 p31

277 Krutnick 1991 p190

278 Krutnick 1991 p190

279 Maltby 1983 p164

280 *Motion Picture Herald* Mar 26 1949 p4550

281 *American Classic Screen,* Jul/Aug 1978 p16

282 Williams in *Quarterly Review of Film and Video* 2001 p315

283 Cohan 1997 p166; *Village Voice,* Mar 7 1995

284 Director of photography was Frank Planer who had worked prolifically in his native Germany through the silent film era, coming to Hollywood in the early 1930s

285 Douglas 2007 p113

[286] Just two years later, Foreman was to be blacklisted following his appearance before HUAC and admitting that he had been a Communist Party member in his youth

[287] *Monthly Film Bulletin* Aug 31 1949 p139

[288] Lardner in *Esquire* magazine, July 1 1949

[289] Kirkham and Thumim 1997 p82

[290] Despite the talk of 'dirty tricks', Haley turns out to be a wise manager and a contrast to the wealthy but corrupt 'businessman' who will later manage Midge. Haley''s personality is enhanced by the sympathetic qualities that Paul Stewart brings to the role: he was to go on to portray a similarly sympathetic confidant, newspaperman Ted McGeehan, in *The Joe Louis Story* (1953)

[291] Another contrasting use of the darkened corridor occurs near the end of the film, where Connie, beaten to the floor by his brother, limps painfully along it to the strains of the celebratory music from the arena - the very antithesis of the fighter's body

[292] *American Classic Screen*, Jul/Aug 1978

[293] Zucker and Babich 1987 p71

[294] Baker 2006 p123

[295] *Today's Cinema* Jul 13 1949 p22

[296] Bergan 1982 p30

[297] *Motion Picture Herald* Mar 19 1949 p4537; *The Cinema* Jul 13 1949

ON THE ROPES - FILMS OF THE 1950s

'They call me Dirty Mex' is the tagline used on all the posters, but it is not borne out in the film itself

'They call me Dirty Mex'
The Ring (1952)

*T*he *Ring* is an underrated 'social problem' B-movie that deserves more critical recognition, for its incisive portrayal of the daily struggles undergone by 'Pachuco' Mexicans living and working in Los Angeles, the desire for assimilation by the younger generation and the nostalgic yearning by the older generation for a 'Mexico' that probably never existed. Its use of location shooting, especially for night-time scenes, was probably due to budget constraints but gives the film a gritty documentary feel. It is also notable for well-filmed, realistic boxing action - and for an early appearance by Rita Moreno, who would go on to spend another 50 years as a Hollywood star.

It was Rita Moreno as the protagonist's girlfriend Lucy Gomez and Gerald Mohr as his manager Pete Ganusa who received top billing, yet the real star is Lalo Rios, the 25-year-old who played boxer Tomas Cantanios (and who would go on to appear as Risto in *Touch of Evil* (1958)). He is completely plausible in the role and his naturalistic acting reinforces the documentary feel of the film. *The Ring* was directed by Kurt Neumann and was a low-budget production by the King brothers based on the novel 'The Square Trap' by

Shulman, who also wrote the screenplay. Shulman, who was born in 1913 in Brooklyn, New York, is probably best known for having written the screenplay for *Rebel Without a Cause* (1955), based on his book 'Children of the Dark'. He used his knowledge of Brooklyn to launch his literary career, his first novel - 'The Amboy Dukes' (1947) about juvenile street gangs - sold five million copies. When he was hired as a screenwriter by Warner Brothers, he adapted 'The Amboy Dukes' into the film *City Across the River* (1949); and 'The Square Trap' - originally called 'Pachuco' - into *The Ring*.

The Ring tells the story of Tomas' desire to raise enough money to enable his jobless father to buy a stall in Olvera Street ('a street forgotten by time' says the narrator) and therefore to avoid the only demeaning job on offer - impersonating a 'lazy Mexican' asleep on a street corner as an 'attraction' for tourists.[298] The only route open to Tomas seems to be to become a fighter, and to do so under the Anglo name of Tommy Kansas. Leger Grindon says that taking on this ringname is a means of 'evoking the American heartland and setting aside his Hispanic heritage'[299] though it is his manager's pragmatic choice of name, not Tommy's. Always pushing to rise higher in the rankings, but not listening to the advice of his manager and trainer, Tommy has one defeat too many and realises he will never make it to the top. Through the kindness of his manager, he does acquire enough money to buy a stall for his father, who is seen at the end of the film in traditional Mexican costume, selling a hand-tooled leather bag to an Anglo couple.

As with many boxing films about first- and second-generation immigrants, a contrast is made between Tommy's father (Martin Garralaga), who is authoritarian and old-fashioned, with a distinct Mexican accent (though the family all speak in English when at home), and Tommy - who dresses and speaks like all young American men - and is prepared to defy his father, even if it is only over the purchase of new furniture for their home. Tommy's 'difference' can never be elided, however: all his friends, including his girlfriend Lucy, are from a Mexican background, jobs are hard to find and he constantly runs into discrimination by Anglos. He lives in what is obviously - though not explictly stated - Chavez Ravine, a Mexican enclave of about 1,800 families close to downtown LA, where he knows everyone, greeting neighbours by name as he sits out on the stoop.[300] Crossing this divide is Pete Ganusa who (in a trope familiar from so many boxing films) witnesses Tommy punching someone on the street, realises his potential - and signs him up. Other than giving him an Anglo fighting name, Pete shows no discrimination and goes against the cliche of the crooked boxing manager, treating Tommy fairly and paternalistically and giving him the entire 350 dollars that he manages to shake out of a dodgy manager in return for Tommy going into the ring against Art Aragon, so that Tommy can achieve his dream.

Aaron Baker argues that black boxers, such as Ben Chapin in *Body and Soul*, and Joe Louis (*The Joe Louis Story*) share a common situation with Tommy: they 'have athletic ability, but they must accept the control of white mentors because of a lack of strategic skills'.[301] Their mentors, he says, tend to direct them towards compromise, leading to insults, threats and exploitation, Chapin accepting money from a crooked promoter, Louis overspending and Tommy unable to 'navigate in the dangerous waters of professional prizefighting'. In Tommy's case, however, that's not really accurate: his youth means that he is overly optimistic about his abilities and inclined to feel that he knows better than Pete, but he is not exploited or asked to compromise or to throw a fight.

Race or ethnic origin is often elided in boxing films but here it takes centre-stage, both as the motivation to fight and in the depiction of everyday discrimination. The reason Tommy's father loses his job is because he's deemed to be too old. 'When an Anglo becomes old,' says the father, 'he's promoted to a boss - when a Mexican becomes old he's laid off.' Tommy - young and fit - can't even get a job at all. At the 'clubhouse', a wooden shack where he meets his friends to talk or play cards, police pay a visit for no reason and when Tommy protests that they are always checking on them, one of the cops says 'that's the trouble with you Pachuco kids - you've always got a chip on your shoulder'. Tommy wants to take Lucy skating but it's a Wednesday and, as the man in the booth points to the sign, 'colored nite is Tuesday' and 'Mexican nite is Thursday'. It's on leaving the rink in disgust and going into a bar that Tommy's fighting career begins: as they enter the bar, two Anglos sitting on barstools make disparaging comments, and Tommy socks them when they emerge. Driving by at the time, Pete Ganusa spots the altercation.

The crucial scene about Mexican discrimination occurs towards the end of the film, when Tommy has lost a fight and his friends drive him to the beach to cheer him up. At an upscale diner, where lush music is playing, Tommy leads them to a table, but the staff are already phoning the police and other diners look very uncomfortable at the arrival of six young Mexican lads. After banging a water jug down on the table, spilling some, the waitress ignores the group. The patrolman who arrives initially expects trouble, questioning the large plaster that Tommy is wearing above his eye and the bruise on his cheek. When one of his friends explains that this is the fighter Tommy Kansas (the patrolman doesn't recognise the name Tomas Cantanios, until his friends explain), his attitude changes: he's heard of Tommy. He asks the diner to serve them.[302] 'I guess it pays to be somebody,' say his friends. Throughout these confrontations, Tommy is unfailingly polite (he leaves a tip at the diner) but firm, and not afraid to challenge authority, whether in the shape of his father, his manager and trainer, or of other Anglos. The scene in the diner is all the more poignant in contrast with an early scene in which Tommy is driven by Pete in his large car to his favourite drive-thru diner, where he knows all the waitresses - and is dating one of them. This is a vision of assimilation (after all, 'Ganusa' is an Italian or Spanish name) that lures Tommy. He can be 'as good as any Anglo' by fighting, Pete tells him; he can feel proud and have people look up to him. Tommy's transition into this new world is indicated through costume: when he first meets Pete and is still Tomas Cantanios, he is wearing baggy trousers, a bomber jacket, white socks and loafers - the kind of outfit worn by all his friends. When he becomes 'Tommy Kansas' and is rising up the ranks, he wears a white double-breasted suit.

It was perhaps precisely this foregrounding of ethnicity (despite its bland title) that led *Variety* to comment that *The Ring* lacked marquee appeal and would 'have to reply on exploitation and word of mouth for its b(ox) o(ffice)'.[303] As it was a B-picture, however, much would have depended on the A-feature that it accompanied, in terms of audience draw, as well as where the film was shown - in areas with a large population of people from south of the border - and surely, Los Angeles was one of these - it may well have had considerable 'marquee appeal'. Both *Variety* and *Monthly Film Bulletin* praised the film for its authenticity, which lifted it above the 'usual American B-picture'.

If reviewers felt the film was 'authentic', then the book offers a more gritty realism particularly in terms of race (black people are referred to as 'chocolates' throughout the book) and in terms of sexuality (homosexuals are referred to as 'fruits' and there is reference to 'syph' and to abortionists). In the book, Tommy's father is a hopeless drunk who whiles away his days drinking wine in the park. In the film he is portrayed as being nostalgic for the parks in Mexico, though in the book when Pete drives into Mexico, the local park conveys nothing but 'enervated depression and aimlessness, of sick animal living, of slow human decay'.[304] This is absent from the film and thus misses the opportunity to point up the contrasts between the US and Mexico - and the differences between the real Mexico and the remembered Mexico of Tommy's father. The difference is one of generation, too. In the book, Pete says Tommy's

At the gym, Tommy has to borrow boxing gloves and shoes

father "is like all our fathers ... Asleep in a little village in Sinaloa or even in Yucatan. It doesn't make any difference."[305] This is the immigrant's story that is familiar from *Golden Boy* and a number of other boxing films, where the older generation are closer to their native customs, morals and language but the younger generation have assimilated more into a generic American identity: a route that is shown as still closed to Tommy because he is Latino.

When Tommy first goes to the gym, he has to borrow boxing shoes and gloves, and as he doesn't own a pair of shorts, he rolls up his trouser legs to spar, swinging wild punches. Pete tells him he could be 'an important fighter' so Tommy starts training and we see - in a montage that will be repeated later in the film - him skipping, punching the heavy bag and using the speedball. At his first fight, he is bottom of the bill in a four-rounder against Billy Smith (Robert Arthur) who greets him in a friendly way - there seems to be no racial animosity between boxers. In Round One, the camera stays low, as if in a ringside seat. Tommy punches well and keeps his head low, but receives a hard punch that knocks him against the ropes, only to be saved by the bell. In Round Two, he is told 'box, don't slug' but forgets that when Billy lands a punch. The camera moves close to their distorted faces as the punches land and Tommy wins on a knockout. All the fights in the film - and there is plenty of boxing action - are well-staged and have a tension and an authenticity. Director of photography Russell Harlan captures well the atmosphere of the smoke-filled arenas and excited crowds. After more fights, in which Tommy is still slugging rather than taking his trainer's advice, he moves up the bill to box in a six-rounder against a black fighter, Chocolate Ganz, who punches hard, rocking Tommy's head back. The fight is lost and Tommy's optimistic smile is gone. His mood is indicated by the shadows of the banisters on the wall of his house as he climbs the staircase to the room he shares with his little brother, Pepe - they are like prison bars. Pepe doesn't want to go to school the next day, because he will have to tell his friends that Tommy lost.

Tommy keeps on pushing, even after two defeats

After two more defeats, his trainer tells him he has gone as far as he can, but Tommy keeps on pushing, his mind set on buying the stand for his father, the father who told him that as a fighter he has become 'a brute, a man without dignity'. He insists he will follow Pete's advice from now on, but again he immediately forgets.

Where Tommy's hands are the key, he feels, to his future success, in the book they are contrasted with those of his father: the hands that are a symbol or stigmata of defeat, 'swollen, scarred and ugly hands, the thumbs spatulate by falling railroad ties, misdirected hammer blows, dropped rocks, the nails broken and bent by coarse earth, tough roots ... the fingers scarred by brambles and gravel ... and in the seams of both hands the grime of years, as indelible as tattoos, was etched deep into the flesh.'[306]

Tommy's final fight is not one that his manager or trainer intended, but Art Aragon's opponent in the 10-round final at the San Diego Arena has pulled out and there is pressure on Tommy to step up instead of fighting further down the bill. In a tense dressing-room scene the evening's promoter says he won't pay anyone at all unless Tommy fights, because he has a stadium full of people waiting to see action. Eventually a deal is done whereby Pete wrings 350 dollars for Tommy out of the manager of the missing fighter ('for your father's stand') and the promoter agrees that Aragon (a Mexican lightweight boxer playing himself in this film) will not hurt Tommy but will 'make it look good'. Stock footage of Aragon is cleverly woven into the fight scene which begins with both fighters crossing themselves before the start of Round One. Aragon is light on his feet, dancing and dodging; the camera closes in as Tommy forgets it is supposed to be a show and starts punching hard. Taken by surprise, Aragon is in trouble and Tommy foolishly believes he can win. In Round Two, betrayed by Tommy, Aragon stops holding back: Tommy is soon on the ropes and then is knocked out.

Back home, sitting outside on the stoop and hearing the lively dance tunes that his sister is playing on the record player and which are such a contrast to his mood, Tommy eventually goes upstairs to his room and we see a shadow silhouette on the wall of his little brother Pepe, boxing an imaginary opponent and wearing his brother's gloves. He says he wants to be 'Young Kansas' but Tommy takes the gloves and the 'Tommy Kansas' dressing gown and burns them in the incinerator in the yard. In the book, the final scene with Pepe is very different: Tommy takes him for a try-out at the gym and the onlookers jeer. It is clear that Pepe will never make a fighter and will be just another failure (like Tommy). It's a downbeat ending that makes the reader wonder where exactly is the way out for boys like Tommy and Pepe.

The film ends with Tommy walking past the incinerator and down the slope into downtown LA, the train whistle mournfully blowing below. There, on Olvera Street, he and Lucy watch his father - dressed to the nines and essentially 'performing' as a Mexican - outside the stall that Tommy's money has bought. Tommy declares he's 'washed up' and will never fight again, but Lucy tells him that he will go on fighting for the rest of his life: for what's right. They link arms and walk away together.

The very section of US society who experienced anti-Mexican prejudice were not presented with this as a theme on the Spanish-language posters

It is both the toughness of the film and the ethnicity that is emphasised on the promotional posters. 'Here's a movie that speaks plain - and hits hard - like a punch in the gut!' reads the poster's tagline alongside a painting of a bare-chested Tommy in boxing gloves, a woman clinging to his arm, but the main slogan is 'They call me Dirty Mex but still they chase my women!' The same combination appears in another poster, showing Tommy slumped on the ropes, a jeering crowd behind him. 'I was slaughtered to please the crowd!' runs the main tagline, while underneath it says 'They call me Dirty Yellow Mex ... I'm not good enough for them - but my women are!' None of these ideas or slogans are borne out in the film itself.

The ethnicity element is missing in the Spanish-language posters for the film, which is called Aurora de Rebeldia ('Dawn of Rebellion') and which uses the same image of Tommy slumped on the ropes and a similar main tagline ('El publico pedia sangre y yo la di!'), but the other wording reads 'Lo obligaron a pelear como hombre antes de saber amar como hombre!' - 'I had to fight like a man before knowing how to love like a man'. So, the very section of society who experienced the anti-Mexican prejudice in the US were not presented with this as a theme on the Spanish-language posters.

Looking at the first two pages of the campaign book, which are the ones with suggestions of how the exhibitor can promote the film to potential audiences, you'd be hard-pressed to know that this was anything other than a run-of-the-mill boxing film featuring a young American fighter. Exhibitors were urged to set up a lobby display and borrow boxing gloves from a local athletics store; or to set up a display on the back of a lorry and drive it around town, urging people not to miss 'the greatest fight film of all time': these are techniques recommended for every film in the boxing genre.The only time the 'dirty Mex' line appears in these pages is as one of a list of 'catchlines', most of which are about the fact that the film is 'hard-hitting'. The Mexican-American angle only appears in the second double-page spread of the campaign book, which is given over to articles that the exhibitor can place in his local newspapers.

Leger Grindon believes that The Ring 'affirms the reality of prejudice, but it also portrays boxing as an ineffective response' and 'a misguided, self-indulgent quest'[307] and that loyalty to the ethnic community is the only solution. It is ironic, therefore, that shortly after this film was made,

Chavez Ravine would become the subject of great controversy, as the Mexican community was evicted and their houses razed to the ground to make way for the new Brooklyn Dodgers stadium to entice the team to move to Los Angeles.

'Your Face is Old. It's Atavistic. It's Almost Prehistoric'
Kid Monk Baroni (1952)

In *Kid Monk Baroni* the struggle familiar from a number of films in the genre - how to become a man who can hold his head up proudly - is told through the metaphor of evolution. Paul Baroni begins as a primitive creature and ends as a civilised human being, the outward sign of his inner progress being the transformation of his face from monkey-like deformity (the reason for his 'Monk' nametag) to handsome, clean-cut features. Although other films such as *The Harder They Fall* have played on the boxer-ape analogy, what makes the film different is that the catalyst for his evolution is the Roman Catholic Church.

Kid Monk Baroni was a cheaply made 'programmer' and if it is remembered today it is largely because it marked the first screen appearance of Leonard Nimoy who was later to achieve lasting fame as Vulcan/human hybrid Mr Spock in the *Star Trek* film and TV series.[308] The film was produced by Jack Broder, a Russian who had emigrated to the US in 1920, setting up first as a film distributor in Detroit and then branching out into B-movie production when he moved to Los Angeles and rented space at the General Service Studios. Funding for the move into production was made possible through a lucrative deal that Broder struck in 1947 which gave his company, Realart Pictures, a ten-year licence to re-release the entire Universal back-catalogue. It is perhaps no coincidence, therefore, that the films that Broder produced were aimed at much the same audience at the Universal films of the previous decade had been, mixing comedy and horror with films like *Bride of the Gorilla* (1951) and *Bela Lugosi Meets a Brooklyn Gorilla* (1952).[309]

Broder made an interesting and commercially shrewd choice of cast and crew for *Kid Monk Baroni*. He used a screenplay by Aben Kandel who

The poster for Kid Monk Baroni *tags 'The Billy Goat Gang' above the title, although it is only referred to as this on one occasion in the film*

had written the novel on which *City For Conquest* was based, and who had also written the screenplay for *The Fighter*. As director he appointed Harold Schuster, an editor-turned-director who was known for his ability to adhere to tight shooting schedules, and as director of photography, he chose Charles van Enger, a highly experienced cinematographer who had worked for Ernst Lubitsch in the 1920s and had had a prolific career with credits that included *Spider Woman* (1944), a Sherlock Holmes film, and *Abbott and Costello Meet the Killer* (1949). Although the 21-year-old Leonard Nimoy was new to the screen, having come from a background of stage acting, the supporting cast - who enjoyed the top billing - included Bruce Cabot who had starred as John Driscoll in *King Kong* (1933) and had appeared in around 60 films since, Richard Rober who had been tipped as 'another Bogart', Allene Roberts who was fresh from starring in tough thrillers *The Hoodlum* (1951) and *Union Station* (1950), and Mona Knox who, until playing in the Bowery Boys film *Hold That Line* (1952), had only appeared in bit-parts. Broder kept a tight rein on costs by filming exclusively on the back lot, yet clever camera angles, imaginative lighting and a large number of sets disguise the economies: the film was even completed under schedule, in nine days.[310]

The film opens in the hallway of a condemned tenement in the Little Italy district of New York, where Monk Baroni and his fellow pennyless gang-members (billed as 'The Billy Goat Gang' in above-the-title credits) are sawing up the banisters for firewood. Monk's ugliness and his sensitivity about it are established immediately: he threatens to punch one of the gang for staring at him: 'next time you wanna look at me', he says, 'line forms to the right: two bits admission.' The difficulty for the viewer in this, and indeed for much of the duration of the film, is that Broder had shied away from distorting Nimoy's face too much - 'they didn't want to do a monster movie because people would be uncomfortable looking at me', Nimoy later explained.[311] The result was some very minor make-up work on his forehead, nose and lip, leaving Baroni still essentially good-looking and making it hard for the central premise of the film - his anger and resentment at his face that he calls a 'curse from God' - to be entirely believable.

The gang are interrupted in their thieving by Father Callaghan (Richard Rober), the new young priest from St Dominic's on East 106th Street, who suggests that they keep warm by making use of the boxing equipment in the basement of the church. Fr Callaghan - whose good looks interestingly go unremarked throughout the film - will become its moral centre and the 'tough love' route through which Baroni develops into a civilised and cultured man.[312] The priest is a competent boxer himself and, while coaching Baroni to 'fight like a man and not an ape', he also tells him to drop his Italian-American street-talk and pronounce words properly. Soon Baroni is asking if he can join the church choir, but he runs into mockery and derision from his former gang-members when they see him wearing his surplice. In the ensuing fracas, Baroni accidentally delivers a knockout punch to Father Callaghan and runs away. He will not see the priest for another year but will be haunted by the need to be reconciled with him.

Baroni, accompanied by former gang-member Angelo (Jack Larson), becomes an amateur fighter, forgetting Father Callaghan's advice to 'fight like a man' and hammering his opponents to the ground as if he is banging in a nail. When he becomes tired of winning fake gold watches for prizes -

Early boxing prizes are fake gold watches, which Baroni pawns so that he can buy food, but when the syndicate calls for a 'dirty fighter', the money starts rolling in

immediately pawned so he can buy food - he turns professional, signing up with with the cynical, book-reading promoter Hellman (Bruce Cabot). Successful fight-tours ensue and soon a boxing syndicate become interested in promoting him. In the same way that film moguls understand every film needs a 'label', the syndicate needs a 'really dirty fighter'. Baroni is happy to oblige. His financial success enables him to have plastic surgery to fix his face, and to ditch his church girlfriend in favour of a follow-the-money glamour-girl, but there's just one problem: he is so proud of his new face that that he doesn't want to spoil it by fighting, plus he has lost the anger and resentment that drove him to fight.[313] 'I start out with a tiger, wind up with a pussycat', complains Hellman as the crowd boos another cautious performance from Baroni. In a last-ditch attempt, Hellman tries emotional blackmail, convincing Baroni that he can 'square himself' with Father Callaghan by fighting in his old way against the Seattle Wildcat: in this way he can donate the winner's purse to the St Dominic's Recreation Center appeal. Baroni fights hard but clean, his face is battered by the Wildcat and he loses. The syndicate and Hellman have lost 20,000 dollars in bets, but 'the way you fought carries its own victories', Father Callaghan assures Baroni. Baroni donates the loser's purse, marries his church sweetheart and is hailed as a hero.

The film received mixed reviews ('it's a routine lowercase' said *Variety*) with the trade and consumer press all commenting on the moral message but with *Kinematograph Weekly* expressing the view that 'religion, romance and fisticuffs do not make ideal bedfellows'.[314] Nimoy's performance was favourably commented on by *Today's Cinema* and *Variety*, but most reviewers felt the script to be overly sentimental and the action scenes weak.[315] They also felt the film was over-long at 80 minutes: the usual running time for a B-movie was 60-70 minutes, and the longer length meant that it bridged the gap between A- and B-feature, able to be shown at the top or bottom of the bill. *Kid Monk Baroni* was implicitly promoted by the studio as a film in the mould of *Angels With Dirty Faces* (1938) which featured the Dead End Kids and the tension between the criminal who is their idol and the priest who was his childhood friend. One of the poster taglines for *Kid Monk Baroni* read 'the screen's toughest rough necks and a two-fisted priest', and the youths were positioned as 'the Billy Goat Gang', a name that appeared above the title in the credits, but which is only mentioned briefly in the film itself. Perhaps Broder had initially planned a series of 'Billy Goat Gang' adventures, or simply wanted to ally the film in the public's mind with other youth-gang films.

While *Kid Monk Baroni* would appear to be a film about 'inner beauty' - Aben Kandel's original script was entitled 'The Face' - David Kopple interprets it as being about the assimilation of an immigrant family into America, with the 'old' deformed face representing the 'Old World'. The fact that this is a monkey-like face, he says, is because 'the simian is a sign for the individual who is outside the mainstream of society'.[316] Kopple's reading is coloured by the fact he is the grandson of Jack Broder, a man who endured 'hard-scrabble early days as a Russian-Polish immigrant trying to make ends meet on the mean streets of Detroit' and who tried to walk a line between an honest life and the neighbourhood's Purple Gang who ran liquor from across the Canadian border during Prohibition. He remarks on the 'emotional authenticity' of the film's scenes in Paul Baroni's family home, and although it is not clear whether Broder actually influenced the storyline or script, Kandel's own experience as a Romanian immigrant might have been brought to bear on these scenes. As in *Golden Boy* and *Body and Soul*, the parents are shown to be tied to the ways and customs of the 'old country' and the son of the family to be already well-assimilated as an American. Paul Baroni's parents Gino (Joseph Mell) and Maria (Kathleen Freeman) address their son as Paulo, have strong Italian accents and speak a mixture of Italian and English in the family home. Maria is traditionally dressed in a woolen shawl, cooks vast quantities of spaghetti and ensures grace is said before the meal. Gino expresses the view that he doesn't want his son to 'become no bandido' and, though he is pleased that Paul is being taught by a priest (Paul conceals exactly what it is that Father Callaghan is teaching him), cannot help showing his disapproval that the priest is Irish and not Italian. The picture painted of Italian-American life is one of respectable poverty: the fire in the apartment is unlit because they cannot afford fuel, and though the family is close-knit - all dining together at the kitchen table - the generational split is beginning to show.

If the simian is indeed a sign for otherness, then it is a metaphor that runs throughout the film, not just in Paul's nickname of 'Monk' but in many lines of dialogue, most strikingly in his first meeting with Hellman when the promoter questions his declared fighting name of 'Young Baroni': 'young Baroni? Your face is old, it's atavistic. It's almost prehistoric', he says, suggesting that 'ape Baroni' or 'gorilla Baroni' might be more appropriate. Though convinced by his potential, Hellman's parting shot to Angelo shows that he will never regard Baroni as anything more than an animal: 'don't overfeed him', he says, 'I want him hungry'. The fact that these lines are all spoken by Bruce Cabot has added resonance, as Cabot would have been best remembered by audiences for his role as dashing hero Jack Driscoll in the 1933 *King Kong*. Thinking of boxers as animals helps distance Hellman emotionally from his fighters and this distance is highlighted by the way he is portrayed as an intellectual. When Baroni and Angelo first meet him in the gym's office, Hellman is wearing horn-rimmed glasses and reading a copy of the *Saturday Review*, an American magazine that until 1952 was called the *Saturday Review of Literature*. 'He's reading; he's always reading', say the gym staff and the contrast between his intellectual life and his life as a fight-promoter mirrors the contrast between Baroni's hate-filled boxing career, with its emphasis on physicality, and his love of church choral music, with its emphasis on spirituality.

228

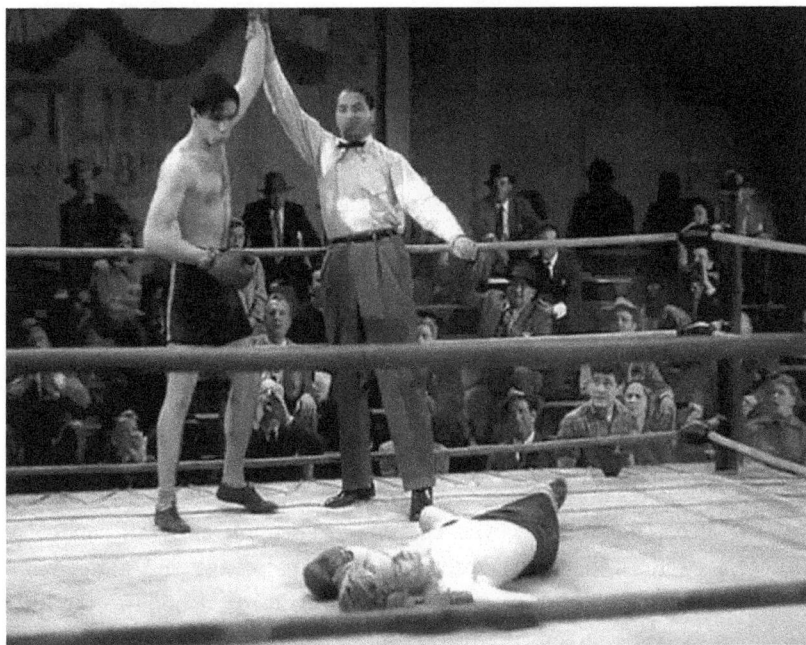

Baroni (Leonard Nimoy) is proud of his new face, achieved through plastic surgery, and doesn't want to spoil it by fighting

These polarities in Baroni's life are shown in scenes that juxtapose his fierce fighting style in the ring with the quiet interludes in which he visits St Dominic's or listens to the record he has had especially imported from Italy. He is shown to be ashamed of his 'finer' side, quickly switching the record over to a dance track when he hears someone knocking on the door. His two sides are also highlighted through the two women in his life: Emily Brooks (Allene Roberts), the demure young church-worker who wears tailored suits and encourages Baroni to read, enjoy music and speak properly with 'long words'; and June (Mona Knox) the fur-clad glamour-girl who makes it plain that she trades 'dates' (in other words, sex) for expensive presents. Emily never looks away from Baroni's deformed face: June only notices him after he has acquired handsome features. The tug-of-war between good-girl and bad-girl is a conventional trope of the boxing genre, with good-girl repelled by the fighting and bad-girl urging a killing. In *Kid Monk Baroni*, however, the characterisation is given a slightly different twist in that Emily represents not just virtue and a steadying influence on the hero, but specifically a church-based notion of virtue. Hellman exploits the tension that he knows Baroni feels between being a 'dirty fighter' and a 'saintly youth' when he asks the boxer to meet him at St Dominic's in order to persuade him to take on the Seattle Wildcat. The two men sit side by side in the pew, organ music playing in the background, whispering to each other

It is surprising, therefore, that the film does not seize the chance for a church wedding scene as its finale: when Baroni loses his final fight and donates the loser's purse to St Dominic's, both Baroni and Emily are absent from the final scene of the Sunday service, Father Callaghan merely alluding to the fact that 'Paul and his bride Emily' will soon return to see the Recreation Center that Baroni's money has made possible. This may have been a budget consideration: the prospect of wrapping the film up in nine days may have encouraged Broder to pull the plug on a final scene. A similar sense of anti-climax is experienced in some of the fight scenes. The pressbook for the film emphasises the training that Nimoy did with 'such former fight greats as Benny Goldberg, Harvey Perry and Joe Gray' who acted as technical advisors, but little of this translates into the finished film. Baroni's trademark hammer blows are shown a number of times, notably in a standard montage sequence of punches, town names and headlines, charting his rise to fame, and his comeback fight is nicely filmed through the ropes, the low angle revealing the overhead lights as well as the fighters in an atmospheric sequence. But after two rounds, the rest of the fight is shown only through short clips and changing round-numbers, a technique repeated in the final fight.

'All Kids and Has-Beens'
The Square Ring (1953)

O f the 130 or so boxing films made in the 1930s, 1940s and 1950s - the heyday of the genre - only a handful are British: *The Third String* (1932), *The Bermondsey Kid* (1933), *Excuse My Glove* (1936), *Mannequin* (1934), *Keep Fit* (1937), *There Ain't No Justice* (1939), *The Square Ring* (1953) and *The Flanagan Boy* (1953). The rest are almost all US productions, which perhaps would indicate that the themes explored by the genre (the rags-to-riches, anyone-can-make-it-big stories, for example), and the visceral presence of the fights themselves, are more relevant to the American psyche. American boxing films were of course on widespread release in the UK, but the market was not often a mutual one - British films found it hard to get US distribution and had to rely largely on the home market. If anyone was to make a successful British boxing film, it surely had to be Ealing, with its sure direction (this time from Michael Relph and Basil Dearden), reliable stars and strong track-record of tapping into (some may say even creating) British national identity, an identity that stood for 'decency, democracy, community, pluck and fair play.'[317] And what could be more British than a film about a fight programme at a second-rate London boxing hall, Adams Stadium, used in its off-nights for dancing and rollerskating? Plenty of scope for colourful characters, humour, the interweaving of different stories and personalities, and some dramatic boxing action. Ealing billed the film as being 'richly comic, tensely dramatic, romantically moving'.[318]

The combination is both the film's strength and its downfall. Based on a stage play, *The Square Ring* retains its unity of time, with the whole of the action taking place during one evening, from the moment 'handler' Danny Felton (Jack Warner) arrives at the stadium to his departure after the fights. *To-day's Cinema* felt that the film 'completely succeeds in disguising its theatrical origin', though the limited number of sets (dressing-room, stadium, tea-shop) induce a certain claustrophobia and the heavy emphasis on dialogue, rather than on action, lend it a staginess or static quality that it never quite shakes off.[319]

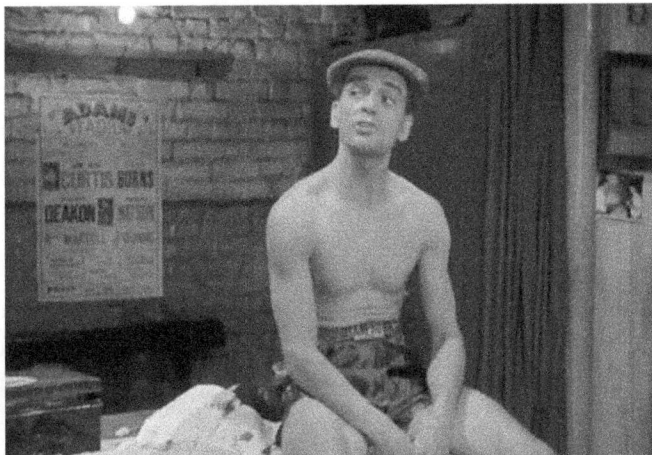

Bill Owen as Happy Burns, the cheeky-chappy Cockney who only takes off his flat cap when he's ready to go into the ring

Another difficulty with *The Square Ring* is its even-handedness in the way it deals with its half-dozen different fighters and their stories, seeming to give equal weight to the tale of the young, nervous Welshman fighting for the first time as it does to the cheeky-chappy Cockney whose main concern is ensuring his nose doesn't get broken. This parade of different characters is strangely un-engaging, and it is only halfway through the film that it becomes obvious that the intended focus of attention is Kid Curtis (Robert Beatty), the veteran boxer who wants to win back his wife, but just can't give up the fight business. Because of the number of characters jostling for attention, mostly in a humorous way, the empathy we should feel for Curtis is late in arriving and this undermines the dramatic climax of the film, in which Curtis dies in the dressing room after his come-back fight.

These criticisms aside, the film is, as *Monthly Film Bulletin* said on its release, 'slick and unpretentious entertainment', the Britishness of the setting and the characters giving a new perspective on the familiar themes of the boxing picture.[320] At its centre, and holding the whole film together, is the figure of Danny - perfect, if too-typical, casting for Jack Warner as the reassuring, caring paternalistic figure who presides over the fighters, tending their wounds, binding their hands and soothing their troubled brows. Indeed, as Pat Kirkham and Janet Thumim point out, in their article on 'Dearden and Gender' Danny combines 'motherly solicitude and fatherly wisdom'.[321] As well as offering philosophical insights into the world of boxing (which Kirkham and Thumim would categorise as fatherly), his motherly qualities are exhibited through the physical contact he has with the boxers (his job requires him to touch their faces, their hands), and through the way he witnesses almost none of the fighting himself, trapped in the dressing room waiting anxiously for the boxers to return 'home'. The motherly analogies can be extended to the clothes he wears - a shawl-necked jumper which softens his appearance - and actions such as sweeping the dressing-room floor with a broom. The pressbook insisted that despite Warner's strong screen persona, 'each part he portrays is always quite different', though each is imbued with 'warm humour' and a down-to-earthness characteristic of the 'common man'.[322]

With Danny as a gravitational centre, the boxers one by one arrive at Adams Stadium to prepare for their fight. This is a one-sided representation of the evening, because we only see one dressing-room - the boxers' opponents clearly have their own room and they remain faceless and largely unnamed. The characters, which *The Square Ring*'s press-book describes as 'strongly drawn' (for 'strongly drawn' read 'stereotypes') are all culturally recognisable social types. They include Lloyd (Ronald Lewis), a naïve Welshman facing his first fight; Happy (Bill Owen), a bright and bubbly Cockney with an eye for the ladies; Rick (Maxwell Reed), a good-looking fighter who agrees to take the money for just one last fixed fight; Whitey (George Rose), the punch-drunk pug who can't see why he shouldn't go on fighting; Rowdie (Bill Travers), the dopey eccentric whose science fiction stories mean more to him than the real world; and Kid Curtis, the top-of-the-bill veteran played by Robert Beatty

Opposite: Danny 'mothers' the fighters, massaging them, tending their wounds - and sweeping out the dressing-room at the end of the night

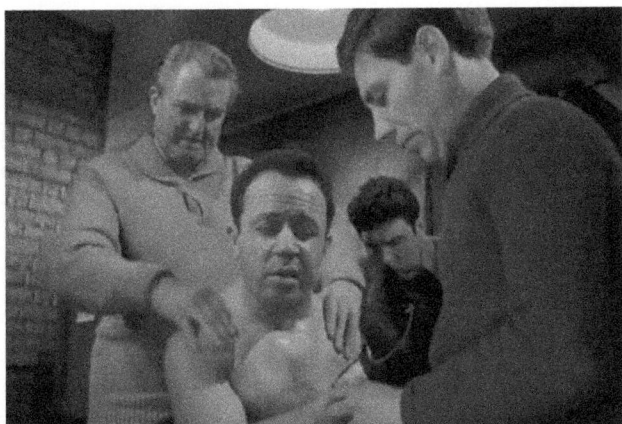

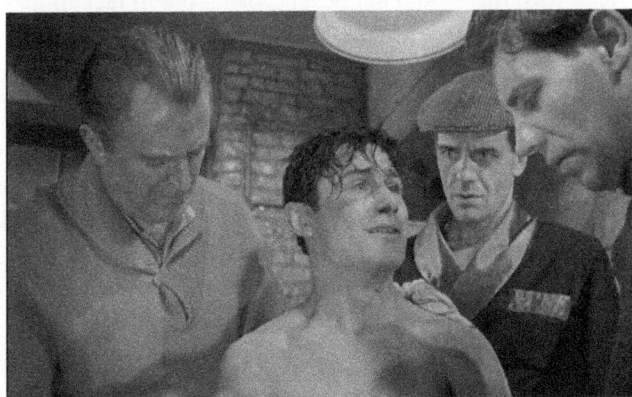

(the name 'kid' is ironic) who wants to make a come-back. The evening's programme, as Rick sharply observes, is 'all kids and has-beens.' The way in which the boxers are contrasted with Danny, the still and calm centre of the film, is strongly in the British tradition which Christine Gledhill says sets restraint (the lead player) against character-acting (the supporting cast); and an 'actorly' approach against expression through the body.[323]

Part of the film's difficulty in building dramatic momentum, is that - with so many main characters - it has to keep swapping back and forth between the individual storylines, so that even the briefest fight-action or piece of plot-dialogue is cut short in order to move to across to another character's tale (given that this is the ploy used by today's soaps, it is surprising that it is not more effective). If the individual characters' stories meshed in some way, this would not be a problem, but in fact all they have in common is their presence in the stadium and their role as fighters: although there is dialogue between them, it is mostly light-hearted and inconsequential. *The Square Ring* has some telling moments of dark melodrama which are unsurpassed in their chill realism, but sandwiching these highly involving scenes between humorous ones (such as the realisation by Adams (Sid James) that the crowd has made off with the charity box) makes it hard to maintain any kind of equilibrium (*They Made Me a Criminal* (1939) had the same difficulty).

One of the most affecting scenes takes place when Rick goes out to fight, having agreed with his manager that he will lose the match. Rick is under no illusions about the business: when newcomer Lloyd remarks on the 'sport', Rick replies: 'sport? You'll learn.' He has been told that members of the Boxing Board are in the audience and has to weigh his options - if he loses the fight, the Board might spot it's been fixed, but if he wins 'they' will be after him. 'Who are they?' asks Rick's glamorous girlfriend Frankie (Joan Collins). 'I've never seen them,' Rick replies, the facelessness and anonymity of the fixers making them all the more deadly. Rick decides: he'll take the fall. We see only about two seconds of action of Rick's fight against his nameless opponent before we learn that he has accidentally won - and now must run for his life, throwing on his clothes and rushing out of the dressing-room into the surging crowd. Buffeted by the press of people is his girlfriend who, in her white coat, stands out (almost as a target) against a surrounding sea of dark suits. As she is swirled into the vortex of the crowd, with Rick unable to reach her, every push or shove is interpreted as a potentially murderous attack until the pair, united at last, make it through the doors of the stadium and out into the night.

Frankie (Joan Collins) is swirled into the vortex of the crowd, fearful of the faceless people who will punish Rick for not taking the fall

An equally tense and dramatic scene constitutes the climax of the film. Kid Curtis, despite the protestations of his estranged wife Peg (Bernardette O'Farrell) - note the recurrence once again of the name 'Peg' for the 'moral-force' woman of the picture - goes ahead with his fight because, he says, 'I can't stop now'. His motives regarding Peg are ambivalent: although he visits the teashop where she works with her father to beg her to come back to him, he is soon making a dubious deal with Eve (Kay Kendall), an old flame who is now married to a boxing manager. Eve makes it clear that winning the fight may bring him more than just new management, but he is warned off by her husband: 'Eve and I will still be here tomorrow and you'll be gone,' he says. 'And there'll be another and another.' In other words, boxers are replaceable commodities and they're all the same. When Kid Curtis enters the ring, for the only sustained fight action of the film, the ring is bleached almost white by the strength of the stadium lights, so the fight takes place in a kind of halo of brilliance. For the first time (and following the time-honoured conventions of the genre), we hear the fight announcement and witness the handshake between opponents. Although the camera stays well outside the ropes for much of the fight, it moves in close when a hard punch floors Kid's opponent. But the punch is just a fluke - the Kid is clearly getting a pasting (and we see gold-digger Eve leave the stadium when she realises: she's not interested in losers). By Round 10, the demeanor of the crowd has changed. No longer are they good-natured and friendly, but are - as *The Times* said in its review of the film - 'sitting in the safety of ringside seats and howling for blood.' Their predatory behaviour is emphasised by the extreme close-ups, first of faces, then just of mouths, open and shouting (a technique used a few years earlier in *The Set-Up*). To highlight the brutality, the camera closes in on the fighters, in a series of blurry action shots which dramatically convey the disorientation of the failing fighter. Exhausted but determined, Kid Curtis finally delivers the knockout punch and staggers out of the ring to carnivalesque music. As the excited crowd makes for the exits, we focus on the figure of Peg, Kid's wife, sitting on alone in the stadium, a centre of stillness around whom the crowd swirls and eddies. Kid, barely alive, makes it back to the dressing room - and dies there on the couch.

The camera stays well outside the ropes for much of the Kid Curtis fight, then closes in to highlight the brutality

As Danny emerges into the night, the ambulance having taken Kid's body away, he looks across the street to a brightly lit pub, full of laughter and singing. Out of the door emerges Happy, dressed to the nines and surrounded by girls. Unknowing, he spies Danny and gives him a cheery wave before driving off into the darkness.

In *The Square Ring*, there's no way a boxer can win. Like Lloyd, he may believe sport is about fairness, but he can still be defeated by a dirty punch from a sand-encrusted boxing glove. Like Whitey, he may believe you can go on and on fighting, but eventually he has to stop being in denial about that double-vision and the doctor's warnings that he will die if you carry on. Like Rick, he can fix every fight 'they' want, but his life will never be his own again. And like Kid Curtis, he may hope for a come-back, but even if he survives, a year from now he'll still end up a loser. In fact, perhaps it is only Happy who wins in the end, his career still on the up-and-up, his nose (his most valued asset) unbroken despite a hard punch and his optimism still keeping pace with his name.

To look for realistic, sustained boxing action in this film is to look in vain, even though Robert Beatty as the Kid was said to have undergone 'many weeks of ring tution'.[324] No sooner has even the briefest boxing sequence got underway, than the film frustratingly cuts away to another aspect of the story. As well as borrowing the 'mouth' close-ups from *The Set-Up*, the film also replicates its shot of two pairs of feet in the ring, moving and dancing to their own rhythm: both these shots are effective in their own right, but do indicate a certain lack of originality (and a turning towards Hollywood for ideas, rather than seeking them closer to home). The lack of boxing action partly follows the convention of saving any sustained coverage for the final fight, but also partly betrays the stage-play origins of the story. Its saving grace is in the way it helps us identify with Danny, back in the dressing room, unable to see the action, but only to hear the crowd and imagine what's happening inside the ring.

Despite the recurrence of some familiar themes (the fixed fights, the danger of death, the gold-digging women), *The Square Ring* is identifiably British. The stadium is seedy, all bare brick and dreary corridors; the fighters are pale and thin (Lloyd's ribs are clearly visible); the audience resolutely working-class; and the staff poor (Danny's assistant wears a jumper with holes at the elbows). There is no big-city glamour here, no big money: the parochial nature of the place is demonstrated by the charity nominated for an audience whip-round - the local Boys' Club. Yet this is a ring in which the essential issues are still fought out, 'the tension between ambition, integrity and competition set against deceit, avarice and self-delusion' as Kirkham and Thumim observe.[325] The quality of self-delusion they cite may be directed at Kid (for thinking he can make a comeback) or Whitey (thinking he can live forever), but really it concerns Danny in his willingness to believe the best. 'We all know it's the people who talk about rackets that muck boxing about,' he says, implying that - if boxing is under a cloud - then it's merely an image-problem. Perhaps unless he truly believes this, he could no longer go on.

Boxing forms the centrepiece of the poster, but much of the film stays in the dressing-room

'A credit to the human race'
The Joe Louis Story (1953)

*T*he *Joe Louis Story* should have been a breakthrough picture, featuring a black fighter in the starring role for the first time, tapping into the popularity of Joe Louis in the public imagination, and using a real boxer with an uncanny resemblance to Louis - heavyweight Coley Wallace - to portray him.[326] Unfortunately, the film is dull and plodding, partly because of the need to integrate large amounts of existing documentary footage of Louis' fights with new studio-shot material; partly because of the 'sanitising' of his life in this biopic; and partly because the fact that he was known to have a 'poker face' (something that Wallace accurately mimics) makes it difficult for the viewer to engage emotionally with him. As for the fights, the documentary footage is all in long-shot and the grainy texture means that it's hard even to distinguish which fighter is which: from the moment cinematographers stepped through the ropes to film boxers up close, viewers' expectations changed and this footage - while having the stamp of authenticity - does not have the impact that is needed.

The film tells the story of Louis' rise and fall through the eyes of reporter Tad McGeehan (Paul Stewart)[327], opening with the final Madison Square Garden fight where Louis loses to Rocky Marciano and with McGeehan vowing to write the 'real story' of his life. The credits roll and the rest of the film is a flashback, beginning with Louis as a young man in Detroit and then charting his rise as a boxer, his love of Marva (Hilda Simms), his war service, money troubles, and then finally into the present-day with his last fight. Along the way, McGeehan's presence or voice reminds us that we are seeing Louis' life through the reporter's eyes.

A United Artists release, *The Joe Louis Story* was directed by Robert

Gordon, an actor-turned-director who had only directed a handful of films before this one, and scripted by Robert Sylvester who had been a newspaperman for 20 years (and author of a novel based on his experience - 'The Second Oldest Profession' - which was published in 1949). Sylvester clearly tapped into his experience in writing the sympathetic character of McGeehan, who is the emotional centre of the film and whose motivations are very different from those of sportswriter Eddie Willis in *The Harder They Fall* (1956). McGeehan befriends Louis - they play golf together - and advises him on the best promoter to choose, even though Louis ignores his advice.

Race turns out to be the 'elephant in the room'. Louis' nickname of 'The Brown Bomber' is never used and race is only referred to twice in the film, first when one of the promoters' team says 'we got to remember that Joe's a coloured fighter and as a coloured fighter he's got two strikes against him already' and second when his trainer refers to 'a lot of trouble in Harlem tonight, gangs picking fights, turning over taxicabs'.This lack of emphasis is in marked contrast to *The Ring*, where race is the central issue and motivating factor, and means that *The Joe Louis Story* cannot be categorised as a 'social problem' film. Leger Grindon argues that the opposite is the case, bracketing *The Joe Louis Story* with *The Ring* and with *Right Cross* (1950) in 'developing the Hispanic or African American boxer as a protagonist who suffers from discrimination and expresses his social anger in ring battles'.[328] That might have been the case in Louis' own life, but it is not present on the screen and McGeehan's voiceover at the end of the film says that there were 'those among us who saw in his rise a bright and permanent hope for all kids who start on backstreets', thus making Louis aspirational for all poor children, rather than singling out race as a factor. Certainly, there are more black characters than in other films of the boxing genre at the time: when Louis turns professional, his base is the Southside Gym in Chicago, where all the men including his trainer Chappie Blackburn (James Edwards) is black. When he's ready to sign up with a big-time promoter, the scene takes place in a black nightclub, where he watches black couples dancing and his eye falls on Marva, who will become his wife and whose love-story is foregrounded in the film.

If race is not a motivating factor, then money certainly is. The film elides Louis' poor beginnings (he came from an Alabaman sharecropper family and his father was a cotton picker) by opening with him as a young adult factory-worker in Detroit (wrapping oranges for a dollar a day), walking through the streets with a friend and swinging his violin case.[329] His mother pays for his music lessons but although his friend enthuses about boxing and encourages him to join the gym, Louis doesn't have the necessary 50 cents. When he does start fighting, he tells his mother it will make them all rich, but as he rises in his career he turns down promoter Jimmy Johnson's promise to make him a million dollars in favour of Mike Jacob's vow to make him a champion. Later in his career, it is implied he is giving money away: he ends up owing 200,000 dollars to the IRS, forcing him to carry on fighting when he knows he is past his prime.

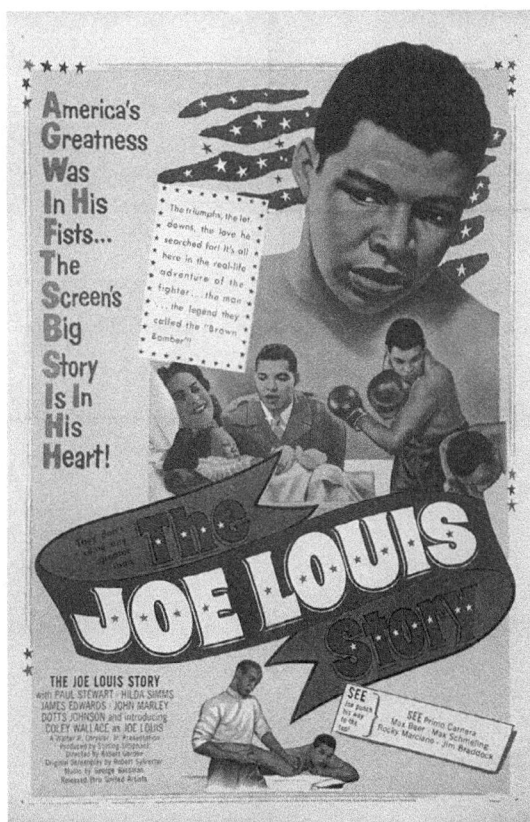

The poster promotes Louis as representing America with its stars-and-stripes design and tagline of 'America's Greatness'

Coley Wallace bears an uncanny resemblance to the character he plays on screen. The studio's campaign book for the film makes much of the fact that he was not an actor but a fighter who, at 24 years old, had risen 'to the rank of Number Seven among contenders for the heavyweight title owned by Rocky Marciano.' He accurately mimics Louis' well-known 'poker faced' expression but unfortunately this means, unless he is smiling, it is hard for the viewer to read his emotions and to engage with them.[330] At 6 ft 2 ins tall, he is around the same height as Louis and his size is emphasised in the opening scene of the film where he swings the violin case casually as he walks - and it looks tiny in his hand. When he and his friend go to a boxing gym, he dwarfs everyone else there. He changes into tight shorts and enters the ring, where he is taught how to jab.

At the gym, Louis (Coley Wallace) is taught how to jab

Having a boxer in the lead role should have made for exciting fight scenes in the film but director of photography Joseph Brun (who was nominated for an Oscar for the film *Martin Luther*, released in the same year as *The Joe Louis Story*) had the difficult job of integrating rather poor and grainy stock footage of Louis' fights, all filmed in long-shot, with new footage of Coley Wallace. This resulted in consistently sooty, shadowy scenes that made the fights uninvolving and makes it hard to distinguish which fighter is Louis and which is his opponent. There is little boxing action: even his fight against Primo Carnera is dismissed in about three seconds in order to concentrate on his courting of Marva. The fight against Max Baer blends longshots of documentary footage with cutaways to Chappie, but the static camera is strangely distancing; and when Louis is knocked out by Max Schmeling, the scene cuts immediately to the aftermath, with Louis - face battered and swollen - facing Marva and his mother.

A rare close-up - nearly all the fight scenes are in longshot and the static camera makes it hard to even see which fighter is which

It is not until the championship fight against James Braddock at Comiskey Park that there is any sustained footage. Boxing films often use cutaways to show the spectators or the trainers because the up-close shots of the fights call for some relief of the tension: that is not needed in the

Braddock fight because the long-shots do not convey the visceral detail that other films do. Although Louis has won the championship title, he does not consider himself the champ until he has won a re-match with Max Schmeling, who arrives from Germany 'with the blessings of Hitler and the Third Reich'. The much-anticipated fight is actually an anti-climax: there are none of the tropes that we are used to seeing in the boxing genre: no announcements, no round numbers, just the restless pacing of the referee. When Louis wins, after just two minutes, we don't even see his hand held up as champion. Louis keeps on fighting but these fights (including those against Billy Conn and Jersey Joe Walcott) occur off-screen: all that is shown is hand-binding then a cut to Louis having a post-match talk with his mother. 'More fights' says McGeehan's voiceover but we see nothing other than billboard posters being put up until the fight against Rocky Marciano. Even this fight has less impact than it should have because there are constant cutaways to McGeehan, who is watching the fight on a tiny TV screen in a bar, having refused to see the fight in person because he believes Louis is past his prime. Louis goes down - in a repeat of the scene that opened the film - and McGeehan leaves the bar.

Hollywood was probably nervous about the reception that a mainstream film with a black boxer in the lead role would receive - in the decade that Louis was champion, during which the boxing genre was at its heyday, there was not a single film released with a black boxer playing the lead role. But the profession itself had had similar difficulties with Louis being black, so Hollywood was able to lean on the inoffensive persona that Louis' promoters had developed for him. Early in the film, when he leaves his Detroit home to go to Chicago the narration tells us 'he was carrying a cardboard suitcase, one change of clothes and the family Bible'. Thus his morality is established, reinforced by his mother telling him that if he wants to box, he needs to put his whole being into it - to 'do it right'. His love affair with Marva, which is foregrounded more than audiences might have expected in this film - portrays him as a faithful husband, eliding the fact that they divorced, re-married and then divorced again, and also failing to mention 'Louis's wolfish libido and his trysts with singer Lena Horne and ice-skater Sonja Henie.'[331] The only subtle reference is when Marva and Louis are at a nightclub, listening to Anita Ellis singing 'I'll Be Around When She's Gone' and holding hands across the table - but then again, this might just be an interlude with an opportunity for a hit song.[332]

Louis is also portrayed as symbolic of American values - a 'credit to the human race' as McGeehan describes him. When Max Schmeling comes to America it is said to be 'with the fuehrer's best wishes' and McGeehan says that if Schmeling wins the championship 'they'll never stop yelling about Aryan supremacy'. So, Louis' war service is emphasised - joining the services and making patriotic speeches to motivate the troops - as is the fact that when he does a radio interview, he says he is donating his fight money to army relief. Thus, as Romano notes in his *Boxing Filmography,* the picture was 'sanitised and then wrapped in sentiment'.[333]

To overcome any qualms Hollywood had about a mainstream film with a black boxer in the lead role, they emphasised his inoffensive persona, making much of his army service

Louis does not escape the trope of boxers being portrayed as childlike. He is unable to manage his money, running up huge debts. When he wins the 'boxer of the year' trophy, he cuts himself a vast slice of the celebratory cake, looking at Chappie as he eats it. Louis is often on the golfcourse when he should be training and Chappie reprimands him for practising putting in his hotel room: 'what you doing playing with those kids' toys?' he asks, ordering him to go to bed to prepare for the fight. Chappie has become a father-figure (Louis' own father is absent and unmentioned in this film though in reality was in a mental asylum) and we see him caring for Louis between rounds, checking his cuts and giving him water. Chappie eventually becomes ill, with Louis being assigned another trainer, a white man called Manny Seaman (John Marley), to prepare him for the Schmeling fight. Chappie dies during Louis' war service.

Although the film was a mainstream A-picture, United Artists clearly realised there was a profitable black audience to be targeted. The pressbook advised exhibitors that 'the most intensive campaigning should be undertaken among the Negro population', suggesting obtaining sponsorship from local 'Negro organisations' for a motorcade through 'the coloured section of town' and approaching 'Negro newspapers in your town' to get publicity. United Artists took out an eight-page advertising section in *Ebony Magazine*, which had a 500,000-circulation, specifically to promote *The Joe Louis Story*.[334]

Despite its drawbacks, reviews for the film were favourable: the trade publication *Film Daily* felt it was 'penetrating and vivid, compassionate and understanding' with first-class direction and script.[335] *Kinematograph Weekly* was equally enthusiastic, praising Coley Wallace's 'incredibly real, sympathetic and vital portrayal'[336] and *Variety* said it rated 'high on sincerity' and was 'heartpoundingly exciting'.[337]

'Money's Money, No Matter Where You Get It'
The Harder They Fall (1956)

*T*he Harder They Fall, along with *Somebody Up There Likes Me*, released the same year, serves to mark the end of the heyday of the boxing film. In the 60s, the genre all but disappeared with only around a dozen films being released - none of them memorable. Joan Dean, in her article 'The Soul in the Machine', believes the reason for the decline was the domination of the sport in the 1960s by Afro-Americans, which meant that 'white America, and with it the film industry, grew uneasy with the now familiar formula'.[338] Whatever the reason, if Hollywood wanted a memorable marker to end an era, then there could be no better vehicle than *The Harder They Fall*, a cynical, tough picture from Columbia which revolves around money: getting it, stealing it, spending it. The poster for the film prepared the audience: featuring a striking graphic of a boxer's gloved hand as he lies prone on the floor of the ring, the tagline reads 'if you thought 'On the Waterfront' hit hard, wait till you see this one'. That it was not simply referring to violence was spelt out in the above-the-title copyline: 'the only thing that's on the square...is the ring itself', thus setting out its stall as an unflinching portrayals not just of boxing but of its endemic corruption.

Despite some hard-hitting pictures in the 30s and 40s, *The Harder They Fall* pushed the limits just too far for many reviewers. *The Times* said it 'revels in scandal and brutality' and *Monthly Film Bulletin* claimed it exploited 'savage boxing material for the maximum sensation effect'.[339] Even *The Cinema,* a trade magazine, accustomed to giving favourable reviews, had to admit the film was 'blunt and uncompromising'.[340] One of the factors that influenced this uncompromising nature was that the film

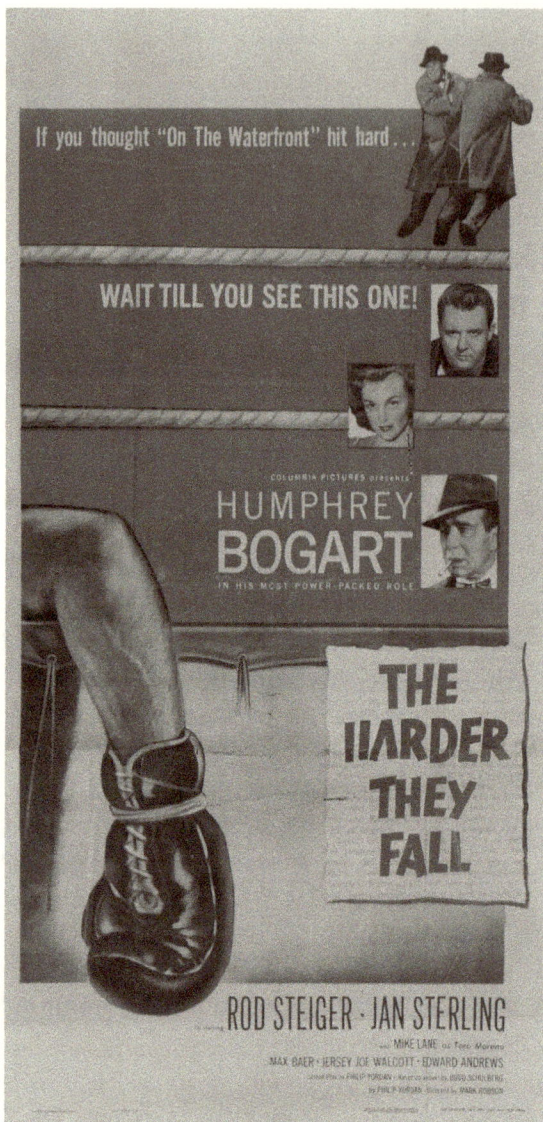

The poster makes it clear that the violence will not just be confined to the ring. Rod Steiger's photograph and the reference to On the Waterfront is an attempt to target the same audience

was made at the time of the liberalisation of the Production Code, which had regulated filmmaking during the 30s and 40s and had ensured, among other things, that gratuitous violence was kept out of pictures, and that criminals got their comeuppance (though watching some of the classic gangster/film noir movies made during that time, you would have been hard-pressed to see exactly where the Code had intervened). Another factor was the increasing domination of the crime-film genre by the social-problem thriller. Frank Krutnik suggests that 'the foregrounding of the social issue became a means of overtly differentiating these films from the classical studio productions of the old-style, supposedly escapist Hollywood'.[341] Escapist is certainly not a term you could apply to *The Harder They Fall*.

Sportswriter Eddie Willis (Humphrey Bogart), unemployed since the paper he wrote for folded, is hired by Nick Benko (Rod Steiger), a corrupt boxing promoter, to promote a new find: the gigantic Toro Moreno (Mike Lane), who he discovered working in a circus in Argentina as a strongman. But Moreno can't fight and all his bouts are fixed, right up until a fight against heavyweight champion Buddy Brannen, which will net Eddie and the promoter a lot of money. Eddie is eventually forced to tell the confident Toro that all his fights so far have been fixed: 'you're just a bum,' he tells him, 'you couldn't break an egg with your punches.' Out of a sense of family honour, and because he needs the money, Toro goes ahead with the fight only to be badly beaten, his jaw broken. Despite a million-dollar gate, Benko claims Toro is only due 49 dollars and 7 cents (the exactness of the amount serving to drive home Benko's villainy and heartlessness). Benko plans to sell Toro to a two-bit promoter and send him off on another round of punishing, countrywide fights, but Eddie intervenes to put Toro on a plane home. Eddie's fee is rather different to Toro's: 26,000 dollars. In a moment of compassion (or, more realistically, disgust at Benko), Eddie gives all the money to Toro, pretending it is what he is owed. As the film ends, Eddie sits down at his typewriter to write an expose of the boxing rackets, with a plea to clean up the fight game, or close it down.[342]

The film was based on the book of the same name by Bud Schulberg, who had drawn some of his material from the life of 1930s boxer Primo Carnera, 'the 270-pound circus giant from Italy (who) was building his undefeated record over an impressive list of roundheels and overnight pacifists'. The figure of Toro, however, is an amalgam of many such characters who come, as Schulberg says, 'in all colours and nationalities.'[343]

The opening sequence sets the tone for the whole movie. Over an edgy, urgent soundtrack we watch Eddie Willis, nattily dressed with bow tie and trilby hat, emerge from his apartment in Peter Cooper Village and hail a cab. Other men - soon revealed as Benko and his henchmen - get into cars and 'hurtle through the empty New York streets to an early morning rendezvous' in a scene that 'evokes brilliantly the ugliness of the milieu and the ruthlessness of the racketeers before disclosing the squalid operation they are embarked upon'.[344] On the way to Feldmans Gym, Benko's car stops to pick up George (heavyweight boxer Jersey Joe Walcott), a black trainer, and the poorer neighbourhood, with its sidewalks cluttered with metal dustbins, indicates his status. A very different vision of New York is shown in the same opening sequence, as Moreno disembarks from the ship that has brought him from South America, his eyes full of wonder at everything that he sees - especially the skyscrapers which, like him, are larger than life. Reality kicks in for Moreno when he arrives at the Gym, which is scruffy, litter-strewn and run-down, and where in his first bout of sparring with George, he immediately collapses when punched in the belly. This is of no consequence to Benko. 'The fight game today is like showbusiness,' he says. 'There are no real fighters any more.'

As well as the star presence of Bogart and a hard-hitting story, the film benefited from Mark Robson's sure touch as director (he had also directed *Champion* (1949)) and from Burnett Guffey's crisp and atmospheric cinematography with its deep noirish shadows. Location shooting gives the film a real sense of place. The Columbia pressbook for the film says that Robson wanted to film the fight scenes at a well-known fight venue, but that everyone 'from New York to Chicago to Los Angeles' refused because of the film's 'scathing indictment of the sport'. Columbia built its own area. Romano, in his *Boxing Filmography*, quotes this pressbook story, and many others, as straightforward historical facts, but in reality these stories were just as likely to have been invented by the studio's publicity department with the aim of maximising editorial coverage for the film, as they were to have been based on any reality.[345]

In what was to be his final film (he discovered shortly afterwards that he was suffering from throat cancer), Bogart plays a man who subscribes to a familiar Bogart philosophy: like Rick in *Casablanca* (1942), Eddie 'sticks his neck out for nobody' but eventually finds his limit - and his compassion. Until the closing moments of the film, Eddie's sole motivation has been money ('You sell a fighter, you sell soap - what's the difference?' he says to his wife when she says she doesn't like the business). When Benko first approaches him about a job, he wants to know what he'll be paid before he even takes a look at Toro, and he is quick to negotiate a higher fee in return for a few extra favours. Making a buck is 'the only reason I'm here,' he says, and it does not seem to bother him that Benko is a gangster. After all, his philosophy is that 'money's money no matter where you get it'. Eddie is not the only character in the film to think like this: even society ladies are shown to have their price. Benko offers 25,000 dollars to the upper-crust Mrs Harding (Lillian Culver) to boost the Crippled Children Fund, if she will make the Toro fight top-of-the bill at the forthcoming benefit-fight. Mrs Harding makes a token resistance but is quickly persuaded that it doesn't matter where the money comes from - after all, Al Capone provided soup-kitchens for the poor and they didn't turn away his money.

Money dominates the life of every single boxer in the film - all that changes higher up the scale is the price, though somewhat obscurely they all agree that a championship fight is the one match that can't be fixed. The boxers are vocal about their pride, though in reality this turns out to be more about saving face. Once offered a good way to lose a fight without seeming to (for example, using the chicken-wire routine), they quickly agree. Even the crowd is motivated by money and have a habit of booing or throwing their programmes if the fight is won too easily: 'they've got to get their money's worth,' says Eddie, explaining why a fight couldn't be stopped even though one of the boxers was injured.

For Benko, of course, money is everything. He may be a gangster, but his language is always the language of business: fighters are 'merchandise', boxing is 'like showbusiness' and his accounts ledgers are almost meticulously kept. He is happy to hype Toro in the press in the build-up to the championship fight, but sees no contradiction in placing his bet on Toro's opponent, Buddy Brennan. How, then, could Benko understand Eddie's motives for giving away all his money to Toro? 'A man who can give away 26,000 dollars, you can't talk to,' he says. It's simply beyond his comprehension. The motivation for Eddie's change of heart is not articulated and is hard to read: *The Times* said that 'neither Mr Bogart, nor the script nor Mr Mark Robson, the director, can make (it) convincing'.[346] There is some earlier indication that Eddie has his limits, occurring when Benko wants to send Toro's Argentine manager home without any money. Eddie insists he is paid - and puts his job on the line for it. Ronald Bergan, in his book *Sports in the Movies*, felt that the cynical message of the film - that everyone has their price - 'smacks of special pleading' and questioned whether so many faked fights could be staged in a row, or whether millions of fans be so taken in. The plot, he says, 'leaves too many questions unanswered', though he concedes that 'the film is so gripping and well-acted that these questions don't arise until one has emerged into the light'.[347] In the final scene, when Eddie has whisked Toro onto a plane to Argentina and is then threatened by Benko who says 'you stole my merchandise', money seems to have lost its power over him entirely. 'You can't scare me and you can't buy me,' Eddie tells him, as he sits down at his typewriter to write an expose of the boxing racket.[348]

Eddie Willis (Humphrey Bogart) hands over his entire 26,000-dollar paypacket to Toro Moreno (Mike Lane), in a change of heart that Benko does not understand and indeed is not articulated

There is no such change of heart in Schulberg's book. In the book, Eddie does toy with the idea of giving Toro his money, then whittles it down to just a percentage, and in the end gives him nothing at all. Eddie knows he is a heel, but he just can't change: there's no sitting down to write about the game in the book - he is a loser and he knows it.

Toro Moreno's promotional bus bills him as the 'Wild Man of the Andes' and features a giant cut-out of the fighter

In the film, boxers are portrayed as simple-minded, docile and childlike - as one of the managers says of his charge: 'he couldn't even go out and buy a pair of shoes without me'. They use phrases like 'nursing' their fighters or 'being like a father' to them. Toro - who has few lines of dialogue in the film - is portrayed as naive, innocent and trusting, and his body is never sexualised or displayed as the object of the 'gaze'. There are strong analogies with King Kong throughout the film, as there are throughout the book, which talks of Toro as a 'trained monkey of nightmare proportions', and a strange throwback to the giants of prehistoric time'.[349] Toro's promotion exploits an association with the primitive, with his tour-bus featuring a giant cut-out of the fighter captioned 'The Wild Man of the Andes',[350] in contrast to his polite and obliging manner. Even his name is (presumably) a circus name rather than his own: Toro Moreno means 'Brown Bull'. He is described as a 'giant' or a 'Goliath'and begins his tour in California because, as Eddie says, 'they like freak attractions out there.' If Toro is King Kong, then Benko is akin to Carl Denham, the entrepreneur bringing the 'monsters' to civilisation but, like King Kong, they are destined to be broken by that same civilisation. In a telling insight into Toro's potential future, Eddie watches some footage a TV colleague has prepared. The programme features interviews with old fighters: every one of them is on skid row, sleeping in cars, old and confused before their time, with no work and no prospect of getting any. It is a chilling picture, made more so by the device of showing the footage within the frame of a TV set to emphasise its documentary nature. King Kong is even mentioned explicitly once in the film, when Toro - unaware that all his fights are fixed - protests that he's a good fighter. 'He thinks he's King Kong,' says Eddie. It is only Eddie's actions that prevent Toro from sharing the same fate.

As if to underline the King Kong analogies, all the camerawork in *The Harder They Fall* works to emphasise Toro's size, with low-angle shots that make him tower above everyone else: actor Mike Lane was 6 ft 8 ins tall and (like the character he plays) an ex-circus strongman. When Toro first emerges from the dressing room at Feldmans Gym, he is so tall that he bumps his head on the ceiling light; then when he enters the ring at the gym, he steps over the ropes, not through them. Unusually for a star in Hollywood pictures, therefore, Bogart spends the entire film looking up at him. In the book, Schulberg writes that 'when you saw Toro ... for the first time he was so big you had to focus on him in sections, the way a still camera photographs a skyscraper'.[351] Toro may be a 'gentle giant', easily manipulated by people he thinks are his friends, but he is the only character who is shown to wrestle with moral questions and the only one to exhibit any religious beliefs.[352] When he believes, mistakenly, that he has killed another fighter in the ring, he goes to a Catholic priest for advice about a letter he has received from his mother who is in mourning for the man Toro has 'killed' and does not want him to fight any more. He wants to please his mother and his priest back in Argentina, but is in a double bind: if he goes home before the title fight, he will be penniless, which will bring disgrace on his family. We never see Eddie debating moral questions like these: when Benko offers him ten percent of Toro to make sure that coverage of a chaotic fixed fight is not reported on network TV, Eddie is happy to visit his old friend at the network and ensure the story is killed.

The fight scenes are as punchy as the plot, with crisp images that contrast the dark background of the arena with the lights illuminating the fighters. After the first fight, a ten-rounder against Sailor Rigazzo during which rosin in rubbed into Rigazzo's face when he disobeys the instruction to throw the fight, he is attacked in the shower by Benko's henchmen. The attack happens off-camera but is all the more chilling for the camera staying on the water draining out of the shower, only the muffled thuds

There is the customary montage of knockouts with the place-names superimposed on the footage: Bakersfield, Salinas, San Jose, Carson City and Reno

indicating the beating that Rigazzo is taking. Eddie solves the problem of fighters not doing what they are told by making a deal whereby he pays 1,000 dollars direct to every fighter who takes a dive. One more fight, with an opponent pretending to be knocked out but winking at his trainer from his position on the floor of the ring, is followed by the customary montage of knockouts with place-names indicating Toro's rise: Bakersfield, Salinas, San Jose, Carson City and Reno.

Only two fights are shown at length. The first is against Gus Dundee (Pat Comiskey), who has recently fought the title-holder, Buddy Brennan, during which bout he was knocked out and remained unconscious for five hours. His head still hurts and it's clear that there is something wrong with him. Nevertheless, he accepts Benko's offer of 100,000 dollars to take a dive against Toro at the Chicago Arena - as long as they can make it 'look good'. The camera stays low and close as in Round One, Toro connects with Dundee's face again and again. In Round Two, Dundee goes down; and by Round Three the crowd are booing because Dundee is not even trying. In Round Four, Dundee is knocked out and carried off on a stretcher to hospital where he dies as a result of the injuries in the earlier Brennan fight. Benko spouts a lot of sentimental claptrap about Dundee to the press, but actually only cares about whether the death will look bad for his own reputation. After Dundee dies, Benko throws a party to celebrate. After all, 'fighters ain't human,' he says.

The championship fight is not one that can be fixed. Brennan (Max Baer, world boxing heavyweight with one of the heaviest punches in the business, who gained the title by winning against Primo Carnera in June 1934) regards Toro as a 'big joker' and although he has been asked to carry him for six rounds, he refuses, saying: 'I'm gonna butcher your guy'. Benko is unmoved: in that case, he figures he will just put big bets on Brennan winning. Before the fight, Eddie tells Toro the truth about how all his fights were fixed, warns him that Brennan is a mean fighter, and that he should stay just long enough to make it look good - then go home with the money. Toro ignores the advice to use his long reach to keep his distance and clinch, not fight. In Round One, Toro is down almost straightaway; he doesn't even have his gloves up and is being battered in the face by uppercuts. In Round Two he is reminded to clinch, not fight, and the camera moves in very close, with Toro on the ropes and with cutaways to Eddie looking sick. In Round Three he takes more punishment: Toro's face is shown as distorted by the punches and the camera switches to Toro's point-of-view as his vision blurs. Toro has refused to sell out - and his jaw is broken as a result.

What sets *The Harder They Fall* apart from many other boxing films is that this is exclusively a man's picture with only one female speaking part, that of Beth (Jan Sterling), Eddie's wife. Although she is arguably the 'moral force' in the film, Eddie's strangely detached relationship with her makes this less than credible. Thus the usual dramatic conflicts between the 'good woman' and the 'glamorous blonde' (mirroring the in-ring fights of the men) are missing. For example, Eddie is surrounded by 'camp followers' but shows no interest in any of them, and neither does Toro. This results in a pared-down picture: in *The Harder They Fall* there is no need for money and greed to be personified by a femme fatale. Money has become so powerful that it can stand on its own: it has supplanted the lure of sex.

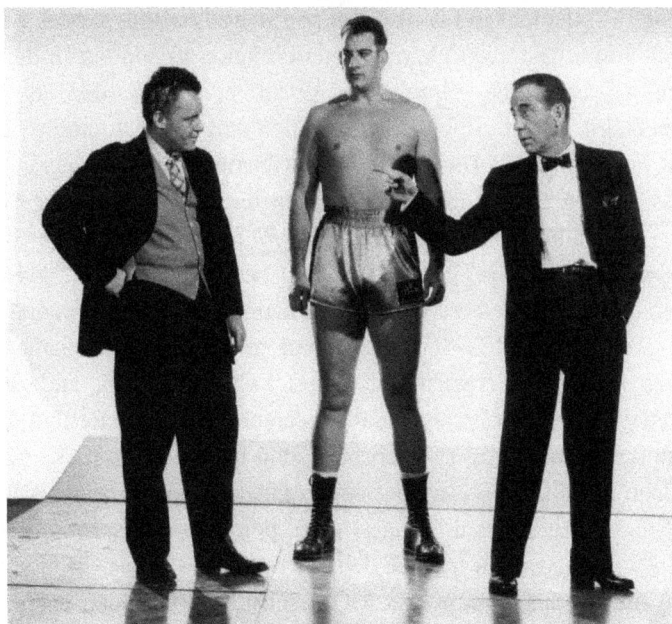

Mike Lane was 6 ft 8 ins tall, and the film - together with publicity stills - work to emphasise his size

'I Don't Know Nothing About No Rules'
Somebody Up There Likes Me (1956)

If Paul Newman's mumbling, shuffling performance as middleweight boxer Rocky Graziano is reminiscent of Marlon Brando's style of acting, it is more than a reflection of the zeitgeist. Brando, in preparing for *On the Waterfront* just two years earlier, also used Graziano as a model for his character. The similarity was to dog every contemporary review of *Somebody Up There Likes Me*, establishing Newman as a star (it was only his second film role) but measuring him against Brando rather than assessing his potential in his own right.[353] It was for this reason, perhaps, that such a tour-de-force in terms of performance missed out in the Oscar nominations, with the film's only Oscar being awarded to Joseph Ruttenberg for his atmospheric art direction and cinematography. By the time of *Somebody Up There Likes Me* Ruttenberg was a veteran of the business, having started in 1917 and been director of photography on a number of notable films including *The Philadelphia Story* (1940), *Dr Jekyll and Mr Hyde* (1941), *Mrs Miniver* (1942) and *Gaslight* (1944).

Despite the lush camera-work, good acting and sharp directing (from Robert Wise), this M-G-M film is hard to like: over-emphatic moral messages hamper the realism of Ernest Lehman's script and Rocky's willful wrong-headedness eventually becomes wearing. Ronald Bergan says the script 'makes every utterance sound like part of a thesis to prove that a man can fight his way out of the ghetto to share in the American Dream' and indeed, it is difficult at some points to remember that this is not a documentary about teenage delinquency.[354] As Leger Grindon points out, the film 'radiates an upbeat MGM sensibility in which every social problem has a solution'.[355] It is interesting to speculate how much of this 'documentary' style was imposed on Lehman by the studio: his many successful scripts include *Sweet Smell of Success* (1957) - for which he also wrote the novel - *North by Northwest* (1959), and *The Sound of Music* (1965) all of which display a lighter touch. In the end *Somebody Up There Likes Me* succeeds more as a homage to New York - arguably the real star of the movie, romanticised in dozens of shots - than it does as a tale of redemption.[356] Many of the scenes were filmed on location in the East Side, lending a necessary grittiness to the film which otherwise, given its somewhat mannered performances and copious amounts of dialogue, might have seemed too 'stagey', a fate that was to befall *The Man With the Golden Arm* (also 1956), despite its similar positioning as a shocking tale of realism. Critics were admiring of *Somebody Up There Likes Me*, which was billed as 'tougher than Blackboard Jungle', but found it unsettling to watch, *Kinematograph Weekly* commenting on how 'squalid and sordid' were the early parts and *Variety* finding Harold Stone's performance as Rocky's wine-sodden father 'almost uncomfortably real'.[357] They were clearly relieved when the film seemed to return to 'normal' Hollywood values and introduce a romantic interest for Graziano in the shape of Norma (Pier Angeli).

Somebody Up There Likes Me tells the story of Rocky Barbello - later to call himself Graziano ('like the wine') - in a linear fashion with no flashbacks, beginning with his childhood experiences and fading out on his moment of glory, a parade through the streets of the East Side as world middleweight champion. In other words, this is a straight biopic which, despite the emphasis on the dark side of Rocky's character, avoids the temptation of a confessional voiceover or any indication that the 'memories' we are seeing might be Rocky's own interpretation of events. Graziano was, as Romano points out, not the greatest middleweight of his era, but certainly the most appealing to filmmakers, who might have found '[Tony] Zale banal, [Jake] La Motta too stand-offish and [Sugar Ray] Robinson the wrong colour'.[358] The film begins with boxing, making the genre clear from the very start. Young Rocky, a puny child, is being forced to spar with his bullying father, failed fighter Nick, in their run-down East Side tenement. As Rocky runs away through the night-time streets - it is nearly always night in this film - two Irish policeman observe the 'little greaseball', confidently predicting that within ten years, he will be in Sing-Sing. Thus Rocky's fate is clearly mapped out for the audience: in contrast to many earlier Hollywood boxing films, however, his eventual triumph over his background will be a long time coming.

From this opening scene, the film now cuts to Rocky as an adult, but the continuity is clearly marked: it is still night and he is still running from the law, this time fresh out of prison. His tenement home is still dirty, his mother (Eileen Heckart) downtrodden, his father still raging, and fisticuffs are still the way to resolve disputes. The only thing that has changed is Rocky's ability to fight back, though the parallels between his 'angry young man' attitude and the defeated bitterness of his father prefigure what might become of him. He seems torn between cementing the ties of his family ('don't worry about a thing,' he frequently tells his mother with seemingly no trace of irony) and severing the only human contact he has ('why don't you give up on me?' he almost begs). This thrusting away of any help or support, together with an implacable hatred of any authority or social institution will become his central characteristic.

Even in this first short sequence, Newman's powerful interpretation of Graziano steals the scene (despite vigorous over-acting on the part of former stage performers Stone and Heckart as his parents). He is intensely mobile, arms waving, head moving, unable to stand still, as if he is already in the ring and is dancing to dodge an opponent. As Michael Kerber in his book on Newman observes, it is this perpetual motion which differentiates Newman's performance from the 'generally listless movement of Brando and Dean' even if his speech patterns are indistinguishable from theirs.[359] During the first half of the film, Rocky elicits no sympathy from the viewer, as he pursues a relentlessly self-destructive course, rampaging mindlessly through the streets with his friends, stealing tyres from cars, robbing a truck, fighting with rival gangs, and sleeping rough on a subway bench. At reform school, where he is sent to have his spirit broken ('we'll see whose spirit gets broken,' he replies), he wrecks his cell, throws his food on the floor and starts a fight with a guard while on ditch-digging duty. He comes within a hair's breadth of murder and of fulfilling the Sing-Sing future predicted for him. It is no better at the penitentiary, despite a sentimental promise to his mother that he will reform. Like all hoodlums, he displays an emotional attachment to his mother, but in this case the portrayal is more realistic than the undying loyalty typical of gangster pictures (such as that displayed by Cody Jarrett (Jimmy Cagney) and his mother in *White Heat* (1949)). Romano feels that that Newman 'expertly balanced' the display of the bad side of the character with a 'believable portrayal of Graziano as a decent, and at times even tender

Rocky pursues a relentlessly self-destructive course, even fighting with a guard while at reform school

individual, related through the fighter's relationships with his mother and wife'.[360] Ma Barbello, however, who has been in the mental hospital because of Rocky, does not always reciprocate this affection, making it clear she has reached the end of the line. 'I've tried to turn a leaf, but I can't make it,' is Rocky's response. 'Something inside me.'

Whatever it is inside him keeps on burning, as his drafting into the army - the only indication in the film that the country is at war - shows. He is contrasted in moralising fashion with other 'squares' who do not relish being drafted but declare their intention to do the best they can, while Rocky refuses to get out of bed, defies orders and fights his captain. By this time, as *Variety* observed, the audience is 'near to the point of hating him'. Rocky runs away from the army and back to New York, determined to find the money necessary for him to buy off the AWOL charge. Remembering a man called Frankie Peppo, who told him that boxing pays good money, he goes to Stillman's gym to see if he can get a 10-dollar fight. Bosley Crowther in the *New York Times* identifies the point where he steps into the ring as being the turning-point of the film: at this moment, Rocky is no longer the no-good hoodlum, but becomes 'a hot-head…a comic, a character', and it is at this moment that the sympathies of the audience probably begin to turn in his favour, sensing where his salvation will lie.[361] Other contemporary critics identify a more conventional turning-point (the entry of Norma into his life) but Crowther correctly cites this as merely reinforcing the direction in which Rocky's life is already heading.

The scene at Stillman's is a familiar one, the huge gym abuzz with conversation and with the spectacle of boxers working out. Learning that Peppo is in Sing-Sing on a '2 to10', Rocky nevertheless secures a sparring match, giving his name as Rocky Graziano. Despite the protective headgear, Rocky knocks out his opponent. Would-be manager Irving Cohen (Everett Sloane) sees the potential, but Rocky is only interested in the money: he'll fight, but he won't train - presumably because training smacks of a discipline which he has demonstrated he finds intolerable. Spotted in his second fight as being AWOL from the army, he is court-martialled and sent to Leavenworth. The scene in which a warder tries to recruit Rocky to the boxing squad is beautifully judged, the harsh lighting and deep shadows emphasising the importance of the decision he must make. It is also the first time that Rocky's chief character failing is identified as something that can be positively channelled: 'you've got something inside you that a lot of fighters don't have - hate,' says the warder. He begs Rocky to put this hate to good use, 'or maybe you'd rather just go on spitting in your own face the rest of your life.' Although the scene is, like much of the film, heavy on moral messages, it works well because Rocky does not answer the plea; the editing does it for him as the scene changes to another fight in the ring, and another win for Rocky. His subsequent successes are charted in the conventional way, through a series of knockout punches, posters heralding the next fight, and - again and again - Rocky's raised arm of victory. We do not see Rocky fight again until the end of the film, and the championship bout.

The humanising of Rocky is told through his romance with Norma, a friend of his sister's from a Jewish family. Initially awkward and as tongue-tied as a teenager (Newman was 32 when he played the part), he confesses that 'fighters ain't got much time for girls' but that through boxing he can 'be somebody'. Like all 'good girls' in the boxing-film genre, Norma does not like him fighting but accepts the necessity. Time is elided as the couple marry, have a baby girl (thus avoiding any indication

*The humanising of Rocky is told through his romance with Norma
(Pier Angeli)*

of fathering a child who will follow in Rocky's footsteps) and Rocky continues to notch up boxing successes. His career nearly comes to a sudden end when jailbird Peppo turns up with a blackmail threat about Rocky's past: if he'll take a dive in the next fight, Peppo will call it quits. Rocky refuses and calls off the fight, but even this seemingly moral stance proves wrong - because he did not report the bribe attempt, the NY State Athletic Commission revokes his licence. When told these are the rules, Rocky says: 'I don't know nothing about no rules', neatly summing up his philosophy of life. He is only saved by the internicene wars between states: Illinois does not see eye-to-eye with the New York authorities and allows him to go ahead with a challenge for the middleweight championship of the world against Tony Zale, the match which constitutes the climax of the film.

A final visit to his old stamping grounds in New York convinces Rocky that he is no longer the hoodlum he once was. The streets of the East Side at night now look scruffy and down-at-heel. Bums sleep on the pavement, couples have sex in doorways and garbage litters the streets. His old pal Ramolo (Sal Mineo) is the only one of his friends not in jail or gone to the electric chair - and it doesn't look as if it will be long before Ramolo will be joining them. Thin and ill, still thieving, his only wish is to get hold of a gun. When he says 'we ain't got a chance, guys like us, do we Rocky?', he does not realise he is bracketing himself with someone who no longer belongs. Even the jerk at Rocky's old soda fountain, delivering more ponderous moral messages, makes Rocky realise he can't just run away: 'You do something wrong, you gotta pay,' he tells the fighter. Just to set the seal on his new-found character, Rocky visits his father, overcoming an initial confrontation to achieve a reconciliation.

The stage is therefore set for the championship fight, which uses the time-honoured conventions (the excited crowd, the procession of round-numbers and the clanging of the bell) but is romanticised through cutaways to the empty night-time streets of the East Side where it seems the whole population has gathered in bar-rooms to hear the fight on the radio. The fight itself is imaginatively filmed with tracking shots following the boxers around the ring, and many punches given direct to camera.[362] Newman looks every inch the authentic fighter, thanks to training by veteran Johnny Indrisano. By round three, Rocky is punched to the floor and a cut over his eye is worsening; by round six, the clock moves so slowly that time seems to have been suspended. Rocky is still talking big, but this time matches his words with renewed vigour - or perhaps hate - and finally gets the better of Zale (Courtland Shepard) with a knockout punch. He's made it: world middleweight champion. But instead of lingering on the moments of his victory, the camera cuts to Rocky's triumphal parade in an open-top car through the crowded streets. It is finally daylight, indicating Rocky's emergence into a new world. As the car moves slowly forward, Rocky acknowledges to Norma that it won't always be this way but 'what I won they can't take away from me in no ring.' This is the scene that it used on the film's poster, the starry-eyed couple, surrounded by ticker-tape and by the outstretched hands of fans who are flinging their hats into the air, look upwards in optimism: a slogan painted across the starry backdrop reads 'a girl can lift a fellow to the skies!'

Had the film ended with this scene, the moral message might have been straightforward - Rocky has overcome his handicaps and changed for the better, the implication being - as Lawrence Quirk states in his Newman biography - 'if I can come out right, then so can you'.[363] But this message is diffused by a charming but curious last line: 'I've been lucky -

The championship fight against Tony Zale (Courtland Shepard) is imaginatively filmed with tracking shots following the boxers around the ring

somebody up there likes me,' says Rocky, thus shifting any responsibility or credit for individual achievement onto a more nebulous concept of luck, or perhaps divine intervention. This last line weakens the notion promoted so hard throughout the rest of the film that individuals can and should 'turn a leaf' by channelling their talents, though even this is not a particularly optimistic message as it presumably condemns the untalented to a life like Ramolo's. The film also seems to absolve society of any responsibility for this new, disenfranchised generation who are instead being encouraged to claw their own way up. *Motion Picture Herald* had no problem with the concept of talent plus a large dose of fate being the only way out of a desperate situation. They saw the bleakness of the film lying more in the notion that 'nothing will curb a life of wanton violence quite as well as a certain amount of material wealth and personal adulation'.[364]

298 This may have led *Motion Picture Herald* to comment - inaccurately - that some of the Mexicans portrayed in the film are 'the shiftless, lazy kind, the stereotype which is responsible for much anti-Mexican feeling'. *Motion Picture Herald*, 30 Aug 1952 p1150

299 Grindon 2014 p9

300 The Gomez home, where Lucy lives, is also in the neighbourhood but Lucy's father's slightly condescending attitude to Tommy when he calls at the house, is indicative that they regard themselves as a better class than Tommy's family. When he visits Lucy, her parents send in the grandmother to chaperone the visit: grandmother (Soledad Jimenez who played Nick Donati's mother in *Kid Galahad*) speaks only in Spanish and wears an ankle length dress more redolent of the nineteenth century than the 1950s

301 Baker 2006 p73

302 The change of heart by the policeman was a requirement of the Production Code Administration

303 *Variety*, 20 Aug 1952; *Monthly Film Bulletin* no 232 April 1953

304 Shulman 2000 p194

305 Shulman 2000 p61

306 Shulman 2000, p107

307 Grindon 2014 p110 and p112

308 At 80-minutes it was longer than the usual format for a B-movie, and though it was exhibited as a second feature, Nimoy remembers it being on the bill with some prestigious films including *Rancho Notorious* and *Singing in the Rain* (DVD audio commentary)

309 The fact that both these films, together with *Kid Monk Baroni*, had 'ape' themes will be discussed below

310 Just one scene was filmed on location in downtown Los Angeles: the steps that lead up to St Dominic's church

311 DVD audio commentary

312 Boxer and priest relationships are common throughout the genre, perhaps trying to encapsulate a 'body vs soul' approach. For example, in *Boys' Town* (1938) Father Flanagan (Spencer Tracy) persuades the delinquents in his school to settle their differences in the ring; *On the Waterfront* (1955) features ex-fighters Terry Malloy and Father Barry; *The Bells of St Mary's* stars Bing Crosby as a boxing priest, Father O'Malley; and *The Big Punch* (1948) has boxer Wayne Morris leaving the ring to enter the church

[313] A similar plotline was used in the James Cagney film *Winner Take All* (1932) in which, anxious to please what Kasia Boddy calls 'a heartless society dame' he rushes off to a plastic surgeon to fix his broken nose and cauliflower ear. She then rejects him because he is now just 'ordinary' and the crowd don't like his new defensive style of boxing aimed at protecting his face (Boddy 2008 p262)

[314] *Variety* 23 Apr 1952; *Kinematograph Weekly* 30 Oct 1952 p25

[315] *Today's Cinema* 24 Oct 1952 p12; *Variety* 23 Apr 1952

[316] Kopple, DVD liner notes

[317] Mark Duguid in Ealing Studios history at BFI screenonline

[318] *The Square Ring* pressbook. It is interesting that the main poster slogan did not mention boxing, but the other nine slogans suggested to promoters all contained the words 'boxing', 'fighting' or 'sport'

[319] *To-day's Cinema* Jun 29 1953

[320] *Monthly Film Bulletin* 1953 p120

[321] Kirkham and Thumim 1997 p98

[322] *The Square Ring* pressbook

[323] Gledhill, unpublished seminar paper 2004

[324] *The Square Ring* pressbook

[325] Kirkham and Thumim 1997 p98

[326] Joe Louis had previously appeared as 'Joe Thomas' in the low-budget picture *Spirit of Youth* (1938) which the Production Code Administration said would be difficult to show in the southern states of the US because it showed a black fighter beating white boxers

[327] Paul Stewart also appeared in *Champion*, as Tommy Haley

[328] Grindon 2011 p55

[329] The contrast between fighting and musicianship (body vs soul) appears in many other boxing films. When Louis leaves his first gym session, it is symbolic that forgets to take his violin with him: he has already made his choice

[330] Wallace would go on to appear as Joe Louis in other boxing films: *Marciano* (1979) and *Raging Bull* (1980)

[331] Romano 2004 p101-102

[332] Studio promotion claims that more than three thousand women applied for the role of Marva before the producers 'gave up in despair and did what they had wanted to do in the first place - cabled Hilda Simms to come home from Paris to do the job', according to the pressbook. This is interesting because, although Hilda Simms was a member of the American Negro Theater, playing the lead in the acclaimed *Anna Lucasta*, she had never appeared in a film before. She was in Paris because the play was touring there - and she was also singing in Parisian nightclubs

[333] Romano 2004 p101-102

[334] *The Joe Louis Story* pressbook

[335] *Film Daily* Oct 5 1953 p6

[336] *Kinematograph Weekly* Dec 10 1953 p15

[337] *Variety* Jan 1 1953

[338] article no longer on Internet

[339] *The Times* Apr 6 1956; *Monthly Film Bulletin* 1956 p56

[340] *The Cinema* April 1946 p10

[341] Krutnik 1991 p213

[342] In his novel, Budd Schulberg based the character on Harold Conrad, a journalist and publicist who campaigned for a clean-up of the fight game over many years

[343] Schulberg 1996 pvii

[344] McArthur 1972 p32

[345] Romano 2004 p83

[346] *The Times* Apr 6 1956

[347] Bergan 1982 p35

[348] This is akin to Charley's oft-repeated remark in *Body and Soul* (1947): 'everybody dies'

[349] Schulberg 1996 p74 and 203

[350] This was not just a Hollywood device: Primo Carnera's nickname in the ring was The Ambling Ape

[351] Schulberg 1996 p73

[352] Toro crosses himself before every fight and before the championship, he kneels in the dressing room and prays

[353] James Dean was said to be lined up to play Graziano. He was already scheduled to star in another Robert Wise production, a TV film based on Hemingway's story 'The Battler', but was killed in a car crash in September 1955 before he could fulfill either role. Newman took the role in both productions

[354] Bergan 1982 p34

[355] Grindon 2011 p176

[356] The city even got equal billing on some of the suggested catchlines for promoters: 'the story of a bad boy...a good girl...and the heart of a city' (*Somebody Up There Likes Me* pressbook)

[357] *Kinematograph Weekly* Oct 25 1956; *Variety* Jul 4 1956; *Somebody Up There Likes Me* pressbook. *Blackboard Jungle*, the story of a teacher in an inner-city school, was released the previous year

[358] Romano 2004 p185

[359] Kerbel 1975 p30

[360] Romano 2004 p185

[361] *New York Times* Jul 24 1956

[362] Leger Grindon notes that seventy-four of the ninety-nine shots of boxing are filmed from inside the ring rather than from the ringside (Grindon 2011 p174)

[363] Quirk 1971 p45

[364] *Motion Picture Herald* Jul 7 1956

BIBLIOGRAPHY OF WORKS CITED

Books:

Algren, Nelson, *Never Come Morning*, Fourth Estate 1988

Altman, Rick, *Film/Genre*, BFI 1999

Atwan, Robert and Bruce Forer (eds), *Bedside Hollywood*, Robinson Publishing 1986

Baker, Aaron, *Contesting Identities: Sports in American Film*, University of Illinois 2006

Barr, Charles, *Ealing Studios*, David and Charles 1997

Bergan, Ronald, *Sports in the Movies*, Proteus 1982

Bernstein, Walter, *Inside Out - A Memoir of the Blacklist*, Alfred Knopf 1996

Blum, Daniel, *A Pictorial History of the Talkies*, Spring Books 1964

Boddy, Kasia, *Boxing: A Cultural History*, Reaktion 2008

Brooke-Ball, Peter, *Boxing: an Illustrated History of the Fight Game*, Hermes House 2000

Buhle, Paul and Wagner, Dave, *A Very Dangerous Citizen - Abraham Lincoln Polonsky and the Hollywood Left*, University of California Press 2001

Cagney, James, *Cagney by Cagney*, Doubleday 1976

Cahn, William, *Harold Lloyd's World of Comedy*, Allen and Unwin 1966

Cohan, Steve and Hark, Ina Rae, *Screening the Male*, Routledge 1993

Cohan, Steve, *Masked Men - Masculinity and the Movies in the Fifties*, Indiana University Press 1997

Cook, Christopher (ed), *The Dilys Powell Reader*, Carcanet 1991

Cripps, Thomas, *Hollywood's High Noon*, John Hopkins University 1997

Christopher, Nicholas, *Somewhere in the Night*, Henry Holt and Co 1997

Curtis, James, *There Ain't No Justice*, London Books 2014

Douglas, Kirk, *Let's Face It*, John Wiley 2007

Dyer, Richard, *White*, Routledge 1992

Eames, John Douglas, *The MGM Story*, Octopus 1979

Etling, Laurence, *Radio in the Movies: A History and Filmography*, McFarland 2011

Fernett, Gene, *American Film Studios: an Historical Encyclopaedia*, McFarland 1988

Gledhill, Christine, 'Women Reading Men' in Kirkham and Thumim (eds), *Me Jane*, Lawrence and Wishart 1995

Grindon, Leger, *Knockout: the Boxer and Boxing in American Cinema*, University Press of Mississippi 2011

Hands, Stuart, 'Body and Soul' in *CineAction*, 22 December 2010

Hansen, Miriam, *Babel and Babylon*, Harvard 1991

Hanson, Patricia (ed), *American Film Institute Catalogs*, University of California Press 1993

Hazlitt, William, 'The Fight' in Essays, University Tutorial Press 1927

Jones, G William, *Black Cinema Treasures*, University of North Texas Press 1991

Kandel, Aben, *City for Conquest*, Routledge 2017

Kennedy, Paul F, *Billy Conn: The Pittsburgh Kid*, AuthorHouse 2007

Kerbel, Michael, *Paul Newman*, W H Allen 1975

Kirkham, Pat and Thumim, Janet, 'Men at Work: Deardon and Gender' in Burton, O'Sullivan,Wells (eds), *Basil Deardon and Postwar British Film Culture*, Flicks 1997

Krutnik, Frank, *In A Lonely Street - Film Noir, Genre, Masculinity*, Routledge 1991

Krutnik, Frank, 'Something More Than Night' in David Clarke (ed), The Cinematic City, Routledge 1997

Lacey, Nick, *Narrative and Genre: Key Concepts in Media Studies*, Macmillan 2000

Landy, Marcia, *British Genres*, Princeton 1991

Loukides, Paul and Fuller, Linda K (Eds), *Beyond the Stars Vol 4: Locales in American Popular Film*, Bowling Green University Popular Press 1993

McArthur, Colin, *Underworld USA*, Secker and Warburg 1972

McCabe, John, *Cagney*, Knopf 1997

McGrath, Patrick, *John Garfield - The Illustrated Career in Films and on Stage*, McFarland and Co 1993

Mailer, Norman, *Fight,* Penguin 1991

Maltby, Richard, *Harmless Entertainment - Hollywood and the Ideology of*

Consensus, Scarecrow Press 1983

March, James Moncure, *The Set Up*, Martin Secker 1929

Mellon, Joan, *Big Bad Wolves - Masculinity in the American Film*, Elmtree 1977

Millhauser, Bertram, and Dix, Beulah Marie, Hot Leather, Bantam 1948

Mullan, Harry, *Ring Wars - A Pictorial History of Boxing*, Parragon 1997

Neale, Steve, *Genre and Hollywood*, Routledge 2000

Neve, Brian, *Film and Politics in America: A Social Tradition*, Taylor and Francis 2005

Oates, Joyce Carol, *On Boxing*, Bloomsbury 1987

Parkinson, David (ed), *Mornings in the Dark - the Graham Greene Reader*, Carcanet 1993

Perry, George, *The Great British Picture Show*, Pavilion 1985

Quirk, Lawrence, *The Films of Paul Newman*, Citadel Press 1971

Rainsberger, Todd, *James Wong Howe, Cinematographer*, A S Barnes 1981

Rode, Alan K, *Michael Curtiz: A Life in Film*, University of Kentucky Press, Lexington 2017

Romano, Frederick, *The Boxing Filmography*, McFarland 2004

Sampson, Henry T, *Blacks in Black and White*, Scarecrow 1995

Sarris, Andrew, *You Ain't Heard Nothing Yet*, Oxford University Press 1998

Schatz, Thomas, *Hollywood Genres*, Random House 1981

Schulberg, Bud, *The Harder They Fall*, Chicago, Elephant Paparbacks 1996

Schulman, Irving, *The Square Trap*, iUniverse 2000

Schultheiss, John, *Body and Soul - The Critical Edition*, California State University 2002

Sklar, Robert, *Movie-Made America*, Vintage 1994

Sklar, Robert, *City Boys: Cagney, Bogart, Garfield*, Princeton 1992

Swindell, Larry, *Body and Soul: The Story of John Garfield*, William Morrow and Co 1975

Tasker, Yvonne, *Spectacular Bodies*, Routledge 1993

Turim, Maureen, *Flashbacks in Film*, Routledge 1989

Williams, Tony, 'Movies and the Enemy Within' in Winston Dixon Wheeler (ed) *American Cinemas of the 1940s*, Berg 2006

Wood, Michael, *America in the Movies*, Columbia 1989

Wright, Basil, *The Long View*, Secker and Warburg 1974

Zucker, Harvey Marc and Babich, Lawrence, *Sports Films: A Complete Reference*, McFarland 1987

Academic journals:

American Classic Screen:

Keenan, Richard, 'Fight Films Go to Court', v2n6 July/Aug 1978

Parker, Jeff, 'Joe Palooka from Ringside', v7n4 July/Aug 1983

Welsh, J M, 'Knockout in Paradise', v2n6 July/Aug 1978

CineAction:

Hands, Stuart, 'Body and Soul', 22 December 2010

Cinema Journal:

Grindon, Leger, 'Body and Soul: Structure of Meaning in the Boxing Film Genre', v35n4 1996

Journal of Sport and Social Issues:

Grindon, Leger, 'Getting into Shape: Classic Conventions Make Their Move into the Boxing Film 1937-1940', v22n4 1998

Labour:

Wayne, Mike, 'A Very Dangerous Citizen - Abraham Lincoln Polonsky and the Hollywood Left' (book review), Fall 2004 pp314-315

Quarterly Review of Film and Video:

Williams, Tony, 'I Could Have Been a Contender: the Boxing Movie's Generic Instability', v18n3 2001

The Hudson Review:

Hunter, Jefferson, 'Joseph Moncure March: Poem Noir Becomes Prizefight Film', Summer 2008

FILMOGRAPHY
FILMS DISCUSSED IN THE BOOK

Palooka (1934)

Reliance. Director Benjamin Stoloff; producer Edward Small; screenplay Jack Jevne, Arthur Kober and Gertrude Purcell; based on comic strip by Ham Fisher; director of photography Arthur Edeson; editor Grant Whytock; art director Albert D'Agostino; music Joseph Burke and Burton Lane. Running time: 86 minutes. Cast includes: Jimmy Durante (Knobby Walsh), Lupe Velez (Nina), Stuart Erwin (Joe Palooka), Marjorie Rambeau (Mayme), Robert Armstrong (Pete Palooka), Mary Carlisle (Anne), William Cagney (Al McSwatt)

Country boy Joe Palooka is signed up to be a fighter when trainer Knobby Walsh sees him swing a punch in a dispute. Fixed fights lead him to a match with champion Al McSwatt, who is so drunk that Joe wins. Seduced by easy money and glamorous women, Joe loses a rematch, quits boxing and returns to the country to marry his sweetheart.

The Milky Way (1936)

Paramount. Director Leo McCarey; producer E Lloyd Sheldon and Adolph Zukor; screenplay Lynn Root, Harry Clork, Grover Jones, Frank Butler and Richard Connell; adapted from play by Lynn Root and Harry Clork; director of photography Alfred Gilks; editor LeRoy Stone; music Tom Satterfield and Victor Young. Running time: 89 minutes. Cast includes: Harold Lloyd (Burleigh Sullivan), Adolphe Menjou (Garry Sloan), Verree Teasdale (Ann Westley), Helen Mack (Mae Sullivan), William Gargan (Speed McFarland), George Barbier (Wilbur), Dorothy Wilson (Polly), Lionel Stander (Spider), Charles Lane (Willard)

Milkman Burleigh Sullivan is mistakenly believed to have floored the champion, Speed McFarland, in a dispute and is groomed as a boxer despite his weedy stature and inability to fight. In challenging McFarland's title, Sullivan wins because McFarland has been drugged. He returns to the dairy to become a partner, having discovered a talent for self-promotion.

Kid Galahad (1937)

Warner Brothers. Director Michael Curtiz; executive producers Hal Wallis, Jack Warner and Samuel Bischoff ; screenplay Seton I Miller; adapted from the *Saturday Evening Post* story by Francis Wallce; director of photography Tony Gaudio; editor George Amy; art director Carl Jules Weyl; music Max Steiner and Heinz Roemheld. Running time: 102 minutes. Cast includes: Edward G Robinson (Nick Donati), Bette Davis (Fluff), Humphrey Bogart (Turkey Morgan), Wayne Morris (Ward Guisenberry/Kid Galahad)

Boxing promoter Nick Donati signs up Ward Guisenberry, a bellhop, when he sees him punch the current heavyweight champ in an argument over a woman. Ward wins all his fights on a knockout but is dragged into a dispute between Nick and rival promoter Turkey Morgan which eventually ends in a shootout. Both promoters die shortly after Ward wins the heavyweight title.

They Made Me a Criminal (1939)

Warner Brothers. Director Busby Berkeley; executive producers Benjamin Glazer and Hal B Wallis; screenplay Sig Herzig; adapted from novel (*The Life of Jimmy Dolan*) and play (*Sucker*) by Bertram Millhauser and Beulah Marie Dix; director of photography James Wong Howe; editor Jack Killifer; art director Anton Grot; music Max Steiner. Running time: 92 minutes. Cast includes: John Garfield (Johnnie Bradfield), The Dead End Kids, Claude Rains (Phelan), Ann Sheridan (Goldie), May Robson (Grandma Rafferty), Gloria Dickson (Peggy), Robert Gleckler (Doc), Frank Riggi (Gaspar Rutchek)

Hard-drinking, womanising, amoral boxer Johnnie Bradfield goes on the run when he is mistakenly thought to have murdered a journalist at a post-match party. Bradfield takes refuge at a date farm, where he attempts to seduce Peggy, and befriends a gang of New York kids sent to the farm to reform. Tracked by policeman Phelan, Bradfield is forced to change his distinctive southpaw boxing style in order to escape capture. Phelan arrests him nevertheless, but lets him go at the last moment.

Kid Nightingale (1939)

Warner Brothers. Director George Amy; producer Bryan Foy; screenplay Charles Beldon, Lee Katz and Raymond Schrock; director of photography Arthur Edeson; editor Frederick Richards; art director Ted Smith; music Howard Jackson, MK Jerome, Bert Reisfeld and Jack Scholl. Running time: 57 minutes. Cast includes: John Payne (Steve Nelson), Jane Wyman (Judy Craig), Walter Catlett (Skip Davis), Ed Brophy (Mike Jordan), Charles D Brown (Paxton), Max Hoffman (Fitts), John Ridgely (Whitey), Harry Burns (Strangler Columbo/Rudolfo Terrassi), William Haade (Rocky)

Singing waiter Steve Nelson impresses boxing manager Skip Davis when he punches an unruly customer in a restaurant. He's signed up by Skip and acquires an ardent female following because of his good looks and his tendency to burst into song in the boxing ring, but he never loses sight of his real ambition - to become a professional opera singer.

There Ain't No Justice (1939)

Capad, UK. Director Penrose Tennyson; producer Sergei Nolbandov; screenplay James Curtis, Sergei Nolbandov and Pen Tennyson; adapted from novel by James Curtis; director of photography Mutz Greenbaum; editor Ray Pitt. music Ernest Irving. Running time: 83 minutes. Cast includes: Jimmy Hanley (Tommy Mutch), Edward Rigby (Pa Mutch), Mary Clare (Ma Mutch), Phyllis Stanley (Elsie Mutch), Edward Chapman (Sammy Sanders), Jill Furse (Connie Fletcher), Richard Ainley (Billy Frist), Gus McNaughton (Alfie Norton), Sue Gawthorne (Mrs Frost), Michael Hogart (Frank Fox), Michael Wilding (Len Charteris)

Garage mechanic and small-time boxer Tommy Mutch signs up with promoter Sammy Sanders who promises Tommy well-paying matches: he needs the money to help out his sister, whose boyfriend has stolen money from the milk bar where she works. Tommy's pride in winning a series of bouts is dented when he discovers that the matches were fixed: he has been duped by Sanders, is expected to take a fall but decides to defy him.

Golden Boy (1939)

Columbia. Director Rouben Mamoulian; producers Rouben Mamoulian and William Perlberg; screenplay Lewis Melzer, Daniel Taradash, Sarah Y Mason and Victor Heerman; adapted from play by Clifford Odets; directors of photography Karl Freund and Nick Musuraca; editor Otto Meyer; music Victor Young; fight adviser Abe Roth. Running time: 99 minutes. Cast includes: William Holden (Joe Bonaparte), Barbara Stanwyck (Lorna Moon), Adolphe Menjou (Tom Moody), Lee J Cobb (Mr Bonaparte), Joseph Calleia (Eddie Fuseli), Sam Levene (Siggie), Edward S Brody (Roxy Lewis), Beatrice Blinn (Anna)

Joe Bonaparte would like to fulfill his family's wish that he play the violin professionally, but finds that boxing for money offers a faster way to get rich. Joe is corrupted by a gangster, kills an opponent in the ring, breaking his hand in the process, and returns chastened to the bosom of his family.

City for Conquest (1940)

Warner Brothers. Director and producer Anatole Litvak; associate producer William Cagney; screenplay John Wexley; adapted from novel by Aben Kandel; directors of photography James Wong Howe and Sol Polito; editor William Holmes; art director Robert Haas; music Max Steiner. Running time: 104 minutes. Cast includes: James Cagney (Danny Kenny), Ann Sheridan (Peggy Nash), Arthur Kennedy (Eddie Kenny), Frank Craven (Old Timer), Donald Crisp (Scotty MacPherson), Frank McHugh (Mutt), George Tobias (Pinky), Anthony Quinn (Murray Burns)

Truck-driver Danny Kenny only takes up professional boxing in order to get enough money to put his brother Eddie, a talented composer, through music school. His ties are to his family and the neighbourhood, but his childhood sweetheart Peggy is burning with ambition to become a top dancer.

The Pittsburgh Kid (1941)

Republic. Director Jack Townley; associate producer Armand Schaefer; screenplay Houston Branch and Earl Felton; adapted from novel *Kid Tinsel* by Octaius Roy Cohen; director of photography Reggie Lanning; editor

Ernest J Nims; art director John Victor Mackay; music Ross Di Maggio, Cy Feuer, Mort Glickman and Paul Sawtell. Running time: 76 minutes. Cast includes: Billy Conn (as himself), Jean Parker (Pat Mallory), Dick Purcell (Cliff Halliday), Alan Baxter (Joe Barton), Veda Ann Borg (Barbara Ellison), Jonathan Hale (Max Ellison), John Harmon (Morrie)

When heavyweight fighter Billy Conn's manager dies, his daughter Pat takes over. With the aid of reporter Cliff Halliday, she grooms Conn for the championship while trying to steer him away from predatory females.

Ringside Maisie (1941)
Loews. Director Edwin L Marin; producer J Walter Ruben; screenplay Wilson Collison and Mary C McCall Jr; director of photography Charles Lawton; editor Frederick Y Smith; art director Cedric Gibbons; music David Snell. Running time: 95 minutes. Cast includes: Ann Sothern (Maisie Ravier), George Murphy (Skeets Maguire), Robert Sterling (Young O'Hara), Virginia O'Brien (as herself), Natalie Thompson (Cissy), Margaret Moffatt (Mrs Dolan), Jack La Rue (Ricky Du Prez)

En route to a dancing engagement at the Cedar Lawns Hotel, Brooklyn girl Maisie Revere bumps into Young O'Hara, an up-and-coming fighter, and becomes his confidante and right-hand-girl, falling in love along the way with his manager, Skeets Maguire.

Gentleman Jim (1942)
Warner Brothers. Director Raoul Walsh; producer Robert Buckner; screenplay Vincent Lawrence, and Horace McCoy; adapted from novel *The Roar of the Crowd* by James Corbett; director of photography Sidney Hickox; editor Jack Killifer; art director Ted Smith; music Heinz Roemheld; fight adviser Mushy Callahan; boxing doubles Ed Lewis (for Ward Bond) and Freddie Steele (for Errol Flynn). Running time: 104 minutes. Cast includes: Errol Flynn (Jim Corbett), Alexis Smith (Victoria Ware), Jack Carson (Walter Lowrie), Alan Hale (Pat Corbett), John Loder (Carlton De Witt), William Frawley (Billy Delaney), Ward Bond (John L Sullivan), Madeleine LeBeau (Anna Held), Rhys Williams (Harry Watson), Dorothy Vaughan (Ma Corbett), Wallis Clark (Judge Geary), Sammy Stein (Joe Choynski)

Jim Corbett wants to rise above his Irish origins to become a gentleman, so uses his boxing prowess to ingratiate himself with nineteenth century San Francisco society and in particular with the atractive Victoria Ware. His arrogance and pretensions annoy Nob Hill, but he rises to become champion, defeating John L Sullivan.

Body and Soul (1947)

Enterprise Productions. Director Robert Rossen; producer Bob Roberts; screenplay Abraham Polonsky; director of photography James Wong Howe; editors Francis D Lyon and Robert Parrish; art director Nathan Juran; music Hugo Friedhofer; fight adviser John Indrisano. Running time: 108 minutes. Cast includes: John Garfield (Charley Davis), Lilli Palmer (Peg), Hazel Brooks (Alice), William Conrad (Quinn), Anne Revere (Anna), Lloyd Gough (billed as Lloyd Goff) (Roberts), Canada Lee (Ben Chaplin)

Against the wishes of his mother, Charley Davis takes up boxing as a way of escaping from the East Side and earning big money, but though revered by his old neighbourhood, he is corrupted by booze, women and easy living, and is manipulated by his manager, the sinister Roberts.

The Set-Up (1949)

RKO. Director Robert Wise; producer Richard Goldstone; screenplay Art Cohn; adapted from poem by James Moncure March; director of photography Milton Krasner; editor Roland Gross; art directors Albert D'Agostino and Jack Okey; fight adviser John Indrisano. Running time: 72 minutes. Cast includes: Robert Ryan (Stoker), Audrey Totter (Julie), George Tobias (Tiny), Alan Baxter (Little Boy), Hal Baylor (Tiger Nelson)

Stoker Thompson is an aging boxer who would rather be running a cigarstand with his wife Julie, but is always 'one punch away' from having enough money to retire. In Paradise City, he wins his fight, unaware that he was supposed to take a dive, and so falls foul of local gangster Little Boy.

Champion (1949)

Screenplays Corp. Director Mark Robson; producers Stanley Krame and Robert Stillman (associate); screenplay Carl Foreman; adapted from short story by Ring Lardner; director of photography Frank Planer; editor Harry Gerstad; art director Rudolph Sternad; music Goldie Goldmark and Dimitri Tiomkin; fight adviser Mushy Callahan. Running time: 99 minutes. Cast includes: Kirk Douglas (Midge Kelly), Marilyn Maxwell (Grace), Arthur Kennedy (Connie Kelly), Paul Stewart (Tommy Haley), Ruth Roman (Emma), Lola Albright (Palmer), Luis Van Rooten (Jerry Harris), John Day (Johnnie Dunne)

Tired of being pushed around, jobless Midge Kelly - always handy with his fists - becomes a successful boxer, but sells his soul in his quest for recognition, money and women. In his rise to champion, he betrays everyone he loves, including his wife, his manager, and his brother Connie.

The Ring (1952)

King Brothers Productions. Director Kurt Neumann; producers Frank, Morris and Herman King; screenplay Irving Schulman; adapted from the novel *The Square Trap* by Irving Shulman; director of photography Russell Harlan; editor Bruce B Pierce; art director Theobold Holsopple; music Herschel Burke Gilbert. Running time: 79 minutes. Cast includes: Lalo Rios (Tomas Cantanios/Tommy Kansas), Rita Moreno (Lucy Gomez), Gerald Mohr (Pete Ganusa)

Young Mexican-American Tommy Cantanios, tired of the prejudice he and his friends face in Los Angeles, and wanting to earn money for his family, becomes a professional boxer under the name of Tommy Kansas. But while Anglo-Americans admire his skill, he still remains an outsider - a 'Pachuco'. He pushes himself to fight more challenging matches but finds himself outclassed. After he is knocked out in the second round of a main event, he decides to never fight again.

Kid Monk Baroni (1952)

Jack Broder Productions. Director Harold Schuster; producers Jack Broder and Herman Cohen; screenplay Aben Kandel; director of photography Charles Van Enger; editor Jason Bernie; art director James Sullivan; music Herschel Burke Gilbert. Running time: 79 minutes. Cast includes: Leonard Nimoy (Paul 'Monk' Baroni), Bruce Cabot (Mr Hellman), Richard Robert (Father Callahan), Allene Roberts (Emily Brooks), Mona Knox (June Travers), Jack Larson (Angelo)

Baroni is a street kid nicknamed 'Monk' because of his facial disfigurement. He is taught boxing by Father Callahan, a priest, enters amateur bouts, pays for surgery on his face and becomes arrogant. He carries on fighting to settle his unpaid debts. Betting syndicates have relied on Monk's use of dirty tactics and resent it when Monk decides to fight cleanly: in a match against the Wildcat, Monk is knocked out ... and the syndicate lose $20,000.

The Square Ring (1953)

Ealing Studios. Director Basil Dearden; producers Michael Balcon, Michael Relph and Basil Dearden; screenplay Robert Westerby; adapted from the play by Ralph W Peterson; director of photography Otto Heller; editor Peter Bazencenet; art director Jim Morahan; music Dock Mathieson; costumes Anthony Mendleson; fight adviser Dave Crowley. Running time: 83 minutes. Cast includes: Jack Warner (Danny Felton), Robert Beatty (Kid Curtis), Bill Owen (Happy Burns), Maxwell Reed (Rick Martell), George Rose (Whitey Johnson), Bill Travers (Rowdie Rawlings), Alfie Bass (Frank Forbes), Joan Collins (Frankie), Kay Kendall (Eve)

A 'portmanteau' story set in the dressing room of a seedy London boxing stadium, where boxers wait to be called: a former champion making a come-back, an amateur stepping up to professional fighting; a fighter being paid to throw a fight; a chirpy flyweight on a winning streak; a punch-drunk old hand; and a simple-minded heavyweight. The evening ends in the death of the former champion at the hands of gangsters.

The Joe Louis Story (1953)

Walter P Chrysler Jnr/United Artists. Director Robert Gordon; producer Stirling Silliphant; screenplay Robert Sylvester; director of photography Joseph Brun; editor Dave Kummins; art director Robert Gundlach; music George Bassman (conductor); costumes Florence Transfield; fight adviser Mannie Seaman. Running time: 88 minutes. Cast includes: Coley Wallace (Joe Louis), Paul Stewart (Tad McGeehan), James Edwards (Chappie Blackburn), John Marley (Mannie Seamon), Hilda Simms (Marva Louis), Dots Johnson (Julian Black)

Biopic about black fighter Joe Louis who as a teenager gives up the violin in favour of boxing, goes professional and chalks up a string of victories to become heavyweight champion of the world. The 'Brown Bomber' lives the high life and, after wartime service, returns to find a mountain of debts which forces him back into boxing. Against advice, he insists on 'one last fight' and loses to Rocky Marciano.

The Harder They Fall (1956)

Columbia. Director Mark Robson; producer Philip Yordan; screenplay Philip Yordan from the novel by Budd Schulberg; director of photography Burnett Guffey; editor Jerome Thoms; art director William Flannery; music Hugo Friedhofer; fight adviser John Indrisano. Running time: 109 minutes. Cast includes: Humphrey Bogart (Eddie Willis), Rod Steiger (Nick Benko), Mike Lane (Toro Moreno), Jan Sterling (Beth Willis), Max Baer (Buddy Brannen), Jersey Joe Walcott (George)

Unemployed sportswriter Eddie Willis is hired by a corrupt boxing promoter to promote a few find: Toro Moreno. But Moreno can't fight and all his bouts will be fixed, right up until a fight against heavyweight champion Buddy Brannen, which will net Eddie and the promoter a lot of money. Moreno is cheated throughout of his fight money and of the knowledge that all his fights were rigged. Eddie tells him just before the championship, not wanting Toro to take a beating. Toro refuses to throw the fight but eventually loses.

Somebody Up There Likes Me (1956)

M-G-M. Director Robert Wise; producer Charles Schnee; screenplay Ernest Lehman from Rocky Graziano's autobiography; director of photography Joseph Ruttenberg; editor Albert Akst; art director Malcolm Brown and Cedric Gibbons; music Bronislau Kaper; fight adviser John Indrisano. Running time: 103 minutes. Cast includes: Paul Newman (Rocky), Pier Angeli (Norma), Everett Sloane (Irving Cohen), Eileen Heckart (Ma Barbella), Sal Mineo (Romolo), Harold J Stone (Nick Barbella)

Based on the life of Rocky Graziano. Young Rocky Barbella is a quick-tempered petty criminal, averse to following rules, whether that be in prison or in the army, from which he receives a dishonourable discharge. He becomes a boxer, marries, and rises to the top, but is blackmailed into throwing a fight. By faking injury, he avoids the fight altogether, refuses to name the blackmailer and has his licence suspended. His manager arranges a fight in Chicago against middleweight champion Tony Zale. Rocky wins.

FILMOGRAPHY
BOXING FILMS MADE 1930-1959

1930

Be Yourself!, dir. Thornton Freeland, United Artists, US
The Big Fight, dir. Walter Long, Sono Art, US
Dumbells in Ermine, dir. John G Adolfi, Warner Bros, US
Hold Everything, dir. Roy Del Ruth, Warner Bros, US
The Leather Pushers, dir. Albert Kelley, Universal, US
Love in the Ring, dir. Reinhold Schunzel, Terra Filmkunst, Germany

1931

The Champ, dir. King Vidor, M-G-M, US
City Lights, dir. Charles Chaplin, Charles Chaplin Corp, US
Iron Man, dir. Tod Browning, Universal, US

1932

The Big Timer, dir. Edward Buzzell, Columbia, US
The Fighting Gentleman, dir. Fred Newmeyer, Freuler Films, US
The Heart Punch, dir. Reeves Eason, Mayfair, US
Lady and Gent, dir. Stephen Roberts, Paramount, US
Madison Square Garden, dir. Harry Joe Brown, Paramount, US
Society Girl, dir. Sidney Lanfield, Fox Film Corp, US
Steady Company, dir. Edward Ludwig, Universal, US
They Never Come Back, dir. Fred C Newmeyer, Supreme Pictures, US
The Third String, dir. George Pearson, Welsh-Pearson, UK
Winner Take All, dir. Roy Del Ruth, Warner Bros, US

1933

The Bermondsey Kid, dir. Ralph Dawson, First National, UK
The Big Chance, dir. Albert Herman, Eagle Pictures, US
King for a Night, dir. Kurt Neumann, Universal, US
The Life of Jimmy Dolan, dir. Archie Mayo, Warner Bros, US
Mickey's Mechanical Man (animation), dir. Wilfred Jackson, Disney, US
The Prizefighter and the Lady, dir. W S Van Dyke, M-G-M, US

1934

Jealousy, dir. William Neill, Columbia, US
Let's You and Him Fight (animation), dir. Dave Fleischer, Paramount, US
Mannequin, dir. George Cooper, Twickenham Film Studios, UK
Palooka, dir. Ben Stoloff, Reliance, US
The Personality Kid, dir. Alan Crosland, First National, US
Punch Drunks, dir. Lou Breslow, Columbia, US
Toboggan, dir. Henri Decoin, Gaumont Franco, France

1935

Cock o' the Walk (animation), dir. Ben Sharpsteen, Disney, US
The Country Mouse (animation), dir. Friz Freleng, Warner Bros, US
The Irish in Us, dir. Lloyd Bacon, Warner Bros, US
Mickey's Kangaroo (animation), dir. David Hand, Disney, US
What Price Crime, dir. Albert Harman, Beacon, US

1936

Born to Fight, dir. Charles Hutchinson, Conn Pictures, US
Cain and Mabel, dir. Lloyd Bacon, Warner Bros, US
Conflict, dir. David Howard, Universal, US
Excuse My Glove, dir. Redd Davis, Alexander Films, UK
Kelly the Second, dir. Gus Meins, M-G-M, US
Laughing Irish Eyes, dir. Joseph Santley, Republic, US
The Milky Way, dir. Leo McCarey, Paramount, US
Never Kick a Woman, (animation), dir. Dave Fleischer, Paramount, US
Prison Shadows, dir. Robert Hill, Mercury/Puritan, US
Rip Roarin' Buckaroo, dir. Robert Hill, Victory Pictures, US
Toby Tortoise Returns (animation), dir. Wilfred Jackson, Disney, US
Two-Fisted Gentlemen, dir. Gordon Wiles, Columbia, US
Wildcat Saunders, dir. Harry Fraser, Atlantic, US

1937

The Duke Comes Back, dir. Irving Pichel, Republic, US
The Fifty-Shilling Boxer, dir. Maclean Rogers, George Smith Prod,, UK
Flying Fists, dir. Bob Hill, Victory Pictures, US
Keep Fit, dir. Anthony Kimmins, Associated Talking Pictures, UK
The Kid Comes Back, dir. Reeves Eason, Warner Bros, US

Kid Galahad, dir. Michael Curtiz, Warner Bros, US
Some Blondes Are Dangerous, dir. Milton Carruth, Universal, US
When's Your Birthday, dir. Harry Beaumont, Renown, US
Woman Wise, dir. Allan Dwan, Twentieth Century-Fox, US

1938

Born to Fight, dir. Charles Hutchinson, Conn, US
Count Me Out (animation), dir. Cal Dalton and Ben Hardaway, Warner
  Bros, US
The Crowd Roars, dir. Richard Thorpe, Loews, US
Hollywood Stadium Mystery, dir. David Howard, Republic, US
The Honduras Hurricane (animation), dir. Rudolph Dirks, Loews, US
The Little Bantamweight (animation), dir. Rudolf Ising, Loews, US
Mr Moto's Gamble, dir. James Tinling, Twentieth Century-Fox, US
Porky and Daffy (animation) dir. Robert Clampett, Warner Bros, US
Spirit of Youth, dir. Harry Fraser, Globe Cinema, US

1939

Dangerous Dan McFoo (animation), dir. Tex Avery, Leon Schlesinger
  Studios, US
Ex-Champ, dir. Phil Rosen, Universal, US
Golden Boy, dir. Rouben Mamoulian, Columbia, US
Invitation to Happiness, dir. Wesley Rugles, Paramount, US
Keep Punching, dir. John Clein, MC Pictures, US
The Kid from Kokomo, dir. Lewis Seiler, Warner Bros, US
Kid Nightingale, dir. George Amy, Warner Bros, US
Pardon Our Nerve, dir. H Bruce Humberstone, Twentieth Century-Fox,
  US
Slapsie Maxie's, dir. Noel Smith, Warner Bros, US
There Ain't No Justice, dir. Penrose Tennyson, Capad, UK
They Made me a Criminal, dir. Busby Berkeley, Warner Bros, US
Winner Take All, dir. Otto Brower, Twentieth Century-Fox, US

1940

City for Conquest, dir. Anatole Litvak and Jean Negulesco, First National/
  Warner Bros, US
Golden Gloves, dir. Edward Dmytryck, Paramount, US

The Leather Pushers, dir. John Rawlins, Universal, US
The Notorious Elinor Lee, dir. Oscar Micheaux, Micheaux Film Corp, US
Pleased to Mitt You, dir. Jules White, Loews, US

1941

Bowery Blitzkrieg, dir. Wallace Fox, Monogram, US
Here Comes Mr Jordan, dir. Alexander Hall, Columbia, US
Knockout, dir. Williams Clemens, Warner Bros, US
The Miracle Kid, dir. William Beaudine, Producers Releasing Corp, US
The Pittsburgh Kid, dir. Jack Townley, Republic Picture, US
Pride of the Bowery, dir. Joseph H Lewis, Monogram, US
Ringside Maisie, dir. Edwin Marin, Loews, US

1942

Footlight Serenade, dir. Gregory Ratoff, Twentieth Century-Fox, US
Gentleman Jim, dir. Raoul Walsh, Warner Bros, US
Right to the Heart, dir. Eugene Forde, Twentieth Century-Fox, US
Sunday Punch, dir. David Miller, M-G-M, US

1943

Kid Dynamite, dir. Wallace Fox, Monogram, US
The Girl From Monterey, dir. Wallace Fox, Producers Releasing, US
The Man From Down Under, dir. Robert Leonard, M-G-M, US
To Duck...or Not to Duck (animation), dir. Chuck Jones, Vitaphone, US

1945

The Great John L, dir. Frank Tuttle, United Artists, US

1946

Gentleman Joe Palooka, dir. Cy Endfield, Monogram, US
Joe Palooka, Champ, dir. Reginald Le Borg, Monogram, US
The Kid from Brooklyn, dir. Norman McLeod, RKO, US
Mr Hex, dir. William Beaudine, Monogram, US

1947

Body and Soul, dir. Robert Rossen, Roberts Productions, US
First Glove, dir. Andrey Frolov, Mosfilm, Russia

Joe Palooka in The Knockout, dir. Reginald Le Borg, Monogram, US
Killer McCoy dir. Roy Powland, Loews, US

1948

The Big Punch, dir. Sherry Shourds, Warner, US
In This Corner, dir. Charles Reisner, ARC Productions, US
Joe Palooka in Fighting Mad, dir. Reginald Le Borg, Monogram, US
Joe Palooka in Winner Takes All, dir. Reginald Le Borg, Monogram, US
Leather Gloves, dirs. Richard Quine and William Asher, Columbia, US
Whiplash, dir. Lewis Seiler, Warner Bros, US

1949

Champion, dir. Mark Robson, Screenplays II, US
Duke of Chicago, dir. George Blair, Republic, US
Fighting Fools, dir. Reginald Le Borg, Monogram, US
Joe Palooka in the Big Fight, dir. Cy Endfield, Monogram, US
Joe Palooka in the Counter Punch, dir. Reginald Le Borg, Monogram, US
Ringside, dir. Frank McDonald, Lippert Prod, US
The Set-Up, dir. Robert Wise, RKO, US

1950

The Golden Gloves Story, dir. Felix Feist, Eagle-Lion, US
Joe Palooka in Humphrey Takes a Chance, dir. Jean Yarbrough,
   Monogram, US
Joe Palooka Meets Humphrey, dir. Jean Yarbrough, Monogram, US
Joe Palooka in the Squared Circle, dir. Reginald Le Borg, Monogram, US
Right Cross, dir. John Sturges, Loews, US

1951

Abbott and Costello Meet the Invisible Man, dir, Charles Lamont,
   Universal, US
Iron Man, dir, Joseph Pevney, Universal-International, US
Joe Palooka in Triple Cross, dir, Reginald Le Borg, Monogram, US
Navy Bound, dir. Paul Landres, Monogram, US
Punch and Judo (animation), dir, Izzy Sparber, Paramount, US

1952

Breakdown, dir. Edmond Angelo, Realart, US
The Fighter, dir. Hebert Kline, GH Productions, US
Flesh and Fury, dir. Joseph Pevney, Universal-International, US
Glory Alley, dir. Raoul Walsh, M-G-M, US
Kid Monk Baroni, dir. Harold Schuster, Jack Broder Productions, US
The Ring, dir. Kurt Newmann, United Artists, US
Sock a Doodle Do (animation), dir. Robert McKimson, Warner Bros, US

1953

Canvas Back Duck (animation), dir. Jack Hannah, Disney, US
Champ for a Day, dir. William Seiter, Republic, US
City of Bad Men, dir. Harmon Jones, Twentieth Century-Fox, US
The Flanagan Boy, dir. Reginald Le Borg, Hammer, UK
The Joe Louis Story, dir. Robert Gordon, United Artists, US
Off Limits, dir. George Marshall, Paramount, US
Second Chance, dir. Rudolph Mate, RKO, US
The Square Ring, dir. Basil Dearden, Ealing, UK
Tennessee Champ, dir. Fred M Wilcox, M-G-M, US

1954

The Good Die Young, dir. Lewis Gilbert, Romulus Films, UK
Tennessee Champ, dir. Fred M Wilcox, M-G-M, US

1955

Fling in the Ring, dir. Jules White, Columbia, US
Killer's Kiss, dir. Stanley Kubrick, United Artists, US
The Square Jungle, dir. Jerry Hopper, Universal-International, US

1956

The Harder They Fall, dir. Mark Robson, Columbia, US
The Leather Saint, dir. Alvin Ganzer, Paramount, US
Somebody up there Likes Me, dir. Robert Wise, M-G-M, US
World in my Corner, dir. Jesse Hibbs, Universal, US

1957

The Crooked Circle, dir. Joseph Kane, Republic, US
Monkey on my Back, dir. Andre de Toth, Imperial, US

1959

The Defeated Victor, dir. Paolo Heusch, Serena, Italy

* (Note that this list does not include many comedy shorts, or films that are only peripherally about boxing)

INDEX

INDEX OF NAMES

INDEX OF FILMS

www.ingramcontent.com/pod-product-compliance
Lightning Source LLC
Chambersburg PA
CBHW021218090426
42740CB00006B/266